Dedicated to Janett, Anne and Christopher

HUMAN MORAL BEHAVIOR

is a Principle of Nature Discovered by Philosophy and Evolutionary Sciences

Essays from Antiquity to Modern Times
Reedited and Updated

MARIAN HILLAR

ARPress
ILLUMINATING IDEAS.
EMPOWERING VOICES

ARPress
45 Dan Road Suite 5
Canton MA 02021
Hotline: 1(888) 821-0229
Fax: 1(508) 545-7580

Ordering Information:
Quantity sales. Special discounts are available on quantity purchases by corporations, associations, and others. For details, contact the publisher at the address above.

Printed in the United States of America.

ISBN-13:   Softcover   979-8-89676-529-5
                  eBook   979-8-89676-530-1

Library of Congress Control Number: 2024925491

TABLE OF CONTENTS

Acknowledgment

Author expresses his thanks and gratitude to Mrs. Claire Stetler, Dr. Alistair Sinclair, and Dr. Christopher J. Hillar for their continous support, reading and reviewing the manuscript, and linquistic and stylistic suggestions for improvement.

Introduction

From Natural Moral Law to Moral Capacity.
Moral Philosophy and Modern Science.

This book is a collection of essays published previously on various aspects of moral philosophy and related issues in science, and arranged thematically and in chronological order showing our increasing comprehension of human moral behavior. There is one theory explaining our moral behavior that seems to be meandering throughout the history of ideas and that led eventually to scientific explanation of human moral behavior and postulating the evolutionary biological process as its origin. Natural moral law theory in its modern interpretation may be considered as the culminating point of intellectual attempts to explain moral behavior, today not only interpreted in a very narrow sense of human behavior, but also encompassing other forms of animal life. For life constitutes a continuum of a phenomenon with gradation of properties and characteristics. Thus it seems proper that we attempt in this introduction to give a review of various interpretations of the natural moral law.

Introduction

Since time immemorial humans have been preoccupied with their own behavior and attitudes towards other humans, the rest of the animate world, and the surrounding environment. This is attested by the oldest written documents from the Mesopotamian, Mediterranean, and Far Eastern regions of the World.[1] In every culture we find the

---

1. Joseph Campbell, *The Masks of God: Occidental Mythology*, (Penguin Books: Harmondsworth, U.K.; New York, USA, 1976). Joseph Campbell, *The Masks of God: Oriental Mythology*, (Penguin Books: Harmondsworth, U.K.; New York, USA, 1986). W.Y. Evans-Wentz, compiler and editor, *The Tibetan Book of the Dead*, (Oxford University

practical injunction for moral behavior expressed in the "*Golden Rule*," a universal principle guiding human behavior. This rule is expressed in religious injunctions as well as in philosophical analyses wherever such attempts were made as is attested again by the history of philosophy.[2]

When answering the questions of how to live our lives and treat others, philosophers developed several theories such as hedonism, psychological egoism and altruism, ethical egoism, consequentialism and utilitarianism, deontological theory (Kant's well-being theory), virtue ethical theory, contractarianism and social contract theory, *prima facie* duties theory, natural law theory.[3] The natural law theory seems to be the most fundamental-going to the roots conditioning human behavior and all other philosophical speculations. The idea of a natural law in morality governing our behavior has a long history and was interpreted or understood in a variety of ways. Though it has limited value for a formulation of detailed practical maxims to conduct human behavior, nevertheless, it is still used by contemporary religious leaders to argue in defense of particular moral assumptions based on their theological worldview. It has, however, a great historical value for the evaluation of validity of secular philosophical intuition.

For modern science, starting with Darwin and his insights into evolution of man, has reached a level of sophistication and precision whereby is able to explain the naturalistic basis for the intuition of philosophers.[4] Consequently, the concept of moral law acquires a new meaning and is interpreted as the natural capacity for the moral behavior that forms the foundation of the behavior of living things, especially higher animals and humans.

Press: Oxford, UK, 1960). *The Texts of Taoism*, translated by Jmaes Legge, Part I, II, (Dover Publications, Inc. : New York, first published, 1962). James B. Pritchard, ed., *The Ancient Near East. Anthology of Texts and Pictures*, Vol. 1, 2, (Princeton University Press: Princeton, 1973). *Hindu Myths. A Sourcebook Trasnalted from the Sanskrit*. With introduction by Wendy Doniger O'Flaherty, (Harmondsworth, UK: Penquin Books, 1975*). The Rig Veda*, translated and annotated by Wendy Doniger O'Flaherty, (Harmondsworth, UK: Penquin Books, 1984). *The Upanishads*, translated by F. Max Müller, Part 1, 2, (Dover Publications: New York, first published 1962). Sarvepalli Radhakrishnan, *Indian Philosophy*, Vol. 1, 2 (first publication, George Allen and Unwin Ltd, 1931). James P. Allen, translator and introduction, *The Ancient Egyptian Pyramid Texts*, (Society of Biblical Literature: Atlanta, GA, 2005). Wing-Tsit Chan, translated and compiled, *Source Book in Chinese Philosophy*, (Princeton University Press: Princeton, 1963). Hammurabi, *The Oldest Code of Law in the World. The Code of Law Promulgated by Hammurabi, King of Babylon B.C. 2285-2242* (Hard Press, 2006). W.W. Davies, *The Codes of Hammurabi and Moses with Copious Comments and, Index, and Bible References* (Book Jungle, 2007).

2   Leonard Swidler, "Toward a Universal Declaration of a Global Ethic," in *Dialogue and Humanism, The Universalist Journal*, Vol. IV, No. 4, 1994, pp. 51-64.

3   Russ Shafer Landau, *The Fundamentals of Ethics*, (New York, Oxford: Oxford University Press, 2010). Henry Sidgwick, *The Methods of Ethics* (London: Macmillan and Co., 1901; first edition 1877).

4   R. Paul Thompson, "An Evolutionary Account of Evil." In Michael Ruse, ed., *Philosophy after Darwin. Classic and Contemporary Readings* (Princeton and Oxford: Princeton University Press, 2009). Pp. 533-538.

Early Societies: The Rule of Law

In all early societies the rules governing them were customs based on traditional and conventional beliefs of what was right or true. Subsequently, they were drawn up and codified as obligatory norms backed by the authority of the state or ruler. Thus the rules of the political society mirrored the moral sensitivity of people who formed it. In primitive societies there was no difference between the moral rules expressed in customs and the laws established in codified norms.[5] Such a situation presupposed the existence of an active designer or giver of these laws, and as long as theistic religion was the governing force this designer was god or divinity. Such view was a common knowledge in ancient Greek society and we find expression of it in Heraclitus (540-480 B.C.E.)[6] and Hesiod (b. ca 750 B.C.E.),[7] who declared that Zeus has laid down a law for all men that unlike the beasts they should possess justice.

Sophists and the *Nomos –Physis* Antithesis in the Fifth Century

This outlook was changed in the first half of the fifth century B.C.E. when social and political changes as well as new ideas about the external world developed by the Pre-Socratic philosophers-scientists led to the rise of intellectual ferment, the age of the ancient Enlightenment.[8] Doubts introduced by the Pre-Socratic philosophers about the role of divinity in the natural world led to its replacement by natural necessity as cause and introduction of relativity to social, political, and ethical conceptions. The so-called Sophists who changed the previous focus of interest from the physical reality to the affairs of humans played the primary role in this movement.[9] They contrasted *nomos* with *physis* -

---

5   Herbert Lionel Adolphus Hart, *Law, Liberty and Morality* (Stanford: Stanford University Press, 1963). Adam Krokiewicz, *Moralność Homera i Etyka Hezjoda* (Warszawa: Instytyut Wydawniczy PAX, 1959). Adam Krokiewicz, *Etyka Demokryta i Hedonizm Arystyda* (Warszawa: Instytut Wydawniczy PAX, 1960).

6   Heraclitus, *The Cosmic Fragments*. Edited with an introduction and commentary by G. S. Kirk (Cambridge: Cambridge University Press, 1954). fr. 114.

7   Hesiod, *The Homeric Hymns and Homerica*, with an English translation and by Hugh G. Evelyn-White (Cambridge, MA: Harvard University Press, 1982), pp. 276-284.

8   Jürgen Habermas, contemporary German philosopher calls this age an Axial Age.

9   The words Sophist (*sophistes*) derives from the Greek *sophos* (skilled, wise, clever, learned, subtle, ingenious*)*, *sophia* (skill, cleverness, wisdom, learning), *sophizomai* (practice an art, play tricks, devise skillfully, speculate). The term was widely used in the ancient Greece and designated a poet, as a teacher of men, a knowledgeable and prudent man, a person with a specific skill, expert or adept. In the fifth century this term acquired a specific meaning designating a class of Sophists i.e. of professional teachers, educators, scholars who gave lessons in grammar, rhetoric, politics, mathematics, for money. They taught in small seminars or circles, in public gatherings or private homes. This term became an abusive term in the hands of the satirical writer, Aristophanes, who slandered them and criticized as deceivers. For him Sophists represented an age of decline and breakdown of morals. Athenians were ambivalent about Sophists for they claimed to teach *arete* (virtue) and how to become a good citizen (Plato, *Protagoras* 319a). Athenians in their democratic outlook did not consider that a special training was necessary for this in contrast to learning specific practical skills (*technē*). Their opinion was shared by Plato who named them

they distinguished between the human laws and laws governing the nature of physical reality. They considered our human laws, customs, and religious beliefs changeable because they were not rooted in the natural order.[10] They looked for explanations and guidance to such matters as politics and morals, and they attempted to develop general theories of human nature, metaphysics, and epistemology.[11]

At the same time, Sophists recognized the existence of the unwritten and necessary natural moral law,[12] though considered as originating from gods. They designated an eternal moral principle, universally valid and overruling the positive laws of men. Its conception is well described in Sophocles's *Antigone* or in Euripides's *Hecub*. However, the popular beliefs in gods became undermined by speculation of the naturalists and satirical writers like Aristophanes.

Plato (427-347 B.C.E.) rejected the idea that morals and moral law are changing.[13] He refers us to the unchanging reality, the reality of the Forms (*eidos*), which is accessible only to reason and of which human societies are largely ignorant. Human behavior in societies is not only subject to the rules established by men in societies, but also to the universal law which is unwritten and to which even gods are subject.[14] Thus it seems that Plato laid the foundation for this original concept of the unchanging natural moral law as part of our natural world.

"worthless fellows" primarily for their atheism or agnosticism. In the next century Aeschinus referred to Socrates as "Socrates the sophist" and later Lucian of Samosata (125-180) referred to Christ "that crucified sophist" (*Peregrinus* 13). W. K. C. Guthrie, *The Sophists*, Cambridge UK: Cambridge University Press, 1971, reprint of 1987 edition), pp. 35-54. The texts of preserved Afragments of the Sophists' writings are available in a bilingual collection: *Sofisti. Testimonianze e frammenti. Testo greco a fronte*. A cura di Mario Untersteiner con la collaborazione di Antonio Battegazzore. Introduzione di Giovanni Reale, indici di Vincenzo Cicero, (Milano: Bompiani, 2009).

10   Modern evaluation of the Sophists indicates that they were not the source of decline in Greek thought, as Plato thought, but on the contrary they represented a transitional period in moral and intellectual development leading to the period of great philosophies of Plato, Aristotle, the Stoics, Epicurus and others.

11   The most prominent among Sophists one can list: Protagoras of Abdera (490-420 B.C.E.), Gorgias of Leontinti (485-380 B.C.E.), Hippias of Elis (ca 460-ca 390), Antiphon of Athens (480- 411 B.C.E.), Prodicus of Ceos (465-395).

12   For example Antiphon in Jan Legowicz, *Filozofia Starożytna Grecji i Rzymu* (Warszawa: Państwowe Wydawnictwo Naukowe, 1968), p. 123-124.

13   Plato, *The Republic, Parmenides*, in *The Republic and Other Works*, translated by B. Jowett, (New York: Anchor Book, 1973). Plato, *Complete Works*. Edited with Introduction and Notes, by John M. Cooper. Associate Editor D.S. Hutchinson (Indianapolis/Cambridge: Hachett Publishing Company, 1997).

14   Famous dialogue from *Euthyphro* : "Euthyphro – Yes, I should say that what all the gods love is pious and holy, and the opposite which they all hate, impious. Socrates – Ought we to inquire into the truth of this, Euthyphro, or simply to accept the mere statement on our own authority and that of others? Euthyphro - We should inquire; and I believe that the statement will stand the test of inquiry. Socrates – That, my good friend, we shall know better in a little while. The point which I should first wish to understand is whether the pious or holy is beloved by the gods because it is holy, or holy because it is beloved by the gods." Plato, *Euthyphro* in *The Republic and Other Works, op. cit.*, p. 435.

Aristotle: Changing Nature and Man as a Rational Animal

Next to dwell on the topic of natural law was Aristotle (384-322 B.C.E.), who distinguished in his *Nicomachean Ethics* between conventional or legal justice, and natural justice. However, they are not unchangeable.[15]

Aristotle could arrive at such a conclusion since he viewed nature from the biological perspective of observing natural phenomena. Biological changes are natural because they derive from the inner working of natural reality, from its latent principles. If such a view is correct, the question now arises what is human nature, what is human characteristic or human function and the principle that makes us humans? After a lengthy discussion and comparison with other forms of life, Aristotle states that the proper nature of man is "an active life of the rational element." And he differentiates between "activity" directed by reason and mere passive "possession" of reason:

> The rational element has two parts: one is rational in that that it obeys the rule of reason, the other in that it possesses and conceives rational rules. Since the expression "life of the rational element" also can be used in two senses, we must make it clear that we mean a life determined by the activity, as opposed to the mere possession, of the rational element. For the activity, it seems, has a greater claim to the function of man ... the good of man is an activity of the soul in conformity with excellence or virtue, and if there are several virtues, in conformity with the best and most complete.[16]

The Stoic Philosophy

By stating that reason and rationality is the distinctive human characteristic, Aristotle set the foundations for formulations of the natural law as governing the world and humans, which was postulated by the Stoics and explicitly formulated by Cicero. The Stoic philosophy was the most important and influential development in Hellenistic philosophy, and it affected Christian writers and their moral thinking as

---

15   Aristotle, *Nicomachean Ethics,* translated, with introduction and notes by Martin Ostwald, (New York, London: Macmillan Publishing Company, 1962), Bk V. 7.
16   Aristotle, *Nichomachean Ethics, op. cit.,* Bk I.7.

well as many philosophers.[17] It was revived in the deism and naturalism of the Enlightenment and continues to affect modern thinking as well.[18]

1. Interdependence in nature

The Stoics were the first philosophers who maintained systematically that all things in the world are necessarily interrelated: "from everything that happens something else follows depending on it by necessity."[19] Chance for them was simply a name for undiscovered causes.[20]

This idea may partially correspond to modern concepts of mutual interdependence in social, political, economical, moral, and ecological terms. Thus it had deep significance for the Stoics since it also included a moral and psychological sense of relating to one's self, society, and the world. To be a happy and good man meant for the Stoics to be related to the universe, "to feel at home in the universe," and to other human beings in a manner according to reason. Marcus Aurelius wrote: "Neither can I be angry with my brother or fall foul of him; for he and I were born to work together...,"[21] and, "The chief good of a rational being is fellowship with his neighbors – for it has been made clear long ago that fellowship is the purpose behind our creation."[22]

We find this Stoic principle repeated almost verbatim by Jürgen Habermas as the only and sufficient justification for the morality and ethics. He develops it into his "moral principle of universalizability," whereby an individual is integrated into a social order and his moral obligation arises from the process of socialization. Before Habermas, Immanuel Kant developed the same principle into his logical maxim of "categorical imperative."[23]

---

17 Lawrence C. Becker, *A New Stoicism* (Princeton, NJ: Princeton University Press, 1998).
18 It was founded by Zeno of Citium (333-262 B.C.E.) and developed by his successors Cleanthes (303-233 B.C.E.) and Chrysippus (b. ca 280 -d. ca 208/4 B.C.E.). *Stoicorum Veterum Fragmenta* collegit Ioannes Ab Arnim (Stutgardiae: in Aedibus B.G. Teubneri, MCMLXIV), Vol. 1-4, (abbreviated as SVF). Italian edition with translation of the *Fragmenta: Gli Stoici. Opere e Testimonianze* a cura di Margherita Isnardi Parente, Vol. 1-2. (Milano: TEA, 1994). A. A. Long, *Hellenistic Philosophy. Stoics, Epicureans, Sceptics* (Berkeley: University of California Press, 1986), second edition.
19 *SVF* II. 945.
20 *SVF* II. 67.
21 Marcus Aurelius, *Meditations,* translated by Gregory Hayes (NewYork : Modern Library, 2002), II.1.
22 Marcus Aurelius, *op. cit.,* V.16.
23 Jürgen Habermas, *Moral Consciousness and Communicative Action,* translated by Christian Lenhardt and Shierry Weber Nicholsen (Cambridge, Mass: The MIT Press, 1990). Immanuel Kant *Foundations of the Metaphysics of Morals* and *What is Enlightenment?* Translated with an introduction by Lewis White Beck (New York: Macmillan Publishing Company, twenty-first printing 1988).

Individualism was antithetical to Stoicism. Since all things are interconnected they have one universal cause that was "creative reason" or the *logos,* which is the indwelling cause of all things.[24] This model was applied to human action[25] in which we have to distinguish the external stimulus from the mind's response. The stimulus causes an impression which presents the mind with a possible course of action. It is up to the man how he is to respond.[26] A deliberate act is thus a combination of an impression and an internal response exactly as Aristotle would define it.[27] The Stoics and Aristotle did not look for a criterion of voluntary action as in "being free to act otherwise."[28] Thus the character of an individual was the general cause of one's actions that was a result of heredity and environment.[29] Moral corruption was traced by the Stoics to persuasiveness of external affairs and communication with bad acquaintances.[30] In the last analysis, the *logos* was the determining factor since it was all-pervasive. An individual's *logos,* assuming the particular identity, is the real self of an individual. Its *logos* is the self-determining factor. Thus the Stoic philosophy of nature provided a rational explanation for all things in terms of the intelligent activity of a single entity that is coextensive with the universe.

2. The problem of evil in the universe

In the Stoic worldview the uncreated and imperishable Nature, God, *Pneuma,* or the universal *Logos* exercises its activity in a series of eternally recurrent world-cycles beginning and ending as cosmic pure fire with each world. Within each cycle, Nature disposes itself in different forms: animal, vegetable, and mineral. Man is just one class of animals that is endowed with a share of its own essence, reason, in an imperfect but perceptible form. Nature as a whole is a perfect, rational being; all of its acts are the ones that should commend themselves to rational beings. If the "world is designed for the benefit of rational being" is there nothing bad within it? Here, Stoics approach the problem of

24   Lucius Annaeus Seneca, *Epistulae morales ad Lucilium* (Las Vegas : CreateSpace, Independent Publishing Platform, 2014), *Ep.* 65, 12-15.
25   Marcus Tullius Cicero, *On Fate (De fato), The Consolation of Philosophy: IV 5-7,V* Boethius. Edited with introduction, translation and commentaries by R. W. Sharples (Warminster: Aris & Phillips, 1991). 39-44.
26   *SVF,* II. 1000.
27   Aristotle, Περι ψυχης, *Traité de l'âme (De anima),* traduit et annoté par G. Rodier, III, 10- 11.
28   *SVF,* II. 984. "Being free to act otherwise" is the paradigmatic statement of the concept of free will adopted by the Christian thinkers.
29   *SVF,* II. 991.
30   Diogenes Laertius (abbreviated later as D.L.), *Lives of Eminent Philosophers* with an English translation by R. D. Hicks (Cambridge, MA: Harvard University Press, 1995). Vol 1-2. VII. 89; *SVF* III. 229-236.

evil in the world and showed their utmost ingenuity.[31] Stoics claimed that nothing is strictly bad except moral weakness. Natural disasters are not bad *per se* and they do not undermine Nature. They have their own rationale peculiar to themselves for, in a sense, they occur in accordance with universal reason and as such they are not without usefulness in relation to the whole. They are not Nature's plan but an unavoidable consequence of the good things that are. Thus Nature plays a double role in any causal explanation.[32] This was an optimistic philosophy that oriented life in accord with Nature and the development of virtues - the perfection of human nature that is reason.[33] The moral ideal thus became a virtuous person who knows the good and acts in accordance with it following the rational order.

3. Human Nature

Concerning human nature, the Stoics gave the traditional answer that it is the Mind that distinguished humans from other things, a concept borrowed from Diogenes the Cynic (b. ca 412 B.C.E.). This rationality was understood as the practical wisdom of living in accordance with Nature. Individual human beings share this rational principle with Nature, and thus it is a part of the world. Humans are endowed in varying degrees with "seed powers" (or *spermatikoi logoi*) which were part of the principle or *logos* of God. Cosmic events and human actions are both consequences of one thing, the *logos*. Therefore, humans have the ability to know the rational order governing the world, and this order is conceived as life- supporting breath or *pneuma* by analogy to the individual living creature. In Plato's idealism, mind and body were distinct. Modern psychology, physiology, neurology, and psychiatry provide evidence that there is little reason to deny that mental computations are purely physical processes in the central nervous system.[34] This Stoic concept of rationality acquired a new meaning in Habermas's interpretation as the communicative action in a social context representing a point of convergence for various cultures and societies. This convergence is based on the role played by universal

---

31 Plutarch, *De Stoicorum repugnantiis*, in *Plutarchi Chaeronensis Moralia* (Athens : Akademia Atheniensis, Institutum Litterarum Graecarum et Latinarum Studiis Destinatum, 2008), *p.* 32-37.
32 *SVF* II. 1118.
33 Zeno and Chrysippus defined the goal of man as "to live in accordance with experience of natural events." *SVF* I, 179; III. 5.
34 Edward O. Wilson, *Consilience. The Unity of Knowledge* (New York: Alfred A Knopf, 1998). Marc D. Hauser, *Moral Minds. How Nature Designed Our Universal Sense of Right and Wrong* (New York: HarperCollins Publishers, 2006).

concepts, such as truth, rationality, justification, and consensus that are found in every community. They form a "grammar" for discourse by analogy to Chomsky's universal language grammar:

> We may assume that the know-how informing argumentative practices represents a point of convergence where participants, however diverse their backgrounds, can at least intuitively meet in their efforts to reach an understanding. In all languages and in every language community, such concepts as truth, rationality, justification, and consensus, even if interpreted differently and applied according to different criteria, play *the same grammatical role.*[35]

Stoic theory thus anticipated the modern concepts as mind and matter are two constituents or attributes of one thing, the body. A man is a unified substance, but what he consists of is not uniform. All human attributes, according to the Stoics, are due to the permeation of matter by *pneuma.* The soul of man is a portion of the vital, intelligent, warm *pneuma* (breath) which permeates the entire cosmos[36] and the body. At death, the soul survives for a limited time only. Moreover, *pneuma* does not endow everything with life – only individual things with *pneuma* of a certain kind of tension are endowed with life. Depending on the type of tension, things are endowed with different types of life but only animal life and man have soul.[37] The soul has eight faculties, five of them being the senses while the other three are the faculties of reproduction, speech, and the governing principle – the so-called *hegemonikon* – "capable of commanding," and "the most authoritative part of the soul."[38]

4. The Stoic Ethics

The governing principle *logos* is the seat of consciousness and consists of all the functions which we would associate with the brain. One function is called "impulse," (*hormē*) "a movement of thought towards or away from something"[39] which is initiated by an impression. Impression

---

35 Jürgen Habermas, *Between facts and Norms,* translated by William Rehg (Cambridge, MA: Polity Press, 1998), p. 311.

36 D.L. VII. 156

37 *SVF* II. 714-716.

38 D.L. VII. 59.

39 *SVF* III. 377.

and impulse provide causal explanations of goal-oriented animal movements. Creatures are genetically determined to show aversion and preference. The technical term describing this relationship to the environment is *oikeiōsis,* a self-awareness and the behavior depends on animal or human recognition of the object as belonging to itself by its faculty of "assent."[40] However, we are not impelled or repelled by things that we fail to recognize as a source of advantage or harm.[41] This faculty coerces us to select things necessary for self-preservation and not necessarily by reason. An infant is "not yet rational," and it takes about 7 years to develop the *logos.*[42] Automatic impulse thus governs the behavior of humans in the earliest years, the first thoughts concerning self-preservation. Gradually, as the child develops, its governing principle is modified by accretion of the *logos,* and then "reason [becomes] supreme as the craftsman of impulse."[43] Reason, however, does not destroy the earlier impulses but rather they are taken over by it.

Human nature therefore develops from irrationality to a structure governed by reason, which in turn brings a change in the direction of impulse.[44] In particular new objects of desire develop and virtue becomes a human characteristic.[45] This process is a natural development towards a moral life described by Epictetus of Hierapolis (60 - ca 120 C.E.):

> But God has introduced man, as a spectator of himself and of his works; and not only as spectator, but as an interpreter of them. It is therefore shameful for a man to begin and end where irrational creatures do. He is indeed to begin there, but to end where nature itself has fixed our end; and that is, in contemplation and understanding, and in a scheme of life harmonious with nature.[46]

---

40 *SVF,* II. 171.
41 *SVF,* II. 979, 991.
42 Aëtius, IV. 11.4 in *Dox. graeci. op. cit.;* Sénèque *Lettres à Lucillius* Texte établi par François Préchac et traduit par Henri Noblot (Paris: Société d'Édition "Les Belles Lettres," 1964),. Tome I-VII. T. V. *Ep.* 124.9.
43 D.L. VII. 86.
44 Cicero, *De natura deorum, op. cit.,* II, 29; Sénèque, *Lettres à Lucillius, op. cit.,* T. V. *Ep.* 121, 10.
45 Cicero, *Du bien suprême et des maux les plus graves (De Finibus)* traduction nouvelle avec notice et notes par Charles Appuhn (Paris: Librairie Garnier Frères, 1938). III, 20. Cicero, *On Moral Ends,* edited by Julia Annas, translated by Raphael Woolf (Cambridge, UK: Cambriddhge University Press, 2007), III.20.
46 Epictetus, *Discourse and Enchiridion* based on translation of Thomas Wentworth Higginson with an introduction by Irwin Edman (Roslyn, N.Y.: Walther J. Black, 1944) I.6.19-20.

Attainment of rationality alters the whole structure of a man's governing principle. Human behavior is a mode of rational conduct, which is the use of faculties for the purposes designed by universal natural law.[47] Even the actions that we usually describe as irrational impulses are in fact governed by rational principle in the sense that they produce a judgment (intellectual assent) that moves to action, the movement of the soul. So the distinction is between the right reason (*eulogos*) and the wrong reason (*alogos*).[48] Therefore, everything that we do is rational in a sense, but the sage or the good man is the criterion because he alone has the right reason[49] in a consistent way.[50] We fluctuate between right and wrong reason and make moral progress not by extirpating desires and emotions but by making them increasingly consistent with the right reason.[51]

The interconnection between all events and things in the universe constitutes its determinism, i.e. the sequence between the causes and the effects. The Stoics believed that the universe operates in an orderly fashion and is intelligible, which means that if we knew all the preceding causes we would be able to predict future events. The ordered interweaving of causes and events was termed "fate" (*heimarmēnē*).[52] Their concept of cause (*aitía*) was different from the Aristotelian one, the novelty consisting of the introduction of regularity, a law between cause and effect. Zeno identified this regularity with providence as corporeal intelligence (*logos*) in the cosmic fire (*pyr technikon* or *pyr noetikon*) located within the world and governing it. This theory reflected that of the soul of the universe developed by Plato. The soul appeared to be ordering and performing a providential function in the universe.[53] The major difference from Plato's scheme was that in Zeno's system the order was to be periodically destroyed and renewed according to a cyclic rhythm. Chance (*tēchē*) was, for the Stoics, another word for a situation where the causes are not clearly visible, known, or differentiated.[54]

---

47 *SVF*,II. 899; III. 5, 175, 438, 466, 488.
48 *SVF*,I. 203; III. 468.
49 *SVF*, III. 175, 570-571.
50 *SVF*, III. 459.
51 *SVF* III. 278.
52 *SVF* II. 912, 915-917, 937, 943, 945, 975-976.
53 Plato *Laws*, in *Complete Works*, X. 896d-897c.
54 *SVF* II. 965, 966, 970, 973.

Among causes, the Stoics differentiated between two types: external causes attributed to the working of fate and internal causes related to the particular nature and linked to necessity (*anankē*).[55] Moreover, determinism was the effect brought about jointly by these two sets of causes. Additionally, "living things possess a natural movement, and this is a movement in accordance with impulse (*hormē*)."[56]

A more detailed description of the forces operating in the living organism was given by Origen:

> But of these [creatures] which have the cause of their movement within themselves, some are said to be moved out of themselves, others within themselves; and they are so divided because those which have life but no soul move out of themselves, those which have soul from within themselves. These latter move when there comes to them an image, that is a kind of desire or incitement, which impels them to move towards an object. Again, there exists in certain animals such an image, that is, a desire or feeling, which by a natural instinct impels and excites them to ordered and complex motion; as we see in spiders, which by an image, that is, desire and longing to weave a web, are excited to accomplish in an orderly manner the work of weaving, some natural movement undoubtedly calling forth the impulse to do this kind of work; nor do we find that this insect has any other feeling beyond the natural longing to weave a web. So too, the bee is impelled to fashion honeycombs and to gather, as they call it, aerial honey. But while the rational animal has in itself these natural movements, it has also, to a greater extent than the other animals, the faculty of reason, by means of which it can judge (*krinō*) and discern between the natural movements, disapproving of and rejecting some and approving of and accepting others. So by the judgment of this reason the movements of men may be guided and directed towards an approvable life.[57]

---

55   *SVF* II. 979, 974.

56   *SVF* II.979.

57   *SVF* II.988. Origen (185-ca 254), church father, succeeded Clement of Alexandria in the school of Alexandria. The patriarch of Alexandria who at first supported Origen expelled him later for being ordained without the patriarch's permission. Origen then moved to Palestine and died there. He wrote commentaries on all the books of the Bible. In a treaise *First Principles* (*Peri Archon*) he formulated the philosophical exposition of Christian doctrine in which

Living creatures operate driven by impulse which is generated from sensory presentation. In some animals the transition is automatic, but in humans the impulse is to be produced in a controlled manner due to the operation of the judging power—the reason (*logos*). Man is the only creature endowed with the capacity to understand cosmic events and to promote the rationality of Nature. He also is the only being that has the capacity to act in a manner that fails to accord with the operation of Nature [call it a Kantian freedom] and as such he is a moral agent. Man has "impulses to virtue" or "seeds of knowledge" as tools for his actions, and this is sufficient to direct reason in the right direction.[58]

5. Cicero and His Formulation of the Natural Law

Thus in the Stoic philosophy humans have a natural capacity to act in accordance with the natural law or "right reason" through the impulse to virtue. We find this understanding of the natural law formulated by Cicero[59] in his *Republic*:

True law is right reason in agreement with nature; it is of universal application, unchanging and everlasting; it summons to duty by its commands, and averts from wrongdoing by its prohibitions. And it does not lay its commands or prohibitions upon good men in vain, though neither has any effect on the wicked. It is a sin to try to alter this law, nor is it allowable to attempt to repeal any part of it, and it is impossible to abolish it entirely. We cannot be freed from its obligations by senate or people, and we need not look outside ourselves for an expounder or interpreter of it. And there will not be different laws at Rome and at Athens,

---

he interpreted scripture allegorically. He was a Neo-Pythagorean, and Neo-Platonist and like Plotinus believed that the soul passes through stages of incarnation before reaching God. For him even demons would be reunited with God. He considered God the First Principle, and Christ, the Logos, the secondary principle who was subordinate to him. Origen's views were declared anathema in the VIth century. Origen, *On the First Principles*, translated by G.W. Butterworth, with introduction by Henri de Lubac (New Yoek: Harper & Row Publishers, 1973), Bk. III, I. 2-3, p. 159.

58   *SVF* I. 566.

59   Marcus Tullius Cicero (106 B.C.E.-46 B.C.E.) was a Roman politician, lawyer, philosopher, and linguist, one of the greatest minds on the ancient Rome. Cicero introduced to the Romans knowledge of the Greek schools of philosophy and created Latin philosophical language. His voluminous writings were influential in the subsequent centuries for developing political and legal thought, and especially Christian ethical thought. His philosophy, Stoic in its outlook, is humanist and still serves as a starting point for modern religious and secular elaborations. Among the most cited works of Cicero one must list *On the Nature of the Gods (De natura deorum)*, *On the Chief Good and Evil (De finibus bonorum et malorum)*, *On Fate (De fato)*, *On Laws (De legibus)*, and *On Duties (De officiis)*.

or different laws now and in the future, but one eternal and unchangeable law will be valid for all nations and all times, and there will be one master and ruler, that is God, over us all, for he is the author of this law, its promulgator, and its enforcing judge. Whoever is disobedient is fleeing from himself and denying his human nature, and by reason of this very fact he will suffer the worst penalties, even if he escapes what is commonly considered punishment...[60]

Cicero in the *Laws* explains why this natural law is called law by differentiating understanding of it by the "populace" and by the "learned men":

Well then, the most learned men have determined to begin with Law, and it would seem that they are right, if, according to their definition, Law is the highest reason, implanted by Nature, which commands what ought to be done and forbids the opposite. This reason, when firmly fixed and fully developed in the human mind, is Law. And so they believed that Law is intelligence, whose natural function it is to command right conduct and forbid wrongdoing. They think that this quality derived its name in Greek from the idea of granting to every man his own, and in our language I believe it has been named from the idea of choosing. For as they have attributed the idea of fairness to the word law, so we have given it that of selection, though both ideas properly belong to Law. Now, if this is correct as I think it to be in general, then the origin of Justice is to be found in Law, for law is a natural force; it is the mind and reason of the intelligent man, the standard by which Justice and Injustice are measured. But since our whole discussion has to do with the reasoning of the populace, it will sometimes be necessary to speak in the popular manner, and give the name of law to that which in written form decrees whatever it wishes, either by command or prohibition. For such is the crowd's definition of law. But in determining what Justice is, let us begin with that supreme

---

60   Cicero, *The Republic*, in *De re publica. De legibus*, with an English translation by Clinton Walker Keyes (Cambridge, MA; London: Harvard University Press, William Heinemann, Ltd, 1988). Bk III. XXII.

Law which had its origin ages before any written law existed and or any State had been established.[61]

It is clear that Cicero defines natural law as "law" by analogy to the human positive law, and such is its popular understanding. However, in reality it is natural force – mind and reason inherent in human nature regardless of the underlying and accepted metaphysics – recognized by "the most learned men" that directs our behavior on an individual and social level. It is natural because it is proper for human nature:

> that animal which we call man, endowed with foresight and quick intelligence, complex, keen, possessing memory, full of reason and prudence, has been given a certain distinguished status by the supreme God who created him; for he is the only one among so many different kinds and varieties of living beings who has a share in reason and thought, while all the rest are deprived of it.

And further:

> But those who have reason in common must also have right reason in common. And since right reason is law, we must believe that men have Law also in common with gods. Further, those who share Law must also share Justice.[62]

6. Natural Development of Human Rationality

Thus in the Stoic view, natural law is a function of our human reason which, however, can be corrupted, and which functions both for an individual and for the society. Stoics could not have said much about the biological conditioning of our behavior except to say that Nature works by allowing a stepwise development of rationality, as the development of an individual proceeds, and with it the moral awareness through the mechanism of an "impulse" (hormē):

> An animal's first impulse, say the Stoics, is to self preservation, because Nature from the outset endears it to itself, as Chrysippus affirms in the first book of his work On Ends

---

61 The Greek term for law is *nomos*, which Cicero derives from *nemō*, to distribute, to grant, and the Latin term *lex* Cicero drives from *lego*, to choose. Quote from *The laws*, in *De re publica. De legibus, op. cit.*, Bk I.VI.18-19.

62 Cicero, *The Laws*, in *op. cit.*, Bk I.VII.22-23.

when his words are, 'The dearest thing to every animal is its own constitution thereof,' for it was not likely that Nature should estrange the living thing from itself or that she would leave the creature she has made without either estrangement from or affection for its own constitution. We are forced then to conclude that Nature in constituting the animal made it near and dear to itself; for so it comes to repel all that is injurious and give free access to all that is serviceable or akin to it. As for the assertion made by some people that pleasure is the object to which the first [primary] impulse of animals is directed, it is shown by the Stoics to be false. For pleasure if it is really felt, they declare to be a by-product, which never comes until Nature by itself has sought and found the means suitable to the animal's experience or constitution; it is an aftermath comparable to the condition of animals thriving and plants attaining full bloom. And Nature, they say, made no difference originally between plants and animals, for she regulates the life of plants too, in their case without impulse and sensation just as also certain processes go on as a vegetative kind in us. But when in the case of animals impulse has been superseded, whereby they are enabled to go in quest of their proper aliment, for then, say the Stoics, Nature's role is to follow the direction of impulse. But when reason by way of a more perfect leadership has been bestowed on the beings we call rational, for them life according to reason rightly becomes the natural life. For reason supervenes as the craftsman of impulse.[63]

The first natural impulse of a living creature, e.g. of a child, is directed not towards the outside world, but towards itself; it becomes self-aware and develops an "affection" for itself. This statement about primary impulse is an empirical one and the logical starting-point for Stoic ethics. Self-preservation (searching for food, defense against enemies, procreation) would be the only natural and right thing to follow if humans did not have the faculty of reason.[64] Therefore, the pattern of human behavior changes from a purely animal-like instinctive

---

[63]   Diogenes Laertius *Lives of Eminent Philosophers* with an English translation by R. D. Hicks (Cambridge, MA: Harvard University Press, 1995). Vol 1-2. VII. 85-86.

[64]   Cicero, *De Finibus*, III. 20-21.

pattern to a fully rational one and involves, according to Cicero, five stages. They represent the development of human nature, but only a few people will reach its highest stages because the process is not independent of a man's own effort. The "function" or goal of man in this process is attainment of perfection of his nature. The term used by Cicero is *officium* (corresponding to the English office, duty or task, as the office of an official charged with certain duties) and the Greek term is *kathēkon* (appropriate action). One could not speak about the "duty" of an animal or of an infant but rather of their natural function. The term duty becomes appropriate in stages three through five in human development as the changes in behavior become now functions of a rational being. Similar views on human moral development were formulated by Lawrence Kohlberg[65] and Kazimierz Dąbrowski.[66]

These psychological studies can be correlated with the studies of physical development of brain by Magnetic Resonance Imaging (MRI) and Graph Theory, a mathematical method allowing to measure how different brain regions develop and interconnect allowing correlation between changes in brain development and changes in behavior and cognition.[67]

---

65   Lawrence Kohlberg (1927-1987) developed a theory, based on the philosophical intuition of Cicero, of the moral development of children through three levels – the pre-conventional, conventional, and post-conventional, each subdivided into two stages: **level 1:** stage 1 – morality is understood as obedience and punishment and avoidance of harm to others; stage 2 – morality is understood as satisfying one's own interests and letting others do the same; **level 2:** stage 3 – morality is understood as playing the role of being a good person, i.e., meeting expectations, following the rules, and being concerned for others; stage 4 – morality is understood as doing one's duty, maintaining the social order and the welfare of the society. **Level 3:** stage 5 – morality is understood as basic rights, values, and legal contracts of a society. Laws and duties are calculated on overall utility (utilitarian morality); stage 6 – morality is understood as an accord with universal, self-chosen principles (e.g., justice, equality and respect for the dignity of all human beings) which confer validity to maxims and actions (Kantian morality).

66   Kazimierz Dabrowski, *Positive Disintegration*, edited, with an introduction, by Jason Aronson (Boston: Little, Brown and Company, 1964). Kazimierz Dabrowski, *Personality Shaping through Positive Disintegration*, introduction by O. Hobart Mowrer (London: J. & A. Churchill Ltd., 1967).

67   Neuroscientific studies show progressive maturation of various regions of the brain by increase in connectivity among brain regions as evidenced by increasing volume of white matter; that is the level of myelin wrapping up around the axons. Myelination taking place from childhood to adulthood speeds up the conduction of nerve impulses up to 100 times. It also allows a quicker recovery time, an increase up to 30 times in frequency with which neurons can transmit information. Another effect produced by myelination is strengthening the synapses or connections allowing for neurons to fire at a certain electrical threshold and coordinate better the activities in different parts of the brain on a variety of cognitive tasks. This interconnectivity can now be measured by applying Graph Theory, a mathematical method. Graph Theory allows one to measure how different brain regions develop and interconnect and allow correlation between changes in brain development and changes in behavior and cognition. Brain circuits develop from the stage of an embryo and continue throughout life. The amount of gray matter consisting of neuron cell bodies, dendrites and certain axons, increases during childhood, reaches its maximum around age of puberty and starts declining through adolescence plateauing during adulthood and starts declining again in senescence. The same pattern applies to the density of receptors on neurons. However, its development in terms of myelination of axons and strengthening of synapses occurs at different times in different parts of the brain. It matures faster in the primary sensorimotor areas devoted to sensing and responding to sight, sound, smell, taste, and touch. Gray matter matures latest in the prefrontal cortex which is important in development of our cognition, development of executive functions such as organization, decision making, formulation of hypotheses, planning, regulation of emotions, and of our social cognition: ability to form and analyze social relationships, discern friends from foes, etc. Jay N. Giedd, The Amazing Teen Brain, in *Scientific American*, July 2015, Vol. 312, No. 6, pp. 33-37.

Medieval Interpretation of the Natural Law and Morality

Thomas Aquinas, the most prominent Christian philosopher and a great mind, constructed a comprehensive system of moral philosophy including the concept of the natural moral law.

His starting point was the Aristotelian conception of happiness or moral wellbeing [*eudaimonía*][68] as the ultimate end of human living. [69] He supplemented this concept with religious doctrine: "the human mind's final perfection is by coming to union with God."[70] Our actions as human actions are rational and voluntary, and depend on our choice. Following Origen, Aquinas states that only such free acts based on the will in view of an end and apprehended by reason can be classified as moral actions, good or bad ("acts are called human inasmuch as they proceed from deliberate will" and "moral acts and human acts are the same").[71]

Aquinas' entire theory of justification of morals is an analogy, developed by comparison with the model of positive human law and the legal system. He postulated five laws:

1. The ETERNAL LAW – the deity himself:

    A law is nothing else but a dictate of practical reason emanating from the ruler who governs a perfect community. Now it is evident, granted that the world is ruled by Divine Providence, as was stated … that the whole community of the universe is governed by Divine Reason. Wherefore the very Idea of the government of things in God the Ruler of the universe, has the nature of a law. And since the Divine Reason's conception of things is not subject to time but is eternal…, therefore it is that this kind of law must be called eternal;

2. The positive DIVINE LAW, which is two-fold: the Old Divine Law, imperfect, underdeveloped, of the Old Testament, and the New Divine Law, fully developed, of the New Testament;

---

68   English text of Aristotle's *Nichomachean Ethics*, in *The basic Works of Aristotle*, edited and with introduction by Richard McKeon (New York: Random House, 1941).

69   The text of Aquinas's *"Summa Theologiae"* is that published in Latin-English version by Blackfriars in conjunction with McGraw-Hill Book Company, New York, and Eyre & Spottis- woode, London, 1963-1972. *Summa Theologiae*, 1a 2ae, 1,7; *Ibidem*, 1a 2ae, 90,2.

70   *Ibidem*, 1a 2ae, 3,8.

71   *Ibidem*, 1a 2ae, 1,3.

3. NATURAL LAW (*"lex naturalis"* or sometimes called *"lex naturae"*):
law, being a rule and measure, can be in a person in two ways: in one
way, as in him that rules and measures; in another way, as in that
which is ruled and measured, since a thing is ruled and measured,
in so far as it partakes of the rule or measure. Wherefore, since
all things subject to Divine providence are ruled and measured by
the eternal law, as was stated above… it is evident that all things
partake somewhat of the eternal law, in so far as, namely, from its
being imprinted on them, they derive their respective inclinations
to their proper acts and ends. Now among all others, the rational
creature is subject to Divine providence in the most excellent way,
in so far as it partakes of a share of providence, by being provident
both for itself and for others. Wherefore it has a share of the
Eternal Reason, whereby it has a natural inclination to its proper
act and end: and this participation of the eternal law in the rational
creature is called the natural law… thus implying that the light of
natural reason, whereby we discern what is good and what is evil,
which is the function of the natural law, is nothing else than an
imprint on us of the Divine light. It is therefore evident that the
natural law is nothing else than the rational creature's participation
of the eternal law… Even irrational animals partake in their own
way of the Eternal Reason, just as the rational creature does. But
because the rational creature partakes thereof in an intellectual and
rational manner, therefore the participation of the eternal law in the
rational creature is properly called a law, since a law is something
pertaining to reason, as stated above… Irrational creatures,
however, do not partake thereof in a rational manner, wherefore
there is no participation of the eternal law in them, except by way
of similitude;

4. HUMAN LAW:

a law is a dictate of the practical reason. Now it is to be observed that
the same procedure takes place in the practical and in the speculative
reason… Accordingly we conclude that just as, in the speculative
reason, from naturally known indemonstrable principles, we draw
the conclusions of the various sciences, the knowledge of which is
not imparted to us by nature, but acquired by the efforts of reason,

so too it is from the precepts of the natural law, as from general and indemonstrable principles, that the human reason needs to proceed to the more particular determination of certain matters. These particular determinations, devised by human reason, are called human laws, provided the other essential conditions of law be observed, as stated above ... that 'justice has its source in nature; thence certain things came into custom by reason of their utility; afterwards these things which emanated from nature and were approved by custom, were sanctioned by fear and reverence for the law. ... The human reason cannot have a full participation of the dictate of the Divine Reason, but according to its own mode, and imperfectly. Consequently, as on the part of the speculative reason, by a natural participation of Divine Wisdom, there is in us the knowledge of certain general principles, but not proper knowledge of each single truth, such as that contained in the Divine Wisdom; so too, on the part of the practical reason, man has a natural participation of the eternal law, according to certain general principles, but not as regards the particular determinations of individual cases, which are, however, contained in the eternal law. Hence the need for human reason to proceed further to sanction them by law. ... The practical reason is concerned with practical matters, which are singular and contingent: but not with necessary things, with which the speculative reason is concerned.

wherefore human laws cannot have that inerrancy that belongs to the demonstrated conclusions of sciences. Nor is it necessary for every measure to be altogether unerring and certain, but according as it is possible in its own particular genus; and

5. The bizarre "LAW OF SIN" ("*lex peccati*") or the LAW OF FOMES: Accordingly under the Divine Lawgiver various creatures have various natural inclinations, ... a law for one, is against the law for another. ... And so the law of man, which, by the Divine ordinance, is allotted to him, according to his proper natural condition, is that he should act in accordance with reason: and this law was so effective in the primitive state, that nothing either beside or against reason could take man unawares. But when man

turned his back on God, he fell under the influence of his sensual impulses: in fact this happens to each one individually, the more he deviates from the path of reason, so that, after a fashion, he is likened to the beasts that are led by the impulse of sensuality... So, then, this very inclination of sensuality which is called the 'fomes,' in other animals has simply the nature of a law (yet only in so far as a law may be said to be in such things), by reason of a direct inclination. But in man, it has not the nature of law in this way, rather is it a deviation from the law of reason. But since, by the just sentence of God, man is destitute of original justice, and his reason bereft of its vigor, this impulse of sensuality, whereby he is led, in so far as it is a penalty following from the Divine law depriving man of his proper dignity, has the nature of a law.[72]

The basis for Natural Law is the religious scheme of reality, the human condition, and the governance of the world by God. What Aquinas calls the "Natural Law" is the participation of the rational creature in the Eternal Reason through which it has its own natural aptitude for its due activity and purpose. It includes, however, the principles governing nonrational creatures as well. Following the Stoics and Cicero, Aquinas states that this participation is natural for humans because humans have a rational nature:

> Whatever is contrary to the order of reason is contrary to the nature of human beings as such; and what is reasonable is in accordance with human nature as such.[73]

Thus the Natural Law is "an ordinance of reason for the common good" and "the rule and measure of acts, whereby man is induced to act or is restrained from acting."[74] However, Aquinas goes beyond Cicero by postulating that the light of natural reason by which we discern what is good and evil is the impression of the divine light on us. He describes Natural Law further as the first principles of human moral activity that are self-evident, indemonstrable (*"sunt quaedam principia per se nota"*), and known to all. The first command of law is "that good is to be sought and done, evil to be avoided;" and on this command "are founded all the other precepts of the law of nature."[75] The commandments of

---

72   *Summa Theologiae,* 1a 2ae, 91. 1,2,3,4,5,6.
73   *Ibidem,* 1a 2ae, 71. a.2e.
74   *Ibidem,* 1a 2ae, 90. a.1.4.
75   *Ibidem,* 1a 2ae, 94.2.

the Natural Law are recognized by practical reason as being a human good ("*quae ratio practica naturaliter apprehendit esse bona humana*"). According to Aquinas, the order of natural commandments corresponds to our natural tendencies or inclinations.[76]

Thus, the behavior of nonrational creatures too is governed similarly but not recognized as a law, because only humans are able to recognize and formulate such precepts. Nevertheless, that Aquinas admits that these animals participate in them classifies their behavior as natural inclinations and instincts. Aquinas was not familiar with evolutionary processes in the world, i.e. with the evolution of living organisms and humans. He put very rigid barriers between inanimate, animate, and human worlds. He did not recognize the continuity of forms and substances in the universe. The term "instinct" used by Aquinas in a rigid sense as behavior governed by inflexible rules has no longer an application today to animals in evolutionary terms.

Aquinas next argues that since our activity of reason and will derives from what we are by nature and since all reasoning originates from principles which we recognize naturally as well as the desire for objectives that are subordinate to ends it is only proper that our acts should be primarily directed towards this ultimate end by the Natural Law.[77] Therefore, natural is what is preconscious, predetermined, self-evident, and not reasoned out. On the other hand he seems to accept the definition of Ulpian that what is the natural is what we have in common with animals, or what is "instinctive" or intuitive, according to the definition of Gratian:[78]

> the precepts of the natural law are to the practical reason, what the first principles of demonstrations are to the speculative reason; because both are self-evident principles. ... Consequently the first principle of practical reason is one

---

76   *Ibidem,* 1a 2ae, 94.2.

77   *Ibidem,* 1a 2ae, 91.2.

78   Ulpian (murdered in 223 C.E.) and Gaius (ca 110 - ca 180) were Roman jurisconsults ("jurisperiti") who set in order Roman law. Roman law was systematized by Emperor Justinian in *"Digest" ("Digesta,"* 533 C.E.), *Institutes* (*Institutiones,* 533), and *Justinian's Code* (*Codex Justinianus,* 528, 534). These were supplemented by additional decrees accumulated over the years as *Novellae* (*Novels*). Roman law was adapted to the politics of state and church. Ulpian and Gaius introduced the definition of "natural law" in terms of what we share in common with animals. Gratian published in 1141 a miscellany of texts related to legislation of the Western church entitled *"Decretum"* which became the canon law of the church and the state. *Decretum* I, 1,7: *"Ius naturale est commune omnium nationum, eo quod ubique instinctu naturae, non constitutione aliqua habetur"*. In *Corpus Iuris Canonici, editio Lipsiensis secunda post Aemilii Ludovici Richteri curas ad librorum manu scriptorum et editionis Romanae fidem recognouit et adnotatione critica instruxit Aemilius Friedberg.* Graz: Akademische Druck U. Verlagsanstalt, 1959.

founded on the notion of good, viz. that 'good is that which all things seek after.' Hence this is the first precept of law that 'good is to be done and pursued, and evil is to be avoided.' All other precepts of the natural law are based upon this: so that whatever the practical reason naturally apprehends as man's good (or evil) belongs to the precepts of the natural law as something to be done or avoided. Since, however, good has the nature of an end, and evil, the nature of a contrary, hence it is that all those things to which man has a natural inclination, are naturally apprehended by reason as being good, and consequently as objects of pursuit, and their contraries as evil, and objects of avoidance. Wherefore according to the order of natural inclinations, is the order of the precepts of the natural law. Because in man there is first of all an inclination to good in accordance with the nature which he has in common with all substances: inasmuch as every substance seeks the preservation of its own being, according to its nature: and by reason of this inclination, whatever is a means of preserving human life, and of warding off its obstacles, belongs to the natural law. Secondly, there is in man an inclination to things that pertain to him more specially, according to that nature which he has in common with other animals: and in virtue of this inclination, those things are said to belong to the natural law, 'which nature has taught to all animals,'[79] such as sexual intercourse, education of offspring and so forth. Thirdly, there is in man an inclination to good, according to the nature of his reason, which nature is proper to him: thus man has a natural inclination to know the truth about God, and to live in society: and in this respect, whatever pertains to this inclination belongs to the natural law; for instance, to shun ignorance, to avoid offending those among whom one has to live, and other such things regarding the above inclination.[80]

Only later do we recognize these natural tendencies as laws, precisely because we are rational creatures. Even nonrational creatures participate in Eternal Reason in their own way; however, they cannot perceive it as a law. When referring to them, we may use the word "law"

---

79   Reference to Ulpian; see note 78.
80   *Ibidem*, 1a 2ae, 94,2.

only in a figurative manner. Because of the double nature of humans (rational and animal), some acts of virtue follow Natural Law as they belong to it by the fact that our proper form is the soul. Therefore, our natural tendency is to act according to virtue. Many virtues, however, do not belong to Natural Law but are reasoned out before they are held helpful to the good life: for example, temperance modulates our natural desire for food, drink, and sex. Sins, if they are against reason, are against nature. On the other hand, some special sins run against nature, such as homosexuality, which, as Thomas thought, is against the course natural to all animals.

With this is associated the issue of changeability of the Natural Law which was introduced first by Aristotle. Aquinas recognized that moral conclusions arrived at by human reason can vary. He solved this problem by postulating two types of principles belonging to the Natural Law. He maintains that the first common principles of theoretical or practical reason, "the law of nature," are the same as the truth or rightness for all and are equally recognized. With respect to the specific conclusions of theoretical reason, the truth is the same for all, though not all recognize it equally. With respect to the particular conclusions derived by practical reason, there is no general unanimity as to what is true or right, and even when there is agreement there is not the same degree of recognition. In a few cases, the desire to do right or information may be wanting.

Thus, according to Aquinas, Natural Law with its first principles is a spontaneous, intuitive, "instinctive" reflex of tendency to seek what is good, to preserve natural being, to preserve the species, and to learn about God and venerate him. This "law" has supernatural origin having being created together with human nature and is self-evident. Practical reason next arrives at the common principles of the Natural Law, which may differ in details and in specific conclusions. However, he postulates one most general principle of practical reason quoting it in Gratian's formulation.[81] This principle is supplanted from the Judaic

---

81   *Summa Theologiae,* 1a 2ae, 94.4. "Consequently we must say that the natural law, as to general principles, is the same for all, both as to rectitude and as to knowledge. But as to certain matters of detail, which are conclusions, as it were, of those general principles, it is the same for all in the majority of cases, both as to rectitude and as to knowledge; and yet in some few cases it may fail, both as to rectitude, by reason of certain obstacles (just as natures subject to generation and corruption fail in some few cases on account of some obstacle), and as to knowledge, since in some the reason is perverted by passion, or evil habit, or an evil disposition of nature; thus formerly, theft, although it is expressly contrary to the natural law, was not considered wrong among the Germans, as Julius Caesar

and Greek traditions into Christianity, but is found in all cultures and religions.[82] He summarizes what is a natural right by quoting Gratian that it is that "by which everyone is commanded to do to others what he would have done to himself, and forbidden to do to others what he would not have done to himself."[83]

And it is generally held that all human inclinations should be directed according to reason.

The first principles of the law of nature *("lex naturae")* are altogether unalterable. But its secondary precepts, which are like particular conclusions close to the first principles, though not alterable in the majority of cases where they are right as they stand, can nevertheless be changed on some particular and rare occasion.

Now expanding the scope of Natural Law, Aquinas uses the notion of Natural Law in a double meaning – a narrow one as the very first principle or principles we recognize unconsciously, and the second, in the broader meaning that includes also particular conclusions derived from it in society.

Aquinas' concept of morality is very restricted and applies only to those rational beings who are able to consciously formulate these rules of behavior. This version of moral behavior found its secular parallel in Kant's *categorical imperative* which has a character of a law and operates strictly in humans, and *hypothetical imperative* operating on the principles of feelings, impulses, and inclinations, and thus can be applied to higher animals as well. Moreover, in Kant's thinking the moral sense or obligation, whether in its absolute form or in the hypothetical imperative is inherent in humans and not originated by participation in divine reason. Modern science finds that higher animals behave similarly to humans with similar feelings, impulses, and inclinations that have developed by the evolutionary process of

---

relates (De Bello Gall. vi)… The meaning of the sentence quoted is not that whatever is contained in the Law and the Gospel belongs to the natural law, since they contain many things that are above nature; but that whatever belongs to the natural law is fully contained in them. Wherefore Gratian, after saying that 'the natural law is what is contained in the Law and the Gospel,' adds at once, by way of example, 'by which everyone is commanded to do to others as he would be done by.'

82 Leonard Swidler, "Toward a Universal Declaration of a Global Ethic," in *Dialogue and Humanism, The Universalist Journal,* Vol. IV, No. 4, 1994, pp. 51-64. Michael Shermer, *The Science of Good and Evil* (New York: Times Books/ Henry Holt and Company, 2004), p. 25-26.

83 Gratian, *op. cit., Decretum* I,1: "Ius naturae est, quod in lege et euangelio continetur, quo quisque iubetur alii facere, quod sibi uult fieri, et prohibetur alii inferre, quod sibi nolit fieri."

socialization. This leads to a refinement of our understanding of moral behavior by contemplating its correlation with the evolution of higher animals. Aquinas, as restricted as he was by his religious notions, nevertheless, recognized that even nonrational higher animals might follow rules of behavior similar or identical to humans though they are not able to recognize them as laws. Modern theologians and religious scholars attempt to explain traditional theological speculations and biblical stories using the language and concepts of evolutionary biology.[84]

Foundation of Kant's Moral Philosophy and its Reinterpretation

Kant's writings on ethics[85] are the most important since antiquity. Kant argues, following the ancient Stoics, that our moral obligations in a final analysis derive from reason by recognition of the natural moral law, and not from either god, or communities, nor from inclinations or desires. But being a practical realist, Kant differentiates several levels of motivation and rules of the behavior that preserve human autonomy and free choice in moral decisions. Thus his theory, just as its sources (Aristotle's psychology and the Stoic doctrine), is deeply humanistic.

There are many parallels in Kant's thought with the ideas developed by the ancient Stoics and Eastern traditions developed in Indian culture and in China. His thought is thus an elaboration of the themes of ancient philosophers.[86] It is important for our analysis to keep in mind that the philosophical intuitions we find in various schools in the West and in the East can be reevaluated today in a more precise way due to the progress in the natural sciences, and especially from the evolutionary perspective. This is not to say that such perspectives were absent in previous searches, especially in the ancient Greek or Indian thought. The naturalistic outlook represented in the ancient schools and the philosophical intuition are confirmed today by studies of our biological nature. Yet we humans are not automata which follow the

---

84   Craig A. Boyd, "Thomistic Natural Law and the Limits of Evolutunary Psychology." In Michael Ruse, ed., *Philosophy after Darwin* (Princeton and Oxford: Princeton University Press, 2009), pp. 522 -532. R. Paul Thompson, "An Evolutionary Account of Evil," in *ibidem*, pp. 533- 539.

85   *Foundations of the Metaphysics of Morals* (1785), *Critique of Practical Reason* (1788), *Metaphysics of Ethics* (1797).

86   The ancient moral philosophy of the Stoics is till valid. It acquired in Kant's elaboration more precise generalization. But this philosophy still inspires more detailed elaborations and application to modern conditions of life, especially by combining the concepts developed by Kant with general outlook of the Stoics. Such an approach reached the level of a new height of logical analysis in the work of Lawrence C. Becker, *A New Stoicism* (Princeton, NJ: Princeton University Press, 1998).

prescribed pattern of input/output operating in the mechanical, even highly adaptive systems, defined by science. With the rise of sentient and rational life appeared a new quality in nature, namely, freedom.[87] Still this freedom should be controlled by reason, though we are not always motivated by moral law. Today, modern science provides insight into the mechanisms operating in human behavior at several levels.

1. Condition of Morality

Kant begins his treatise *Foundations of the Metaphysics of Morals* (1785)[88] with the classification of our rational knowledge. Kant specified the task of a moral philosopher as: 1. one of clarifying the "principle of morality" on which the rational agent can act insofar as his action is morally good; 2. to justify this principle, that is, to show that this principle is actually binding upon an imperfect agent such as a human being; 3. to apply this principle to build an exposition of human obligations, i.e., duties. In this first work out of the three treatises devoted to moral philosophy,[89] Kant dealt with the first task of the moral philosopher. He was not interested in constructing an ethical doctrine or writing a casuistry of morals but rather searched for an axiom or principle that might be used for building a general theory of laws of freedom (in contrast to the laws of nature, concerned with physical nature), the science of which he called ethics or theory of morals. In the *Metaphysics of Morals* (1797), Kant defined more precisely what ethics is; namely the science of how one is under obligation without regard for any possible external lawgiving, that is, as doctrine of virtue.[90] Just as natural philosophy (physics) has its empirical part so does moral philosophy because it must determine the human will as it is affected by nature. Kant calls this anthropology.

The laws of moral philosophy are therefore those according to which everything should happen, allowing for conditions under which what should happen often does not. Though the title of Kant's work

---

87   Daniel C. Bennett, *Freedom Evolves* (New York: Viking, 2003). Gregory R.Peterson, "Falling Up: Evolution of Original Sin." In Michael Ruse, ed., *Philosophy after Darwin* (Princeton and Oxford: Princeton University Press, 2009), pp. 539-548.

88   Immanuel Kant, *Foundations of the Metaphysics of Morals and What is Enlightenment?* Translated, with Introduction, by Lewis White Beck (New York: London: Macmillan Publishing Company, Collier Macmillan Publishers, 1988). Onora O'Neill, "Kantian Ethics." In *A Companion to Ethics*. Peter Singer, ed. (Oxford: Blackwell Publishers, 1997), pp. 175-185.

89   Those three treatises are: the *Foundations of the Metaphysics of Morals* (1785), *Critique of Practical Reason* (1788), and *Metaphysics of Morals* (1797).

90   Kant, *Metaphysics of Morals*, introduction, translation, and notes by Mary Gregor, (Cambridge; Cambridge University Press, 1991), XVII, 410.

contains the word "metaphysics," it is not about the understanding of ultimate reality, or the metaphysics of nature, but rather a rigorous search for the establishment of a supreme principle of a possible pure will which cannot be derived from observations of actual behavior of men but by reason. For Kant defines metaphysics as "a system of *a priori* knowledge from concepts alone ... a practical philosophy, which has not nature but freedom of choice for its object," and as such it requires a metaphysics of morals which "every man also has it within himself, though as a rule only in an obscure way."[91]

Kant begins his considerations with an analysis of the conditions for attaining happiness – namely, of being worthy to be happy, i.e., of having a good will that strives for moral perfection. Our moral obligation in the Greek and Judaic traditions is to achieve this "purity of heart" or "kingdom of god," which means good will. "Nothing in the world – indeed nothing even beyond the world – can possibly be conceived which could be called good without qualification except a good will.[92] This statement represents a spontaneous respect for moral law and an innate sense of "ought." It is an empirical postulate derived from observation of universal human nature. Kant next analyzes in quite an evolutionary approach that nature for achieving its end – preservation of life and its welfare – selects instinct rather than reason:

> For all the actions which the creature has to perform with this intention, and the entire rule of conduct, would be dictated much more exactly by instinct, and that the end would be far more certainly attained by instinct than it ever could be by reason. And if, ... reason should have been granted to the favored creature, it would have served only to let it contemplate the happy constitution of its nature, to admire it, to rejoice in it, and to be grateful for it to its beneficent cause. But reason would not have been given in order that the being should subject its faculty of desire to that weak and delusive guidance and to meddle with the purpose of nature. In a word, nature would have taken care that reason did not break forth into practical use nor have the presumption, with its weak insights, to think out for itself the plan of happiness and the means of attaining it. Nature would have taken over

---

91   *Ibidem*, II, 216.
92   Kant, *Foundations, op. cit.*, p. 9.

not only the choice of ends but also that of the means, and with wise foresight she would have entrusted both to instinct alone… Reason is not, however, competent to guide the will safely with regard to its object and the satisfaction of all our needs … and to this end an innate instinct would have led with far more certainty. But reason is given to us as a practical faculty, i.e., one which is meant to have an influence on the will. As nature has elsewhere distributed capacities suitable to the functions they are to perform, reason's proper function must be to produce a will good in itself and not one good merely as a means, for to the former reason is absolutely essential.[93]

The function of reason is thus the establishment of this "good will." Good will is good because of its willingness; that is, it is good in itself without regard to anything else. It is not the sole and complete good but rather the highest good and the condition for all others. "It dwells already in the natural sound understanding and does not need so much to be taught as only to be brought to light. In the estimation of the total worth of our actions it always takes first place and is the condition of everything else."[94] As an example of such situation Kant gives us an interpretation of the scriptural passages that command us to love neighbors and enemies. It is not done from inclination but duty, which resides in the will and not in feelings or propensities, but in principles of action.

Kant here is describing nothing other than common moral consciousness and from it derives principle for moral action. Charles Darwin observed that in the time of Kant the origin of this moral consciousness was questioned and Kant himself wondered about it. Darwin was among the first who gave a naturalistic explanation for its origin. He stated in his *The Descent of Man* (1871):[95]

I fully subscribe to the judgment of those writers who maintain that of all the differences between man and the lower animals, the moral sense or conscience is by far the most important.

---

93   Kant, *ibid.* p. 11-12.
94   Kant, *ibid.* p. 15.
95   Charles Darwin, *The Descent of Man*, in *The Origin of Species and The Descent of Man* (New York: The Modern Library, no date). Chapter 4, pp. 471-472.

This sense as Mackintosh[96] remarks, 'has a rightful supremacy over every other principle of human action;' it is summed up in that short but imperious word *ought*, leading him without a moment's of hesitation to risk his life for that of a fellow-creature; or after due deliberation, impelled simply by the deep feeling of right or duty, to sacrifice it in some great cause. Immanuel Kant exclaims, 'Duty! Wondrous thought, that workest neither by fond insinuation, flattery, nor by any threat, but merely by holding up thy naked law in the soul, and so extorting for thyself always reverence, if not always obedience; before whom all appetites are dumb, however secretly they rebel; whence thy original?'[97]

This great question has been discussed by many writers of consummate ability; and my sole excuse for touching on it, is the impossibility of here passing it over; and because, as far as I know, no one has approached it exclusively from the side of natural history. The investigation possesses, also some independent interest, as an attempt to see how far the study of the lower animals throws light on one of the highest physical faculties of man.

The following proposition seems to me in a high degree probable – namely, that any animal whatever, endowezd with well-marked social instincts, the parental and filial affection being here included, would inevitably acquire a moral sense or conscience, as soon as its intellectual powers have become as well, or nearly as well developed as in man.

We can now add that modern science confirms Kant's intuition and provides a biological, naturalistic, and evolutionary explanation for the existence of this moral consciousness.

---

96   Mackintosh, *Dissertation on Ethical Philosophy*, 1837, p. 231.

97   Immanuel Kant, *Metaphysics of Ethics*, translated by J .W. Semple (Edinburgh, 1836), p.136. This quote comes from Kant's work *Critique of Practical Reason* (1788). The full quote is: "Duty! Thou sublime and mighty name that dost embrace nothing charming or insinuating but requirest submission and yet seekest not to move the will by thretening aught that would arouse natural aversion or terror, but only holdest forth a law which of itself finds entrance into the mind and yet gains reluctant reverence (though not always obedience) – a law before which all inclinations are mute even though secretly work against it: what origin is worthy of thee, and where is the root of thy noble descent which proudly rejects all kinship with the inclinations and from which to be descended is the indispensable condition of the only worth which men alone can give themselves?" Immanuel Kant, *Critique of Practical Reason*, edited and translated with notes and introduction by Lewis White Beck, third edition (New York: Macmillan Publishing Company, 1993), p. 90.

Kant insists that in deciding what we ought to do our variable desires are not important – for an action to be truly moral it has to be done in the belief and because of the belief that it is right, i.e., out of respect for moral law.

It is important to indicate at this point that Kant and all philosophers until Darwin considered as truly (strictly) moral the actions produced by conscious rational and reflective analysis. This view arose from Origen's account of the Stoic analysis of the motion of objects and action of animals and humans.[98] Origen reported that the Stoics differentiated human beings from all other natural things by a particular kind of movement (action) unique to them. What distinguished them from others was that they are had a certain kind of cause (*aitía*) of motion in themselves. Things like plants and animals have an internal cause of motion, "nature" (*logos* for Stoics) and "soul" (in Origen's view); inanimate objects must have an external agency to be moved along; and are moved by thrust of external force. Plants and animals by virtue of having "soul" (and "nature") are capable of self-movement or action. In the case of animals, sensory stimulation is a necessary condition of the impulse to self-movement. Those lacking intelligence move and act according to a prescribed pattern. Human beings do not move or act in a set fashion—because the faculty of reason (*logos*) enables them to judge (*krinō*) their sensory presentations, to reject or accept, and to be guided. Origen calls this third kind of movement (action) self-movement of which only rational animals are capable, motion (action) "through themselves."[99]

We are deserving of praise when we choose the noble and avoid the base, but when we follow the opposite course we are blameworthy. Origen reasoned:

> It is neither true nor reasonable to lay the blame on external things and release ourselves from the accusation making ourselves analogous to wood and stones inasmuch as they are drawn along by external things that move them; such is the argument of someone who wants to set up a

---

98   See note 57.

99   *Stoicorum Veterum Fragmenta* Collegit Ioannes Ab Arnim (Stutgardiae: In Aedibus B.G. Teubneri, MCMLXIV). Vol 1-4. (abbreviated as SVF). *SVF* II.989, 879. Origen, *De principiis*, (*On the First Principles*), translted with introduction and notes by G. W. Butterworth (Gloucester, Mass.: Peter Smith, 1973). III, 1, 2, 3.

counterfeit notion of autonomy. For if we should ask him what autonomy is, he would say that it obtains 'if there are no external causes, when I intend to do something in particular, that incite to the contrary.'[100]

The Stoics believed that human beings are capable of self-movement without actually initiating their own motion. Origen's account of the difference in motion (action) between humans and other animals gave rise to the concept of morality as a behavior conditioned by a rational, reflective act. Origen said:

> We must not forget, however, that the greater part of the nature assigned to every rational creature is in animals in varying degree, some having more and some less; so that the instinct in hunting dogs and in war horses comes near, if I may say so, to reason itself. To be subject, then, to particular external impression which gives rise to such or such image is admittedly not one of the things lying within our power; but to decide to use what has happened either in this way or in that is the work of nothing else but the reason within us, which, as the alternatives appear, either influences us towards the impulses that incite to what is good and seemly or else turns us aside to the reverse.[101]

Many actions, even if they produce good results, that are done in accordance with the law do not belong to the realm of moral actions in this strict sense if they are done with some ulterior motives. Thus truly morally good action is not only in accord with the law but also because the law is acknowledged as absolutely and universally binding. Kant formulated the condition of morality with three propositions: 1. It must be done from duty; 2. Moral value is in the maxim by which action is determined, thus it depends on the principle of volition; 3. Duty is a necessity of an action from the respect of law, i.e., consciousness of the submission of the will to a law. Moreover, the subjective principle of volition must be distinguished from the objective principle of volition which would serve all rational beings also subjectively if they were governed by reason.

---

100   *SVF* II.990.
101   Origen, *op. cit.*, Bk III, 3, p. 160. *SVF* II.992.

2. Moral Law or Categorical Imperative

Kant next derives the concept of moral law from consideration of pure reason and will. Everything in nature works according to laws, but only a rational being has the capacity of acting according to the conception of laws, i.e., according to principles.

This conception of law derives from Stoic philosophy as a natural capacity to act in accordance with "right reason" through the impulse to virtue. We find such a formulation of the "natural law" in Cicero's *Republic*.[102]

Cicero in the *Laws* explained why this natural law is called law by differentiating understanding of it by the "populace" and by the "learned men;" and at the same time he explains the etymology of the term "law" from the idea of "choosing" and fairness implied by the term.[103]

It is clear that Cicero defines natural law as "law" by analogy to the human positive law, and such is its popular understanding. However, in reality it is natural force, mind and reason inherent in human nature regardless of the underlying and accepted metaphysics, recognized by "the most learned men" that directs our behavior on an individual and social level. It is natural because it is proper for human nature.[104]

Kant equates this capacity to act according to the conception of laws with will. But since reason is required for the derivation of actions from laws, will is nothing else but the practical reason that governs human behavior through a conception of law. In human beings, however, reason by itself does not sufficiently determine the will, which is also subjugated to subjective conditions not always agreeing with objective ones. But the pure conceptions of duty and moral law have the highest influence. Kant emphasizes that moral theory that is put together from a mixture of incentives, feelings, inclinations and partially from rational concepts makes the mind vacillate between motives and leads only accidentally to good and often to bad. The conception of

---

102   Cicero, *The Republic*, in *De re publica. De legibus*, with an English translation by Clinton Walker Keyes (Cambridge, MA; London: Harvard University Press, William Heinemann, Ltd, 1988). Bk III. XXII.

103   The Greek term for law is *nomoi* which Cicero derives from *nemō*, to distribute, to grant, and the Latin term *lex* Cicero derives from *lego*, to choose. Quote is from *The laws*, in *De re publica. De legibus, op. cit.*, Bk I.VI.18-19.

104   Cicero, *The Laws*, in *op. cit.*, Bk I.VII.22-23.

an objective principle governing our actions is a command of reason and the formulation of it is an imperative, an expression containing an "ought."

If an action is good as a means to something else, the imperative is hypothetical, and thus is conditional upon circumstances and advisable only. Such a goal cannot be universally held by all men at all times. Further, hypothetical imperatives can be divided into those that are technical (imperative of skill), those that belong to art, and those that are pragmatic (imperative of prudence), belonging to welfare of the being.

Accordingly, Kant differentiated three levels of behavioral rules operating in the living world:

1. The instinctive rules to which belong human urges satisfying our physiological and biological needs, as well as behavior of lower social animals. They are controlled by genes or epigenetic rules.

2. The heteronomous rules (hypothetical imperative, where the action is a means to something else or the will is subjected to extraneous motivations) which Kant divided into two types. A. One type, empirical, is associated with desires, fear, and other motivations. Here belong also the rules produced by the so-called moral sense which is responsible for subconscious or vaguely perceived, non-reflective actions and reactions. They may operate as well in higher animals. Modern science enlarges this intuition of Kant indicating that there is a subconscious, quasi-instinctive component in human behavior which may be controlled genetically and/or a result of habituation.[105] Also behavior of higher animals like apes may be controlled by this unconscious mechanism. It cannot be termed "moral," however, using the Kantian definition of morality (morality in the strict sense). Once these rules are consciously recognized, they constitute the basis for moral reflective behavior (morality in the strict sense). Nevertheless, higher animals have a certain subconscious recognition of rules of behavior common with humans which we prefer to classify as proto-morality. B. The second type, rational, refers to heteronomous rules which are produced

---

105 This aspect of human behavior was amply discussed and elaborated by the Stoics. In modern times Friedrich Nietzsche was one of the early philosophers who recognized the importance of social pressures on a society for the development of moral rules. Friedrich Nietzsche, *The Birth of Tragedy and The Genealogy of Morals*, translated by Francis Golfing, (New York: Anchor Books, 1990).

by reflection; however, they are motivated by extrinsic values such as achieving perfection or theological considerations.

3. The autonomous rules (categorical imperative), which are attained by conscious reflection representing the categorical imperative. These are moral rules in the fullest sense of morality proper only to humans.

Modern Psychological and Philosophical Studies on the Development of Human Morality

This classification of behavioral levels derives from Stoic doctrine[106] and corresponds to the stages of moral development of man through which community life and virtue are recognized as pre-eminently "things belonging to man" in their terminology and are related to autonomous behavior (categorical imperative of Kant). In modern times, Kazimierz Dabrowski[107] (1902-1980) and Lawrence Kohlberg[108] (1927-1987) confirmed the Stoic view of man's moral development. Dabrowski developed a theory of *positive disintegration* which views psychic breakdown as an important step to personality building. This disintegration embraces a variety of processes of emotional disturbance or even complete breakdown. But he considers them natural processes for integration, psychic health, adaptation to the environment, and building of personality.

Kohlberg, following the studies of Jean Piaget[109] (1896-1980), suggested six stages of moral development of children and adults through three levels – the pre-conventional, conventional, and post-conventional, each subdivided into two stages. The first two levels correspond to the heteronomous behavioral level of Kant. Level 1: stage 1 – morality is understood as obedience, punishment, and avoidance of harm to others; stage 2 – morality is understood as satisfying one's own interests and letting others do the same; Level 2:

---

106 *SVF* 1.197.
107 Kazimierz Dabrowski, *Positive Disintegration*, edited, with an introduction, by Jason Aronson (Boston: Little, Brown and Company, 1964). Kazimierz Dabrowski, *Personality-shaping Through Positive Disintegration*, introduction by O. Hobart Mowrer (London: J. & A.Churchill, Ltd, 1967).
108 Lawrence Kohlberg, *Essays on Moral Development*, (San Francisco: Harper & Row, 1981, 1984), Vols. 1, 2.
109 Jean Piaget, *The Moral Judgment of the Child*, translated by Marjorie Gabain (New York: The Free Press, A Division of Mamillan Publishing Co., 1965). Ronald Duska and Mariellen Whelan, *Moral Development. A Guide to Piaget and Kohlberg* (New York, Paramus, Toronto: Paulist Press, 1975). Emile Durkheim, *Moral Education. A study in the Theory and Application of the Sociology of Education*, forward by Paul Fauconnet, translated by Everett K. Wilson and Herman Schnurer, edited, with a new introduction, by Everett K. Wilson (London: The Free Press, A Division of Macmillan Publishing Co., 1973).

stage 3 – morality is understood as playing the role of being a good person, i.e., meeting expectations, following the rules, and being concerned for others (generally defined as group identification); stage 4 – morality is understood as doing one's duty, maintaining the social order and the welfare of the society. This stage is generally defined as recognition of authority. In the third level (Level 3) in stage 5, morality is understood as the basic rights, values, and legal contracts of a society. Positive laws and duties are calculated on overall utility (utilitarian morality). This stage involves critical thinking and choice; in stage 6 morality is understood as an accord with universal, self-chosen principles (e.g., justice, equality, and respect for the dignity of all human beings) which confer validity to maxims and actions. This level involves internalization of the principle of autonomy and corresponds completely to the autonomous behavioral level (categorical imperative) in Kant's classification. This is the level where human internal dialogue elevates moral behavior to a level of abstraction and self-reflection absent until humans entered the evolutionary scene.

Jürgen Habermas Adopts the Kantian Moral Philosophy Model

The Kantian pattern of moral behavior was adopted by Jürgen Habermas (b. 1929), a popular contemporary German philosopher-sociologist, with only a small modification.[110] Habermas develops Kantian ethics into a discourse of social consensus. Habermas considers modernity as a process by which subjects liberate themselves from traditional roles and values, to create a new social order through communication and discourse, a new "normativity." And he understands this "normativity" as new meanings and understandings that are shared and rational, i.e., based on mutual recognition of validity claims. The issue here is the emergence of secular morality from the Judeo-Christian tradition, namely the question of how to live one's life. Habermas contends that gradually a normative ethics as an exposition of detailed norms based on religious tradition was replaced by competing conceptions of the good and transformed from a set of commands to a system of principles and valid norms which are universal and unconditional. Though they are a legacy of the religious tradition,

---

110   Jürgen Habermas, *Moral Consciousness and Communicative Action*, translated by Christian Lenhardt and Shierry Weber Nicholsen (Cambridge, Mass: The MIT Press, 1990 [1983]).

these norms function in a new social order. Such a consideration refers to the existing morality in practice.

Similarly, one could consider the history of a moral theory, and Habermas emphasizes that Kant was the first among moral philosophers who pointed to the modern conception of morality, namely, the "formula of the universal law," maxims which are incorporated into the will: "Act only on that maxim by which you can at the same time will it to be a universal law." In Kant's ethics, moral actions are expressions of a free act and based on establishing the validity of moral norms by each individual. Habermas, as a sociologist, criticizes Kant for this individualistic twist and considers morality a collective process of reaching a consensus: "The emphasis shifts from what each can will without contradiction to be a general law, to what all can will in agreement to be a universal law." But this critique is not justified; he simply overlooked Kant's principle of universality at the same time he contradicts himself by introducing "moral discourse" which is equivalent to the Kant theory of morals and concerns norms which are absolute and are either unconditionally valid or invalid and hold across competing cultural traditions. They are evaluated either as right or wrong, just or unjust, and are deontological, their validity unconditional. But the detailed rules of behavior conditioned by social situations are labeled by Habermas as "ethical discourse," and he claims that in many situations it is difficult to separate these two discourses. Habermas, nevertheless insists on the priority of moral discourse and moral norms to always trump ethical values, confirming Kant's theory of the moral. This is due to the fact that in this discourse values are removed from the justification process: moral norms are not cultural values but they are communicative ideals of universal validity, and moral discourse is not rooted in any particular cultural tradition but belongs to the post-conventional level of the understanding of morality.

Categorical imperatives are possible because the idea of freedom makes man a member of the intelligible world. If one were a member only of this intelligible world, then all actions would be in accordance with the autonomy of the will. But since man is at the same time a member of the world of sense, his actions ought to conform to the autonomy of the will as belonging to the intelligible world, which, according to reason, should dominate the sensuously affected will. Anyone who is accustomed to using reason is conscious of the good will that constitutes the law for his bad will as a member of the world of sense and acknowledges the authority of this law even while transgressing it. The moral "ought" is one's own volition as a member of the intelligible world. It is conceived as an "ought" only insofar as one regards himself at the same time as a member of the world of sense.

Kant next asserts, however, that philosophy has no knowledge of this supersensible world; it only can indicate its possibility and thus philosophy defends the foundations of morality.

Modern Science Provides a Biological Foundation for Human Moral Behavior

As we have seen, the Stoics claimed that the pattern of human behavior changes from purely animal-like and instinctive to fully rational and involves five stages. They represent the development of human nature, but only a few people will reach the highest stages because the process is not independent of a man's own effort. Thus the Stoics recognized a natural biological basis for human behavior from which reason draws conclusions, develops rules, and constructs a moral philosophy.[111] Even Kant wondered about the origin of the moral principle that humans display and which he called "goodwill."[112]

The "function" or goal of man in this process is attainment of the perfection of his nature. The term used by Cicero *officium* (duty or task, as the in the office of an official charged with certain duties) could not be applied to an animal or an infant, so one could not talk about the "duty" of an animal or of an infant but rather of their natural function. The term duty becomes appropriate in stages three-through-six in Kolberg's model of human development as the changes in behavior become the functions of a rational being.[113]

Evolutionary Biology and Cooperation

111 Marian Hillar, "Natural Development, Rationlity, and Responsibility in Stoic Ethics," published in the *Essays in the Philosophy of Humanism*, Robert D. Finch, M. Hillar, F. Prahl, eds., Vol. 6, pp. 44-78. American Humanist Association, Houston, 1998.

112 Immanuel Kant, *Critique of Practical Reason*, edited and translated with notes and introduction by Lewis White Beck, third edition, (New York: Macmillan Publishing Company, 1993), p. 90.

113 Cicero, *On the Good Life*, translated with an introduction by Michael Grant (Harmondsworth, UK: Penguin Books, 1986).

Looking at the principles of evolutionary theory, it seems at first that the existence of cooperation should be contradictory to the evolutionary process. Darwin noticed this difficulty already when he discussed the origin of social moral faculties in "the primeval man." Darwin admitted that such traits as courage and fidelity could increase in competition between tribes: "A tribe rich in the above qualities would spread and be victorious over other tribes."[114] But asking how a large number of members could become endowed with these social and moral qualities within the same tribe, Darwin answered himself:

> He who was ready to sacrifice his life, as many a savage has been, rather than betray his comrades, would often leave no offspring to inherit his noble nature. ... Therefore it hardly seem probable, that the number of men gifted with such virtues, or that the standard of their excellence could be increased through natural selection, that is by the survival of the fittest; for we are not speaking here of one tribe being victorious over another.[115]

Darwin postulated "that though the high standard of morality may give a slight advantage to each individual in a tribe, yet an increase in the number of well-endowed men and an advancement in the standard of morality more generally will certainly give an immense advantage to one tribe over another. A tribe that includes many members who, from possessing in a high degree the spirit of patriotism, fidelity obedience, courage, and sympathy, were always ready to aid one another and to sacrifice themselves for the common good would be victorious over most tribes, and this would be natural selection."[116] Evolutionary scientists classify this as a "between-group selection." Moreover, cooperative and altruistic behavior, understood not in the everyday sense of conscious act but as a behavior which benefits other organisms at a cost to the donor, is widely shared throughout the animal kingdom.[117] It seems from the studies of many biologists that entire organisms like multicellular organisms with specialized cells could also be considered as made up of cooperating cells, and entire

---

114 Charles Darwin, *The Origin of Species* and *The Descent of Man and Selection in Relation to Sex* (Toronto: Modern Library, reprint of the second edition of 1860, no date). p. 498
115 Ibid. p. 499.
116 Ibid. p. 500.
117 Frans de Waal, with participation of Robert Wright, Christine M. Korsgaard, Philip Kitcher, Peter Singer, *Primates and Philosophers. How Morality Evolved* (Princeton and Oxford UK: Princeton University Press, 2006).

colonies of social organisms depend on cooperation and often altruistic sacrifice of some individuals for the sake of the group.[118] Thus, Martin A. Nowak who builds mathematical models for evolution considers cooperation its third fundamental process after mutations and natural selection.[119] The problem puzzled many biologists, economists, and mathematicians. Darwin suggested that natural selection favored families whose members were cooperative and answered Kant's question about the origin of moral rule.[120]

Such predictions by Darwin are confirmed today by scientific investigations that postulate the existence of cooperative behavior in the animal world. Scientists have developed several behavioral models using computer modeling and studies of animals.[121] Most recently, Frans de Waal[122] summarized studies on the primate behavior suggesting that we share our human behavioral traits with higher primates and that our morality, as predicted by Darwin and many philosophers, is a refinement of basic fundamental processes operating in nature.

Modern Science enlarged the Kantian paradigm of behavioral rules into three levels of morality understood in a broad sense (Table 1).

---

118 James H. Hunt, *The Evolution of Social Wasps* (Oxford: Oxford University Press, 2007). Bert Hölldobler and E. O. Wilson, *The Superorganism: The Beauty, Elegance, and Strangeness of Insect Societies* (NEW York: W. W. Norton & Company, 2008).

119 Martin A. Nowak, *Evolutionary Dynamics: Exploring the Equations of Life* (Cambridge, MA: Belknap Press of Harvard University Press, 2006).

120 Charles Darwin, *The Descent of Man and Selection in Relation to Sex, op. cit.* p. 471-472.

121 Elizabeth Pennisi, "On the Origin of Cooperation," in *Science*, 4 September, 2009, Vol. 325, pp. 1196-1199.

122 Frans de Waal, *Our Inner Ape. A Leading Primatologist Explains Why We Are Who We Are* (New York: Riverhead Book, 2005). Frans de Waal, with participation of Robert Wright, Christine M. Korsgaard, Philip Kitcher, Peter Singer, *Primates and Philosophers. How Morality Evolved* (Princeton and Oxford UK: Princeton University Press, 2006).

Table 1

Three Levels of Morality Compared From Animal Studies

Level	Description	Humans and Apes Compared
1. Moral sentiments (Kant's instinctive behavior)	Human psychology provides "building blocks" of morality, such as the capacity for empathy, a tendency for reciprocity,	In these areas, there exist evident parallels with other primates.
2. Social pressure (Kant's heteronomous behavior)	Insisting that everyone behaves a way that favors a group life. Thee tools to this end are punishment, rewards and reputation building.	Community concern and cooperative prescriptive social rules do exist in other primates, but social pressure is less concered with the goals of a society as a whole.
3. Judgment and reasoning (Kant's autonomous behavior)	Internalization of others' needs and goals to the degree that these needs and goals figure in our judgement of behavior including other's behavior that does not directly touch us. Moral judgement is self-reflective (i.e., governs our own behavior as well) and often logically reasoned.	Others' needs and goals may be internalized to some degree, but we do not know this since we are not able to communicate with other species.

According to Frans de Waal, (with modifications), *Primates and Philosophers*

(Princeton and Oxford: Princeton University Press, 2006), p. 168.

Such studies and others led to the formulation of humanity capacity for moral judgment and action as a "moral faculty."[123] This concept of the "moral faculty" or rather "moral capacity" goes back to antiquity when the ancients had a premonition of innate moral principles (moral sentiment, sense of justice, common moral thought), which were working subconsciously.[124] It is the basis for the moral rules which like

---

123 Marc D. Hauser, *Moral Minds. How Nature Designed Our Universal Sense of Right and Wrong*, (New York: HarperCollins Publishers, 2006). Marc D. Hauser, "The Liver and the Moral Organ," in *Philosophy after Darwin*, Michael Ruse, editor (Princeton, N.J., Oxford, UK : Princeton University Press, 2009), pp. 423-433.

124 Among modern philosophers, David Hume suggested that our notions of good and evil derive from very general principles expressed by our "sentiments." David Hume, *Enquiries Concerning Human Understanding and Concerning the Principles of Morals* reprinted from the posthumous edition of 1777 and edited with introduction, comparative table of content, and analytical index by L.A. Selby-Bigge. Third edition with text revised and notes by P.H. Niddith (Oxford: Clarendon Press, 1992), pp 3-9.

rules of logic or of natural sciences are objective truths, outcomes of rational choice. These rules were developed and formulated in various cultures with varying degree of success, and today they are at the foundation of humanistic ethics. John Rawls (1921-2002) in his well known treatise *A Theory of Justice* (1971) suggested that these innate moral principles can be analogized to the "sense of grammaticality" (a "faculty of grammar") described by Noam Chomsky[125] (Table 2).

Table 2

===

Characteristics of the moral faculty (capacity) derived from the principle of fairness postulated by Rawls.

1. Analogous to the faculty of language: from a limited experience comes out a broad range of utterances; from limited set of moral experiences we project intuition to novel cases. Generalization process could be the same for language mathematics, categorization of objects, morality, etc. Moral judgments emerge rapidly without reflection, emotions, and without clear justification or explanation. They are robust and firm. No conscious reasoning is involved here, we know by intuition how to behave. Even having conscious access to some moral principles underlying our moral behavior may have as little impact or none on our moral behavior as knowing the principles of language has on our speaking. (Knowledge comes from a subconscious intuition).

2. Moral conflicts are resolved by considered judgment uniting the subconscious principles with expressed principles: they are rapid, automatic, without reflection, without emotion, and without awareness of specific moral rules or principles. Once such judgments are formed, they are subject to different constraints, revisions, refinement, and rejection.

3. Unconscious principles imbedded in the moral faculty are the original position, e.g., how to evaluate dispensation of compensation for individual actions in the contractarian model of Thomas Hobbes, in the self-interest model of Adam Smith

---

125 John Rawls, *A Theory of Justice,* revised edition (Cambridge, Mass: The Belknap Press of Harvard University Press, 1971, 1999), pp. 40-46. Noam Chomsky, *Aspects of the Theory of Syntax* (Cambridge, Mass: The M.I.T. Press, 1965), pp. 3-9.

where the individual self-interests promote the public interest, or in the justice model of Rawls where they operate under the veil of ignorance or impartiality, i.e., free of knowledge of anyone's age, wealth, religious beliefs, health, ethnicity, or other biases.

===

Finally, a few words should be devoted to the so-called altruistic behavior of animals as contrasted with the so-called selfish behavior. These two terms have different meanings in biological studies of behavior. In popular usage, however, the term selfish is used to mean self-centered behavior. In biology this term means self-serving behavior without motives or intentions implied by "selfish." One cannot say about a spider building a web that he is doing this intentionally for his self-centered interest to catch flies. It seems that insects do not have a capability to predict the results of their actions. So similarly, the term "altruistic behavior" signifies a behavior benefiting the recipient without regard to motives or intentions. Humans behave altruistically most often spontaneously, automatically, and instinctively without previous rationalization, though we are able to act altruistically after cognitive reflection. Primates behave the same way, and we cannot expect that they always plan this behavior anticipating a reward. Thus de Waal differentiated several levels of altruistic behavior: 1. Functional, done without any appreciation of cost or benefit; 2. Socially motivated – a result of distress of others or begging; 3. Intentional – done with awareness how others may benefit (limited to humans and a few large-brained animals); 4. "Selfish" helping – done with expectation of returned benefits.

Table 3

Classification of Altruistic Behavior

==

Functionally Altruistic	Socially Motivated helping	Intentionally Targeted helping	"Selfish" helping
Cost to performer, benefit to recipient	Empathic response to distress or begging	Awareness of how the other will benefit	Intentionally seeking return benefit

←Most animals→

←   Many social animals   →

←   Humans, some large-brained animals   →

←Humans, some large-brained animals→

Frans de Waal, *Primates and Philosophers. How Morality Evolved* (Princeton and Oxford: Princeton University Press, 2006), p. 180.

Conclusion

We may now present a brief exposition of how the natural law should be understood so far. The natural law postulate formulates recognition of a general principle operating in nature which is innate in humans and governs their behavior. It has a character of law because it is binding to humans; it is universal, because it is independent of particular human positive law and applies to all people. Our human understanding of this natural law grows with the development of our rationality; thus, it is a law of human nature, a law of reason. Our behavior changes from an animal-like instinctive pattern to a fully rational one through stages: "The first appropriate function of a creature is to maintain itself, in its natural condition. The second, that it should seize hold of the things which accord with Nature and banish those which are the opposite." Thus we can differentiate in the natural law two types of principles – one instinctive, automatic which directs our behavior unconsciously, and the second one, reflective, rational at which we arrive after some analysis. For as soon as man acquires the capacity for understanding or conceptual reasoning, he draws rational conclusions that the highest human good is that which is worthy of praise and desirable for its own sake.[126]

These principles are classified as law from popular understanding of governing principles in analogy to written laws, that is human positive law which "in written form decrees whatever is it wishes, either by command or prohibition." But in reality "law is intelligence, whose natural function it is to command right conduct and forbid wrongdoing... it is the mind and reason of the intelligent man, the standard by which justice and injustice are measured."

Christian religious thinkers adopted the Ciceronian formulation of the natural law, for Thomas Aquinas stated that reason is the rule and measure of human action: "The good of the human being is being in accordance with reason, and human evil is being outside the order of reasonableness... So human virtue, which makes good both the human person and his works, is in accordance with human nature just in so far as it is in accordance with reason; and vice is contrary to human nature just in so far as it is contrary to the order of reasonableness."[127] It was linked, however, to their religious speculations.

Following Darwin, primatologists and other biologists[128] have long argued that the roots of human morality are manifest in social animals like apes and monkeys. These species express feelings of empathy, expectations of reciprocity and fairness, community concerns,

---

126   Cicero's view on human behavior coincides with that of Immanuel Kant who postulated categorical imperative as the maxim for human conduct. This maxim represents the highest level of understanding of morality and therefore he also postulated hypothetical imperative in which human behavior may be governed by other motifs. Immanuel Kant, *Foundations of the Metaphysics of Morals and What is Enlightenment?* Translated, with an Introduction by Lewis White Beck (New York, London: Macmillan Publishing Company, Collier Macmillan Publishers, 1988). Marian Hillar, "Is a Universal ethics Possible? A Humanist Proposition." In *The Philosophy of Humanism and the Issues of Today.* American Humanist Association, Houston, 1995, pp. 127-148. In the final analysis reason is the basis for morality and philosophy produced very good intuitive theory how it works. Derek Parfit, *Reason and Persons* (Oxford: Clarendon Press, 1987). Jürgen Habermas, "A Conversation about God and the World," in *Time of Transitions*, edited and translated by Ciaran Cronin and Max Pensky (Cambridge, UK: Polity Press, 2006), pp. 149-170. Modern science now grounds this philosophical intuition in evolutionary biological processes providing solid empirical foundations.

127   *Summa Theologiae, op. cit.,* 1a 2ae, 71, a.2c.

128   E. O. Wilson, *Sociobiology: The New Synthesis* (Cambridge, MA: Harvard University Press, 1975). E. Westermarck, *The Origin and Development of the Moral Ideas* (London: Macmillan, 1908 (1912, 1917), Vol. 1-2. Frans de Waal, *Our Inner Ape* (New York: Riverhead Books, 2005). Frans de Waal, *Primates and Philosophers. How Morality Evolved* (Princeton and Oxford: Princeton University Press, 2006). Robert Wright, *The Moral Animal. Evolutionary Psychology of Everyday Life* (New York: Vintage Books, 1995). Robert Trivers, *Natural Selection and Social Theory. Selected papers of Robert Trivers* (Oxford: Oxford University Press, 2002).

and gratitude, which are essential behaviors for mammalian group life and constitute a counterpart to human morality. Marc D. Hauser, summarizing all studies done with animals and in modern psychology and anthropology, proposes that people are born with a capacity for moral judgment (moral grammar of Rawls) wired into their neural circuits by evolution.

This grammar generates instant moral judgments which are instantaneously inaccessible to the conscious mind. Hauser presents his argument as a hypothesis to be proved, but it has solid experimental grounding, including work with primates and young children and in empirical results derived from studies performed by moral philosophers. Hauser argues that moral grammar operates in much the same way as the universal grammar proposed by linguist Noam Chomsky for developing language faculty. This universal grammar is a system of rules for generating syntax and vocabulary but does not specify any particular language. That is supplied by the culture in which a child grows up. By analogy, moral grammar, too, is a system composed of neural circuits which generate moral behavior and not a list of specific rules. Basic rules are the same in every society, but cultural variations are allowed, since cultures can put different emphases on its elements.

This proposal has strong and far-reaching implications. It suggests that parents and teachers do not really teach children the rules of correct behavior; rather, they instill cultural biases and modifications. Also, it demonstrates in a tangible way that religions are not the source of moral codes. On the contrary, moral grammar which operates subconsciously is immune to religious doctrines. At best, religions enforce instinctive behavior, and it seems that they developed for the purpose of enforcing the internalization of rationally recognized "building blocks" of morality: capacity for empathy, tendency for reciprocity, and a sense of fairness.[129] Moral grammar is a product of the evolutionary process because restraints on behavior are necessary for social living and have been favored by natural selection for survival. Friedrich Nietzsche was among those philosophers who argued for societal origin of rules of behavior which developed as cultures evolved.[130]

---

129   Pascal Boyer, *Religion Explained. The Evolutionary Origin of Religious Thought* (New York: Basic Books, 2001). Marian Hillar, "What does Modern Science Say about the Origin of Religion" in *Dialogue and Universalism*, Vol. XXII, No. 4, 2012, pp. 111-120.
130   Friedrich Nietzsche, The Birth of Tragedy and The Genealogy of Morals, translated by Francis Golfing (New York: Anchor Books, 1990).

Moral grammar, now universal among people, is thought to have evolved to its present shape during the hunter-gatherer stage of our past, some 50,000 years ago, through the mechanism of group selection as was suggested already by Nietzsche in a cultural context.

The question now arises, what validity does moral philosophical speculation have in view of scientific theories and the evidence behind them, such as the one postulated by Hauser? The answer which is suggested by Hauser was presented in the form of three models for human behavior incorporating three major themes of philosophical speculation.

The first model, the so-called Humean Model, is based on the entire line of philosophical speculation going back in antiquity to the Stoics, and in modern times has been best expressed by David Hume. Hume assumed that "perceptions" produce feelings and emotional reactions from which follows judgment.

The second model, labeled the Kantian Model, emerges from Kant's moral philosophy as a misunderstanding or single-minded interpretation of his "categorical imperative." Hauser, who noticed this misconception, introduced a double path in the model. Kant accepted the existence of something he called "good will." It has thus a quality of an instinct. We proceed to evaluate events, actions, etc., either on some principles which he classified as: 1. Heteronomous (empirical e.g., from principle of happiness, the so-called *moral sense*, inclinations, etc. or rational e.g., from the concept of perfection, (transcendental or theological) because they derive from the outside of the individual; 2. An autonomous or categorical imperative which is an autonomous moral law, a law for the will of every rational being. He expressed it as a formula or maxim by which we can judge. It has to be universal to be classified as the moral imperative.

But Kant did not go, and in his time it would be very difficult to do so, into the biological foundations of this mechanism. It was anyway an ideal situation if all humans behaved all the time in such a rational way. He knew that humans do not behave all the time in this way and do not always use reason for judgment. Thus these heteronomous principles were valid in practice (and still are).

The third model, the Rawlsian Model, is based on the theory of John Rawls who postulated an instinctive "moral faculty" that allows us to differentiate moral actions and situations from those which have no moral value and to differentiate actions which are allowed, permissible, or forbidden. So in this last model we have perception first, then automatically (unconsciously) we judge them and only then we develop emotions and feelings about them. Of course in the later stage comes also conscious reflection and reasoning which is then the basis for developing cultural rules, laws, etc. The last model is more realistic and it accommodates all previous models as certain approximations while at the same time is confirmed by evidence from scientific studies in many disciplines and provides evolutionary basis for human behavior. Still Kant's model seems to be the most complete though its biological basis could not be developed in his time.

I. VIRTUE ETHICS OF A SAGE

THE STOIC ETHICS: NATURAL DEVELOPMENT, RATIONALITY, AND RESPONSIBILITY[131]

1. Myth and Philosophy.

Understanding of Being: Myth and Philosophy

The Myth (*muthos*) was the early form of human dealing with the "understanding of our way of being in the universe."[132] The word originally meant "a story" and there was no difference here between truth and fable. The problem of differentiation between these ideas did not exist. Moreover, the myth gave rise to magic and incantations as a practical means of controlling events in life. Once, however, the credibility of myth was questioned and people sought answers to their cosmic and existential questions on a rational basis, the crisis arose and a need to develop a better system of explanation.

Thus theories were developed that the myths of Homer and Hesiod were symbols of the truth and later they allowed the Jewish (e.g. Philo of Alexandria, 20 BCE-50 CE) and Christian (Origen ca 185-ca 254 CE) apologists to defend their scriptures by an allegorical interpretation of the fables. In the 20th century studies of the societies in which the myth is still regarded as truth, led to the development of new theories about myth based on the observation of its persistent social functions:

-- sacred stories sustain the life and unity of the community;

-- provide archetypal models for meaningful human activities;

-- provide structure for explanation of the natural/human world.

Myth can be divided into two different types. One is the Central myth, which provides an archetypal model of the structure and function of the community. It is the heart of culture which is

---

131 Published in Houston Freethought Alliance Newsletter, Vols. 101-106, 2008. A version of it was published in Essays in the Philosophy of Humanism, Vol. 6, pp. 43-78, 1998.

132 I owe the concept of "the way of understanding of being" to Howard R. Johnson.

sustained by retelling and re-enacting the story. Such was a myth of "chosen people" in the Jewish culture which sustained the group against all adversarial vicissitudes of their history. The myth outlived itself when it was contradicted by the growing evidence of facts which demonstrated that communities cannot be isolated and explanations of human existence require a more universal basis. Thus the political and social circumstances in the first-century Palestine gave rise to the original Christian myth. The other type is the Peripheral myth, which serves as a model of explanations for details of everyday life in a community; it provides meaning for the existence of individuals, establishes conventions and serves as a basis for philosophical reflection and elaboration of a system of thought.

Thus we may consider that myths are true in the pragmatic sense as effective and useful, but they are not truth in the absolute sense (especially in comparison with modern science). But the argument may be presented that the scientific approach has no regard for the human experience which is expressed by myth. Disregarding the truth of myth leads to a crisis and breakdown of the structure of society (as it happened in Greece at the end of the archaic age, in Europe at the end of the Middle Ages, and in modern times with the myths of Nazism or Marxism). Howard Johnson considers our history as a succession of crises in understanding of our existential meaning. The survival is brought about by reconstruction of the myth and creation of a new understanding. In the process, myths become divested from their supernatural meaning and more and more secularized. That this is true is attested by the fact that people continue to be fascinated with myth. The myth thus is an expression of ontological crisis and a tool to overcome it and preserve a community. To be authentic, however, and perform its function, it must be believed.[133]

The original Christian myth based on Hebrew tradition and mixed with Greek philosophy and Greek and Buddhist moral outlooks, developed from the fourth century into an institutionalized and a rigid, repressive, and morally bankrupt political system. Nevertheless, it is needless to say that the myth will not die, but will be modified and constantly adapted to the sum total of our human experience and knowledge. Myth will not die because there will always be people too

---

133 Howard R. Johnson *The Myth of the Christ and Meaning of Jesus*, in manuscript, 1970

busy, too lazy intellectually or not intelligent enough to reflect and search for intellectual and rational answers. Myth provides an easy, comfortable, and often aesthetically and emotionally pleasing substitute for serious effort.

But the picture of the possibilities of "understanding our way of being" would not be complete without discussing the other way, the way of the reflective mind which existed simultaneously with the myth, though it was not so popular and available to everyone. When we ask questions and try to develop rational answers to them, we practice philosophy that, in a broad sense of the word, also includes scientific inquiry. This way of philosophical reflection was so aptly described by the Stoic philosopher and statesman, Seneca:[134]

> Philosophy is not an occupation of a popular nature, nor is it pursued for the sake of self-advertisement. Its concern is not with words, but with facts. It is not carried on with the object of passing the day in an entertaining sort of way and taking the boredom out of leisure. It moulds and builds the personality, orders one's life, regulates one's conduct, shows one what one should do and what one should leave undone, sits at the helm and keeps one on the correct course as one is tossed about in perilous seas. Without it no one can lead a life free of fear or worry. Every hour of the day countless situations arise that call for advice, and for that advice we have to look to philosophy.

In ancient Greece philosophical reflection existed parallel to myth and religious practice and several philosophical systems vied for acceptance and verification in practical life. The most complete and influential system of philosophy that served as a practical wisdom and guidance in the everyday life was the Stoic philosophy founded by Zeno of Citium (ca 334--262 BCE) and developed further by Cleanthes (303--233 BCE) and Chrysippus (282-- ca 206 BCE). This philosophy was practiced in everyday life by people like Cicero (106-43 BCE), Epictetus (55- 135 CE), Seneca (4 BCE - 65 CE), and Marcus Aurelius (121-180 CE). It is a monistic philosophy in which the universe is

---

134 Seneca *Letters from a Stoic. Epistulae Morales ad Lucilium.* Selected and translated with an introduction by Robin Campbell (Harmondsworth: Penguin Books, 1969, 1987). Lett. XVI.

represented as one entity of many things and events bounded together and governed by universal law—the *logos*. The human individual is but one part of this cosmic reality.[135] Stoic ethics, as built on natural principles, was adopted by early pre-Nicaean Christianity and today it is the foundation of all secular types of ethical systems.

It is worthwhile to mention here, however, why Jürgen Habermas, a leading German sociologist and philosopher of our times thinks that religion will survive probably for a long time. One reason is that it provides a bonding, a uniting element in a society through moral norms. He accepts essentially Kantian outlook on ethics claiming that moral norms must be universally applicable, and must generate feeling of obligation. It can come only through the realization of collective goals of the community:

> The authority of moral norms rests on the fact that they embody a general interest, and the unity of the collective is at stake in protecting this interest. . . The 'ought' quality of moral norms implicitly invokes the danger that any harm to the social bond means for all the members of a collectivity— the danger of anomie, of group identity.[136]

There is no other answer to question Why be moral?

The other reason is inadequacy of philosophical language:

> Philosophy, even in its post-metaphysical form, will be able neither to replace nor to repress religion as long as religious language is the bearer of a semantic content that is inspiring and even indispensable, for this content eludes (for the time being?) the explanatory force of philosophical language and continues to resist translation into reasoning discourses.

> Indispensable semantic potentials are preserved in religious language, potentials that philosophy has not yet fully exhausted by translating them into the language of public

---

135 *Stoicorum Veterum Fragmenta* Collegit Ioannes Ab Arnim (Stutgardiae: In Aedibus B.G. Teubneri, MCMLXIV). Vol 1-4. (abbreviated as SVF). 2.945, 991. *Gli Stoici. Opere e Testimonianze*, a cura di Margherita Isnardi Parente (Milano: I Classici del pensieroTEA, 1998). A.A. Long *Hellenistic Philosophy. Stoics, Epicureans, Sceptics* (Berkeley: University of California Press, 1986).

136 Jürgen Habermas, *The Theory of Communicative Action,* translated by Thomas McCarthy, Vol. 1, Vol. 2, (Cambridge UK: Polity Press, 1981).

reasons, that is, reasons assumed to be capable of commanding general agreement. Taking the example of the concept of the individual person, which the language of monotheistic religions has articulated from the outset with all the precision one could wish for, I attempted to point out this deficit, or at least the clumsiness of philosophical attempts at translation. In my view, the basic concepts of philosophical ethics, as they have been developed up to this point, do not even come close to capturing all the intuitions which already found nuanced expression in the language of the Bible which are learnt only through a halfway religious socialization. Mindful of this deficiency, discourse ethics attempts to translate the categorical imperative into a language that enables us to do justice to another intuition, I mean the feeling of "solidarity," the bond of a member of a community to her fellow members.[137]

2. Fundamentals of Stoic Ethics

The Stoics regarded ethics as an imprecise "science" just as Aristotle did, and sought to establish a set of values and practical principles of conduct that would be as securely based as the laws of Nature. Stoic ethics was developed into a formal and coherent system by Chrysippus who subdivided it into three sections: 1. dealing with classification of ethical conceptions; 2. dealing with the common view, sciences and the virtues thence arising; 3. dealing with things good and evil.[138] The intellectual procedure of the Stoics was later imitated by Spinoza,[139] and Kant,[140] and others.

According to Nature

The Stoic metaphysics requires that the subject of ethics, good and bad, virtue, vice, happiness can be analyzed only from the perspective of accordance with universal Nature. Everything that accords with the

---

137   Jürgen Habermas, "A Conversation about God and the World." In Jürgen Habermas, *Time of Transitions*, edited and translated by Ciaran Cronin and Max Pensky, (Plity Press, Cambridge, UK: 2006).

138   Diogenes Laertius *Lives of Eminent Philosophers* with an English translation by R.D.Hicks. (Cambridge, MA: Harvard University Press, 1995). Vol 1-2. VII. 84, 199-204. (Abbreviated as DL).

139   Benedict de Spinoza *Ethics Preceded by On the Improvement of Understanding* Edited with an introduction by James Gutmann (New York: Hafner Press, 1949).

140   Immanuel Kant *Foundations of the Metaphysics of Morals* and *What is Enlightenment ?* Translated with an introduction by Lewis White Beck (New York: Macmillan Publishing Company, twenty-first printing 1988).

nature of a creature necessarily has positive value and anything that is contrary to a creatures' nature has necessarily negative value. The nature of anything is that structure and pattern of behavior which universal Nature has ordained as appropriate or in the interest of the creature concerned.

Stoics believed that everything that happens is governed by Nature and what is unnatural or contrary to Nature is a description of events that applies only to the particular things still for the benefit of the whole.[141] If Nature's activity is viewed as contradictory it is due only to the limitations of our human vision. Nature does not will the actions of bad people, it only harmonizes the dissonances. Thus according to Chrysippus virtue cannot exist without vice.[142] Man as a Moral Agent

According to Stoics man, by receiving reason from Nature is an active and conscious, autonomic moral agent participating in the processes of the universe. Man has the capability to harmonize his actions with nature: whether he does it or not is left up to him.

Man is equipped by Nature with "impulses" to virtue or "seeds of knowledge" which serve as instruments for building of his character. By using them he is able to direct himself[143] and develop a character which is defined as a sustained disposition. The process requires an internal effort and external influences may prevent him from developing a disposition harmonizing with Nature. This aspect of human behavior is studied today by modern science – psychology, experimental psychology, developmental psychology, ethology, neuropsychological biology, etc. Modern science comes to results amazingly congruent with the outlook and speculation of ancient Stoics by postulating the existence of a "moral faculty," not unlike the language faculty, the universal "language grammar." We have discussed this modern scientific approach previously in a published article (*Modern Philosophy and Modern Science*, Houston Forethought Alliance Newsletter, issue 99, 2008, pp. 5-6).

Man, being an autonomous agent develops his own character even though it is controlled by the law of Nature, the law of cause

---

141 Marcus Aurelius, *Meditations* translated with an introduction by Maxwell Staniforth (Harmondsworth: Penguin Books, 1964). V.8. SVF 1.537.
142 SVF 2.1169.
143 SVF 1.566.

and effect. Man is not responsible for the environment in which he finds himself, but he is responsible for the way he acts in relation to this environment. Man is equipped with the capacity to make a moral judgment on human well-being which is related to his inner attitude and his state of mind. It is illustrated by the simile of a dog attached to a cart. The dog can run willingly and, if he does not do so, he will be compelled to. So the cart represents the man's external situation which he cannot control, but the man himself can determine whether he will run willingly or not. The same is aptly illustrated in the Cleanthes' hymn to Zeus:

> Guide me, O Zeus, and Destiny,
>
> whither I have been appointed by you.
>
> For I will follow freely; and if, grown bad,
>
> I prove unwilling, I shall follow no less.[144]

However, of all the external circumstances only some are the making of Nature, most are of our own doing. Thus we should consider the results of our actions. In order to stress further the active role of man in deciding on his destiny, the Stoics emphasized the importance of education. The initial potentialities of man are such that with training he can achieve the disposition to act in accord with the moral order of Nature.

Development of Rationality and Pattern of Behavior

According to the Stoics, Nature works by allowing a stepwise development of rationality, as the development of an individual proceeds, and with it the moral awareness through the mechanism of an "impulse" (hormē):

> An animal's first impulse, say the Stoics, is to self preservation, because Nature from the outset endears it to itself, as Chrysippus affirms in the first book of his work On Ends when his words are, 'The dearest thing to every animal is its own constitution thereof,' for it was not likely that Nature should estrange the living thing from itself or that she would

---

144   SVF 1.527.

leave the creature she has made without either estrangement from or affection for its own constitution. We are forced then to conclude that Nature in constituting the animal made it near and dear to itself; for so it comes to repel all that is injurious and give free access to all that is serviceable or akin to it. As for the assertion made by some people that pleasure is the object to which the first [primary] impulse of animals is directed, it is shown by the Stoics to be false. For pleasure if it is really felt, they declare to be a by-product, which never comes until Nature by itself has sought and found the means suitable to the animal's experience or constitution; it is an aftermath comparable to the condition of animals thriving and plants attaining full bloom. And Nature, they say, made no difference originally between plants and animals, for she regulates the life of plants too, in their case without impulse and sensation just as also certain processes go on as a vegetative kind in us. But when in the case of animals impulse has been superseded, whereby they are enabled to go in quest of their proper aliment, for then, say the Stoics, Nature's role is to follow the direction of impulse. But when reason by way of a more perfect leadership has been bestowed on the beings we call rational, for them life according to reason rightly becomes the natural life. For reason supervenes as the craftsman of impulse.[145]

The first natural impulse of a living creature, e.g. of a child, is directed not towards the outside world, but towards itself; it becomes self-aware and develops an "affection" for itself. This statement about primary impulse is an empirical statement and the logical starting-point for Stoic ethics. Self-preservation (searching for food, defense against enemies, procreation) would be the only natural and right thing to follow if humans did not have the faculty of reason.

One consequence [of this starting-point] is this primary classification: Stoics say that that has value which is either itself in accordance with Nature or such as to bring about that state of affairs; accordingly it is worthy of being selected because it possesses something of sufficient moment to be valued, whereas the opposite of this is not

---

145   DL. VII. 85-86. Quoting from the biography on Zeno of Citium (333-261 BCE).

to be valued. We have then established as basic principles that those things which are in accordance with Nature are to be acquired for their own sake, and their opposites are to be rejected. The first appropriate function of a creature is to maintain itself in its natural condition. The second, that it should seize hold of the things which accord with Nature and banish those which are the opposite. Once this procedure of selection and rejection has been discovered, the next consequence is selection exercised appropriately, then such selection performed continuously; finally, selection which is absolutely consistent and in complete agreement with Nature. At this point for the first time that which can truly be called good begins to be present in a man and understood. For a man's first affection is towards those things which are in accordance with Nature. But as soon as he acquired the capacity for understanding or rather, a stock of rational concepts, and has seen the regularity and harmony of conduct, he values this far higher than everything for which he had previously felt affection, and he draws the rational conclusion that that constitutes the highest human good which is worthy of praise and desirable for its own sake. In this harmony consists the good which is the standard of all things; and so virtuous action and virtue itself, which is reckoned the only good thing, though later in origin, is the only thing to be desired through its intrinsic nature and worth. And none of the primary objects of natural affiliation is desirable for its own sake.[146]

Thus, the pattern of human behavior changes from a purely animal-like instinctive pattern to a fully rational one and involves, according to Cicero, five stages. They represent the development of human nature, but only a few people will reach the highest stages, because the process is not independent of a man's own effort. The "function" or goal of man in this process is attainment of perfection of his nature. The term used by Cicero is *officium* (corresponding to the English office, duty or task, as the office of an official charged with certain duties) and the Greek term is *kathēkon*. One could not talk about the "duty" of an animal or of an infant, but rather of their natural function. The term duty becomes appropriate in stages three-through-to-five in human

---

146 Cicero *De Fin*. III. 20-21. Cicero, *Du bien suprême et des maux les plus graves* (*De finibus*) traduction nouvelle avec notice et notes par Charles Appuhn (Paris: Librairie Garnier Frères, 1938). In English translation : Cicero, *On Moral Ends*, edited by Julia Annas, translated by Raphael Woolf (Cambridge UK: Cambridge University Press, 2001, 2007).

development as the changes in behavior become now functions of a rational being.

3. Development of the Concept of Values. Moral Development

What has value for the Stoics? They determined that "things according to nature" constitute a particular class of things that have value the opposite of which are things contrary to nature.[147] In that class there were distinguished things which were defined as "primary things according to (or contrary) to nature." The term "primary" specifies the chronological order of things and it refers to the primary impulse towards things necessary for self-preservation (e.g. food of a proper kind, shelter, parental affection etc.) common to all animals.

But human individuals, along the stages of their moral development, find a wider range of "good" things than irrational animals: e.g. health, technical competence, beauty, high repute etc.[148] A child acquires these things and rejects the opposites by trying and learning in its second stage of development. Some things remain indifferent, neither good nor bad.[149]

Things naturally "attractive" or "to be rejected" become, in the third stage, raw material for selection and rejection which will be performed by developing reason which will also modify the pattern of behavior. Now the function of man is to perform appropriate acts (*kathēkonta*) which are impulses directed by reason: "That which reason persuades one to do;" "Befitting acts are all those which reason prevails with to do;"[150] "That which when done admits of reasonable justification."[151] Inappropriate acts are defined as the "opposite way." Among such things to be selected, Stoics listed honoring one's parents, brothers and sisters, native land, taking proper care of one's health, sacrificing one's property etc. Taking care of one's health is unconditionally appropriate, whereas the sacrifice of one's property is only conditionally appropriate. The appropriateness of these things rests in the fact that they remain in accord with the nature of a rational being. The range of appropriate actions grows with the growth of rationality and includes

---

147   SVF 3.140-146.
148   SVF 3.127.
149   SVF 3.118.
150   DL. VII. 108.
151   DL VII.107.

the impulse for "civic association." These social principles derive from the natural impulse for familial and extra familial attraction implanted by Nature[152] and are the starting point for justice. This natural attitude of attraction Stoics called *oikeiōsis*—attitude of attraction to things which belong to oneself, are proper to a thing or person.[153] Through this moral development community life and virtue are recognized as pre-eminently "things belonging to human nature."

Such Stoic view of moral development of man was wholly adopted by modern psychology and philosophy. Lawrence Kohlberg (1927-1987) suggested six stages of the moral development of children through three levels – the pre-conventional, conventional, and post-conventional, each subdivided into two stages: Level 1: stage 1 – morality is understood as obedience and punishment and avoidance of harm to others; stage 2 – morality is understood as satisfying one's own interests and letting others do the same; Level 2: stage 3 – morality is understood as playing the role of being a good person, i.e., meeting expectations, following the rules, and being concerned for others; stage 4 – morality is understood as doing one's duty, maintaining the social order and the welfare of the society. Level 3: stage 5 – morality is understood as basic rights, values, and legal contracts of a society. Laws and duties are calculated on overall utility (utilitarian morality); stage 6 – morality is understood as an accord with universal, self-chosen principles (e.g., justice, equality and respect for the dignity of all human beings) which confer validity to maxims and actions (Kantian categorical imperative morality). This scheme was repeated by Jürgen Habermas with a small modification he expanded the stage six by including his discourse interpretation of moral development.[154]

Disposition, Virtue, and Intermediate Goods

The habit of continuous and consistent selection of appropriate actions (and rejection of inappropriate actions) becomes a disposition characterizing an ideal good man, a sage. His pattern of behavior is now classified as virtue and is in tune with Nature and rationality. He

---

152 Cicero *Du bien suprême et des maux les plus graves (De finibus)* traduction nouvelle avec notice et notes par Charles Appuhn (Paris: Librairie Garnier Frères, 1938). III.66, I.12.

153 SVF 1.197. The term derives from the Greek term for building, house, home – οἰκία. It designates properties or things natural or proper to a person or thing.

154 Lawrence Kohlberg, *Essays on Moral Development*, (San Francisco: Harper & Row, 1981, 1984), Vols. 1, 2. Jürgen Habermas, *Moral Consciousness and Communicative Action*, translated by Christian Lenhardt and Shierry Weber Nicholsen, (Cambridge, Mass: The MIT Press, 1990 [1983]).

selects natural things to do because they are right things to do and they accord with virtue, i.e. the nature of a perfect rational being.

There are natural things which may be "advantageous" or "disadvantageous" but they are not constituents of virtue.[155] For example, wealth by itself has no moral value, though it is preferable to poverty. It acquires moral value only through the agent's principles or manner of acting.

The distinction between virtue and the other things which accord with Nature rests on the specific way in which they accord with Nature. Virtue is a special function or goal of a rational being that applies absolutely to all mature human beings. A rational being is naturally predisposed to prefer wealth to poverty but it is not the special function of a rational being to possess. There is no difference in moral worth whether one is poor or wealthy.[156]

To make a distinction between virtue and everything else, the Stoics described everything else by the term "indifferent" and used the terms good, useful to virtue, and bad, useless to vice. Only virtue is desirable, so it is "choiceworthy"; the rest is selected or taken.

Virtuous Action and the Goal of Life

The goal of life is, according to the Stoics, virtue and virtuous action. To achieve it man must aim at particular goals which can be specified precisely.[157] These are objectively preferable to their opposites. Later Stoics differentiated a comprehensive goal, which is the ultimate goal, namely virtuous behavior regardless of whether or not the intermediate goal is achieved. Diogenes of Babylon, Chrysippus' successor defined the goal of life: "To act rationally [i.e. with right reasoning, *eulogos*] in the selection of natural advantages."[158]

Things naturally "advantageous" and "disadvantageous" are necessary conditions of virtue, but are themselves not constituents of virtue. They are necessary because complete knowledge of that which is good presupposes and arises out of a disposition to select natural

---

155 SVF 3.123.
156 SVF 3.145-146.
157 DL. VII.129.
158 DL VII.88.

advantages and reject the opposites.[159] Moreover, they provide the material for the exercise of virtue and vice.[160] Every virtuous action must aim at bringing about some change in the external world.

The distinction between advantages and disadvantages is valid independently of the agent's intentions and allows specification of a set of intermediate goods that will "normally" (without the presence of exceptional circumstances) include anything aimed at by a good man: "So long as the succession of events is uncertain to me I always cling fast to the things which are better adapted for attainment of natural advantages; for God himself has given me the capacity to select such things. But if I knew that sickness was ordained for me now, I would pursue sickness."[161]

If the pursuit of an intermediate good, e.g. health, is not successful, the moral worth of the action is not affected and the lack of success does not show that the agent was wrong to try. It is preferable to succeed, but not morally more worthwhile. Intermediate goods do not have any moral value in themselves, but they provide the material to exercise rational discrimination which is morally good.

Presumed Difficulty with the Stoic Position on Intermediate Goods

The Stoics were criticized for their attitude towards intermediate goods, e.g. by Carneades, who insisted that the attainment of natural advantages implied acceptance of them as a goal.[162] But he did not maintain that virtue on its own is sufficient to provide well-being.[163] Another objection was expressed by Posidonius, who claimed that life consistent with reason should include "doing everything possible for the sake of the primary natural advantages."[164]

The distinction between the "good" and the "preferable" was also attacked by the eclectic Academic philosopher Antiochus of Ascalon: "The good," so Antiochus argues, "ought to include the satisfaction of these natural impulses from which it is supposedly derived."[165] He

---

159 Cicero *De Fin. op. cit.*, III.23,31.
160 Cicero *De Fin. op. cit.*, III.61.
161 SVF III.191.
162 SVF III.57.
163 SVF III.56.
164 SVF III.12.
165 Cicero *De Fin. op. cit.*, IV.25-28.

criticized the Stoics for treating man as if he were a disembodied mind needing nothing from the physical environment. He asked why these natural advantages are to be selected if the possession of them is not something good?[166] He claimed that virtue is not the only good thing even if it outstrips the worth of everything else. Natural advantages are bodily "goods" which make a difference, however slight, to the sum total of human well-being.[167]

The question thus arises whether the distinction between the "good" and the "preferable" is a valid one and the answer cannot be unequivocal since it depends on the critic's own moral theory. The Stoics, however, were consistent in their position and drew a line between moral value in a strict sense and any material or physical value of things. Difficulty with the Stoic Concept of Virtue

There is one more apparent general difficulty with the Stoic concept of virtue. The Stoics claimed that virtue, being the comprehensive goal of human nature, consists wholly of *eudaimonia* or welfare or well-being. They claimed that a man, in order to fare well, needs nothing but virtue and as virtue is something absolute, welfare admits of no degrees.[168] It seems that Aristotle had a more realistic position when he defined *eudaimonia* as "activity of the soul in accordance with virtue."[169] He recognized also that it required an adequate provision of possessions like health and other "goods." The notion of welfare seems to be logically tied up with notions like profitable, useful, and beneficial, and the Stoics seemed to recognize this themselves. But for the Stoics virtue, constituting moral welfare, is profitable to its possessor in the moral sense. The problem arises when people admit welfare as "the good for man" because then it seems to be arbitrary and false to assert that nothing except virtue identifies the content of welfare. It becomes more visible if we consider the welfare of others. For example if we consider a situation where our action would prevent the death of someone else, the Stoics would admit that a good man would do everything in his power to prevent or avert the disaster. But, we would agree with the Stoics that the virtuous man who so acted would fare

---

166   Cicero *De Fin. op. cit.,* IV.71.
167   Cicero *De Fin. op. cit.,* V.71.
168   Cicero *De Fin. op. cit.,* VII.96.
169   Arsitotle, *Nichomachean Ethics,* translated, with introduction and notes by Martin Ostwald (New York, London: Macmillan Publishing Company, edition 1988) 1100b, 14.

well, if the virtuous acts are beneficial to the agent. At the same time, part of the benefit must consist in the external object which is the goal. Stoics would agree that the object has value, but it is "preferred" and not "good" in the strict moral sense. Many would, however, think that it makes far better moral sense to say that both the action and its external object were "good." Good was done by the virtuous man's efforts to promote another's welfare. Still more good would have come from success.

The Stoics recognized rightly that goodness of intention or the principle of an action must be evaluated independently of a man's achieving some desirable result. This emphasis is one of the most important aspects of their ethics. The intentions or motives are commendable because of the good which the agent sought to produce.

The difficulties discussed arose because of the Stoics' terminological distinction, which introduces more confusion than clarification, and their emphasis on psychological equilibrium i.e. of man's avoidance of all changes in strong emotions.

If we call the "good" the "preferable," following the Stoic terminology, we obscure the relation between the value of a morally good action and the value of the change in the world at which it is aimed. Moreover, we might argue that a man's moral worth depends partly on his attitude towards success or failure at achieving morally desirable results. We might be inclined to think less of a man who felt no sorrow or regret that he was unable to avert the disaster (e.g. accidental death) in spite of all his efforts to do so. But for the Stoics the virtuous man having done everything in his power, does not feel pity or regret.[170] He accepts the result without reacting emotionally. The moral value is not dependent on one's emotional state. This attitude is easily understood and consistent in the context of the whole Stoic philosophy. For the external circumstances are, for the Stoic, in his power only to the extent that he can choose to accept them or not when they occur. He would accept them gladly if he knew that they contribute to the well-being of the universe as a whole. Before the events happen, he may be more favorably disposed to some events than to others and would prefer all manner of things for other people and himself to their

---

170   SVF III.450-451.

opposites and so far as he seeks to bring about these preferable states of affairs, his preferences are perfectly rational, i.e. they fully accord with an objective assessment of the relative merits of external things as determined by Nature itself. But he does not regard the things which he prefers as good (morally), nor does he desire them.

As for the attitude towards the future, the Stoic maintains the attitude of preference or rejection. He is in no position to judge their goodness and therefore views it with indifference and leaves it to Nature.

Moral Well-Being of the Agent

For similar reasons the Stoic's own well-being is to be "in his power" and therefore he cannot depend on the attainment of results which may not be realized. Nature ordained that a man can and should attain well-being solely through what is in his power. His disposition as a rational man is in his power, i.e. through virtue, the only good. Virtue is consequently a rational disposition[171] and its value is something different in kind from natural advantages. These are things which he can take if he encounters them, but virtue is something he can choose irrespective of circumstances. Natural advantages supply man with objective goods at which he can choose to aim and the material for forming his own moral principles. They are necessary to virtue only as means by which it can be exercised and not as things which it needs for their own sake.

4. Development of Virtue, the Paradigm of the Sage, and Philosophical Determinism. Development of Virtue

1. Virtue is one thing to which "good" belongs in a strict and necessary abstract definitions of virtue were given:

2. Virtue is a disposition and faculty of the governing principle of the soul, "or rather reason itself, consistent, firm, and nonwavering."[172]

3. Virtue is the goal which nature has laid down for man.

---

171   SVF I.202.
172   SVF I.202.

4. Virtue arises from the patterns of behavior of the earlier stages of man's development. From them we find that virtue is a kind of "knowledge" or "art."[173]

Thus, in general terms virtue is a disposition of the soul (psychē) which can be subdivided into four primary virtues: practical wisdom, justice, moderation, and courage. Each of them is described in terms of knowledge[174] (as in the Socratic and Platonic tradition) and can still be subdivided further.[175] For example, courage is the knowledge of things which should be endured. It is necessary to have knowledge which belongs to any particular virtue in order to have the knowledge constitutive of virtue as a whole. The virtuous man's knowledge is grasped by his intellect. He uses the evidence of sense-perception as preliminary steps to its acquisition and arrives at the "knowledge of the good:"

> After the mind, by means of rational inference, has climbed up from these things which are in accordance with Nature, it arrives at the idea of the good. But we perceive the good and name it so, not as a result of addition or growth or comparison with other things, but through its own specific nature. Honey, though it is very sweet, is perceived to be sweet by its own taste and not through comparison with other (sweet) things; similarly that good which is our subject, is something of the highest value, but this assessment is valid because of the kind of thing the good is, not because of its size.[176]

Similar language was used by Plato, who said that a philosopher ascends to knowledge of the good by the help of hypotheses about the objects of sight and intellect.[177] Things which accord with Nature are the stepping-stones to reach a principle that cannot be inferred directly from them. They are the preferable objects of instructive, and later, rational selection. The fact that the "good" is not intuited by a simple comparison with these natural advantages does not mean that "the good" falls outside things which accord with Nature. Different things

---

173   SVF III.256, 202.
174   SVF III.285.
175   SVF III.264.
176   Cicero *De Fin. op. cit.,* III.33-34.
177   Plato *Republic* 509c-511e.

provide an idea of being in accordance with Nature, but the "good" accords with Nature in a sense that is beyond anything else. Other things provide the mind a ladder, a help to a position from which "the good" is directly apprehended through its own nature. In practical terms no account is fully adequate. To know "the good" entails discovering the principle of conduct which satisfies the general idea of "accordance with Nature" formed by deduction, introspection, and the particular facts of human nature—that man is a rational being with the capacity to understand and participate in the universal activities of Nature.

Seneca specifies how we attain our first concept of the good and virtue.[178] It is not innate endowment and it would be absurd to suppose that man hit upon it by chance. Antecedents of moral knowledge are "observation" and "comparison of repeated acts": "Our school of philosophers claims that what is good and of moral worth is learned by means of 'analogy.'" He explains that by analogy with physical health (a natural condition which is familiar to us), we have inferred that there is such a thing as health of mind ("something just and good is conceived naturally"[179]). To reason by analogy the Stoics considered natural as well:

> There are certain acts of generosity, or of humanity, or of courage which have amazed us. We begin to admire them as if they were perfect. But they conceal many faults which are hidden by their appearance of something brilliant and we have overlooked these. Nature bids us to augment praiseworthy actions ... From them, therefore, we have derived an idea of remarkable goodness.[180]

From the idea of bodily health we develop a concept of the health of mind. To give a content to it from observation and comparison of behavior of individual men we form an idea of courage. The individual man who is always consistent with himself in every action, good under the direction of a disposition—in him we recognize that virtue has been perfected. Thus according to this theory our general concept of virtue is refined by observation.

---

178 Sénèque *Lettres à Lucillus*. Texte établi par François Préchac et traduit par Henri Noblot (Paris: Société d'Édition "Les Belles Lettres," 1964), Tome I-VII, T. V. *Ep.* 120.
179 DL VII.53.
180 Sénèque, *Lettres, op. cit., Ep.* 120.

The Paradigm of the Sage

Does this mean that the moral concepts that men form are relative to experience ? The Stoics tried to avoid the problem of relativism by setting up the sage as a paradigm and giving a detailed description of his disposition and of the kinds of things that he does. They realized, however, that imitation of the sage, of the paradigm of the actual good man cannot ensure virtue but it can certainly set a man in the right direction to secure it.

The sage is defined by his moral expertise—which includes several tests:

-- steadiness and orderliness, but he may act differently according to changing events;

-- timely behavior e.g. Stoics justified suicide on the ground that in extreme circumstances it may be the rational thing to do. Though the preservation of human life accords with human nature, it is not unconditionally appropriate;

-- absence of passion; the sage does not regard pleasure as something good nor pain as something evil; it does not mean he is insensitive, but they do not move his soul excessively, he is impassive towards them;

-- like Aristotle, the Stoics rejected the emotional attitude that accompanies actions as an index of moral character.[181]

These objective qualities form a canon of excellence, though the Stoic philosophers themselves did not pass it.

Man naturally develops a concept of value and Nature's part is to give man the ability to think analogically. But virtue or knowledge of what is truly good does not follow necessarily from these faculties. To know what is truly good, a man has to consider what is involved in the performance of a virtuous action and to ask himself why a man who acts apparently well in one sphere can fail to do so in another. He has to grasp what is needed if a man is to act well in all spheres at all times.

181　Andreas Graeser *The Stoic Theory of Meaning* in John M. Rist, ed. *The Stoics* (Berkeley: University of California Press, 1978), chap. 3, pp. 77-100.

The conditions indicated by Cicero and Seneca are orderliness, propriety, consistency, and harmony. To know what all of these are is to know what is good. The "good" is prior in value to anything else, but with respect to any individual, it is posterior in time to other valuable things, because a man can recognize "the good" after he has learned to select natural advantages and to reject their opposites in a regular and systematic pattern of action.

Natural advantages include all those states of affairs which, though not constituents of virtue, are objectively (or naturally) preferable to their opposites. They are intermediate goods, but it is not necessary to be a good man to aim at these things. On the contrary, the good man was aiming at them before he became good and all men do so to a lesser or greater degree. It is not a special mark of a good man to select natural advantages, but to do so in a certain way and on the basis of certain principles.[182] Natural advantages are neither good or bad in the final analysis.

Appropriate action considered independently of the character of its agent must be judged as "intermediate." But in terms of the agent's character, every action, whether appropriate or not is either "perfect" or "faulty." The "faultiness" of an appropriate act may have nothing to do with its external object (not that it fails to secure the object aimed at, it does not have to achieve it—it is sufficient in certain circumstances to have tried), only inappropriate acts are faulty in this respect. An appropriate act performed by someone who is not a sage lacks the fundamental characteristic of fitting into a pattern of actions all of which are completely harmonized with each other.

Of a man who advanced so that he only just falls short of perfect wisdom Chrysippus wrote:

He fulfills all appropriate actions in all respects and omits none; but his life is not yet in a state of well-being. This supervenes when these 'intermediate' actions acquire the additional property of firmness, consistency and their own proper co-ordination.[183]

---

182   SVF III.516.
183   SVF III.510.

But most performers of appropriate acts will by no means fulfill all of them. Chrysippus' man is classified a sage with respect to what he does, still with respect to character he is judged as "foolish." (Precepts can lead to right actions if a man's character is compliant—they may tell one what but they do not tell how to live virtuously).[184]

There are no degrees of goodness, though there are degrees of coming closer towards it. Until a man is good, he is bad according to the Stoics.[185] A minute element of disharmony is sufficient to disqualify him. This is a hard demand and there is a big gap between theory and the practical achievement admitted by Chrysippus:

> Wherefore on account of their extreme magnitude and beauty we seem to be stating things which are like fictions and not in accordance with man and human nature.[186]

Stoic ethics are based on striving to achieve an ideal. The sage is not somebody who could be found in everyday life. He is an embodiment of perfection which mirrors the perfection of Nature. Judged by the standard of the sage we are all foolish or bad but through an effort and education the theory is that we can progress to a condition that approximates this perfection.

As a consequence of their concept of the sage the Stoics developed a radical political theory. In Zeno's *Republic* the fundamental Greek social and economic institutions are abolished. In the ideal world the state withers away because each Stoic sage is self-sufficient on his own authority, united with other men by the bond of true friendship.[187]

Philosophical Determinism

The interconnection between all the events and the things in the universe constitutes its determinism, i.e. the sequence between the causes and the effects. The Stoics believed that the universe operates in an orderly fashion and is intelligible, which means that if we knew all the preceding causes we would be able to predict future events. The ordered interweaving of causes and events the Stoics termed

---

184 Sénèque *Lettres, op. cit., Ep.* 95.
185 SVF III.657-670.
186 SVF III.545.
187 SVF III.517, 625.

"fate" (*heimarmenē*).[188] Their concept of cause (*aitía*) was different from the Aristotelian one, the novelty consisting in the introduction of a regularity, a law between cause and effect. Zeno identified this regularity with providence as corporeal intelligence (*logos*) in the cosmic fire (*pur technēkon* or *pur noetikon*) located within the world and governing it. This theory reflected the theology of the soul of the universe developed by Plato. The soul appeared to be ordering and performing a providential function in the universe.[189] The major difference from Plato's scheme was that in Zeno's system the order was to be periodically destroyed and renewed according to a cyclic rhythm. Chance (*tēchē*) was, for the Stoics, another word for a situation where the causes are not clearly visible, known or differentiated.[190]

Among causes the Stoics differentiated between two sets: external causes attributed to the working of fate and internal causes related to the particular nature and linked to necessity (*anankē*).[191] And determinism was the effect brought about jointly by these two types of causes:

> For, they say since the nature of things and events are various and different ... what happens by the agency of any particular thing happens in accordance with its own specific nature. The behavior of a stone is in accordance with the nature of a stone, that of fire with the nature of fire, that of a living thing with the nature of the living thing. None of things that happen by the agency of a particular thing according to its nature can happen otherwise, but they all happen by necessity, though not from compulsion, since it is impossible for something whose nature it is to behave in one way, given that certain circumstances are invariant, to behave differently on some other occasion. If a stone is released from a height, it cannot fail to fall, because it contains weight in itself which is the cause of its natural movement. And when there are also external causes present which contribute to the stone's natural movement, stone by necessity is moved according to its nature ... The same principle applies also to other things. What holds for inanimate things also holds for living things,

---

188   SVF 2. 912, 915-917, 937, 943, 945, 975-976.
189   Plato *Laws*, X. 896d-897c.
190   SVF 2. 965, 966, 970, 973.
191   SVF 2.979, 974.

as they say. For living things possess a natural movement, and this is a movement in accordance with impulse (*hormē*).[192]

A more detailed description of the forces operating in the living creature was given by Origen:

> For sentient creatures are moved from themselves when a presentation (*fantasía*) arises in them and calls forth impulse; moreover in some living creatures this occurs when the presentational nature of the creature prompts the impulse according to a fixed pattern, as in a spider the presentation of spinning occurs and the impulse follows until spinning results—its presentational nature calls forth this behavior in a prescribed manner and nothing else beyond the presentational nature is believed to belong to the animal—and in the bee the same process results in the making of wax. The rational animal, however, in addition to a presentational nature, has reason that judges (*krinō*) the presentation, rejecting some and accepting others, in order that the animal may be guided in accordance with them.[193]

These two examples illustrate how fate and necessity operate in Nature. Behavior thus operates and is determined by two sorts of causal laws—the external causes operating jointly with the intrinsic causes on the body fixed by its nature. Sentient creatures operate driven by impulse which is generated from sensory presentation. In some animals the transition is automatic, but in humans the impulse will be produced in a controlled manner due to the operation of the judging power—the reason (*logos*). Man is the only creature endowed with the capacity to understand cosmic events and to promote the rationality of Nature. He also is the only being that has the capacity to act in a manner that fails to accord with the operation of Nature (call it a Kantian freedom) and as such he is a moral agent. Man, as tools for his actions, has "impulses to virtue' or "seeds of knowledge" and this is sufficient to direct reason to the right direction.[194]

---

192   SVF 2.979.
193   SVF 2.988. Origen, *De principiis*, (*On the First Principles*), translated with introduction and notes by G. W. Butterworth, (Gloucester, Mass.: Peter Smith, 1973). III, 1, 2, 3.
194   SVF 1.566.

5. Moral Responsibility

Since the Stoics considered the laws governing all things including human beings, to be universal, one may question therefore the responsibility of humans for what they do. If all things are directed by fate, and the course of fate cannot be changed, then the faults of men too ought to be considered a result of an unavoidable impulse that comes from fate. Thus, to many the Stoic determinism may seem to be incompatible with the practice of holding people accountable for their actions. The Stoics, however, did not compromise their stance on determinism in Nature and sought to show that it did not rule out moral responsibility for human conduct. They responded to the criticism and justified the use of moral and judicial concepts of praise, blame, responsibility and punishment.

The key element in the answer of the Stoics to their opponents was the assertion that reason sets humans apart from all other animals, and encompasses faculties which we call mental activities, such as judging, deciding, choosing, etc. Reason is subject to the inviolable laws that govern the rest of Nature and whatever happens is governed by the laws of nature and given prevailing conditions.

Aristotle developed the concept of things which are "in our power" and which are "not in our power." The Stoics altered the sense of these two expressions into things which "are or are not attributable to us" and adapted it to their concepts of human nature and action:

> If, they say, those things are attributable to us the opposites of which we are also capable, and in such cases praise and blame, encouragement and discouragement, rewards and punishments are given, then wisdom and virtue (*aretē*) cannot be attributable to those who have them, because they are no longer capable of receiving the vices (*kakíai*) opposed to their virtues; similarly, neither can vices be attributable to those who are vicious, since it is not attributable to them not (any longer) to be vicious. But it is absurd to deny that virtue and vice are attributable to us or that praise and blame

are given for these. Therefore 'that which is attributable to us' does not have the same meaning.[195]

This argument follows from the assertion that virtues and vices, virtuous action and vicious actions are among the things that are attributable to humans and the detachment of this concept from the notion of capability or power. Virtues and vices are the mutually exclusive traits of character which determine conduct.

But, the formulation is not clear and Charlotte Stough,[196] in her article, suggested three ways of interpretation of the assertion that the virtuous cannot be vicious and vice versa: 1. this "cannot" has a logical meaning—the virtuous cannot act viciously inasmuch as they are virtuous; 2. it is a moral "cannot" since those who are virtuous cannot, because their moral character will not permit it, act viciously and vice versa; 3. it is a natural "cannot" since those who are virtuous cannot become vicious and vice versa. The second interpretation becomes relevant for the Stoic assertion because that impossibility of the opposite action rests here on the moral ground of choice—certainly the virtuous can violate his moral principles if he chooses to do so, but he does not want to act unjustly thereby violating his moral principle. For a vicious person, the impossibility of action out of character does not mean that he is prohibited from virtuous action, but there is a certain sense of commitment to his goals. He could do so if he chose, but he does not want to perform actions which are deemed just. Thus, the possibility of a certain action is conditioned by the choice, the desires of a moral agent. And the denial of the opposite action is associated with some kind of stable or relatively permanent disposition to act in a specific way.

Stoics identified the moral dispositions of the human soul with its physical states and considered them to be relatively constant.[197] But they could undergo change to the opposite state, thus inducing change in moral behavior. The morally relevant disposition that was not identical with virtue was termed vice and included also the state in which a vicious person wanted to improve his moral character.[198]

---

195 SVF 2.984.
196 Charlotte Stough, *Stoic Determinism and Moral Responsibility*. In *The Stoics* John M. Rist, ed. (Berkeley: University of California Press, 1978). pp. 203-232.
197 SVF 2.786, 806.
198 SVF 3.237, 238, 459, 560.

Virtue and vice were considered, by the Stoics, acquired dispositions of the soul.[199] They are not innate and they are not determined exclusively by inherited nature. The innate potential develops into moral character which is shaped by training or neglect, and by corrupting influences. The Stoics pointed to the experience that the same bad men can become good, as evidence that virtue can be taught and moral progress made. The moral disposition can be also temporarily lost e.g. through melancholy or drunkenness.[200]

It would seem that this view, that virtue and vice are not permanently fixed traits, does not fit well with Stoic determinism. But since the actions are determined by external and internal causes, moral improvement is not ruled out, even in this deterministic world of the Stoics.

Thus the first interpretation denies that a person can do what is logically impossible. The second that a person can or is willing to do what is incompatible with his moral principles or with his aims or purposes in acting. The third interpretation would have been rejected by the Stoics, because the individual would be totally helpless in his moral character inherited by his particular and fixed nature. He would be denied the capacity to act as a moral agent in accordance with choice.

However, the first two interpretations would deny that a person could be held accountable for his actions and the term "things attributable to us" could not mean "those things the opposite of which we are capable," because the virtuous are not capable logically or morally of being vicious or vice versa. But, at the same time, virtue and vice are the things attributable to us and the moral agent is capable of opposite behavior if he chooses so.

The Stoics thus considered human beings as moral free agents and contrasted them with the Nature's inanimate and animate (plants and animals) beings. The "thing which is attributable to us" is restricted by human intelligence and is defined as "ability to act by impulse (*hormē*) and assent (*sunkatathesis*)."[201] The assent consists of such typically human faculties as formation of opinions, judgment, evaluation and

---

199 SVF 3.223, 237, 224, 225, 238.
200 SVF 3.228.
201 SVF 3.169. 175, 178.

learning (*pasa oun doxa kai krisis kai hupolepsis kai mathēsis*).[202] Thus, human action remains in contrast to events that just happen in nature with a regular consequence to causes, as prescribed (*tetagmos*) by fate. Humans, therefore, from the very nature of "things attributable to us" are responsible for their actions and things they do. But we cannot be held responsible for the things that befall us.[203]

Chrysippus distinguishes two types of causes in order to avoid the imputation of necessity to fated events. All events in nature including human actions are fated but not necessitated by antecedent causes. These antecedent causes are auxiliary and proximate causes e.g. sensory stimuli are auxiliary and proximate causes. Though they are not in our power and not attributable to us, it does not follow that the impulse to action that results is not attributable to us. It would be so if the antecedent causes were "perfect and principal causes." This he asserted to undercut the undesirable consequence of the necessity of fate. Antecedent causes are linked to external causes and are both auxiliary and proximate causes. The perfect and principal causes correspond to internal causes, linked to the nature of the entities in question.[204]

Chrysippus believed that the doctrine of the necessity of fated events had disastrous implications for human actions. He thought that a) if all events were determined by antecedent causes that were perfect and principal, human behavior would be necessitated by antecedent causes, and b) if human behavior were necessitated by antecedent causes, there would be no such thing as autonomous human action.

The distinction thus made by Chrysippus refutes the argument incorporating simplistic assumptions about things attributable to us. If the cause of a certain event is not attributable to us then the effect is not attributable to us. Chrysippus thus repudiates the argument with his distinction between "auxiliary and proximate causes" and "perfect and principal causes" to stop the inference.

This distinction is quite important: if auxiliary causes are necessary causes but not sufficient conditions of behavior and if they are equal to antecedent causes then the latter must be also necessary conditions

---

202   SVF 2.992.
203   SVF 2.984, 974, 994, 997.
204   SVF 2.979.

for behavior. But the antecedent causes will not detract from the status of behavior as action, the type of natural event that is properly "attributable to us" as agents. This is so because the antecedent causes which are external causes of behavior are not the type of things that could be "attributable to us;" they are not a part of human nature nor do they belong to the sphere of things we do.

Auxiliary causes which are internal causes will also fall outside the domain of things we do. From the fact that the external causes of human behavior are not in the category of things attributable to us, given the fact that they are merely necessary conditions of behavior, we can draw no conclusion about the effect of these causes in particular, whether or not certain kinds of behavior can be attributable to us. On the other hand, if the antecedent causes were not only necessary, but also sufficient conditions of human behavior, such behavior could not, in principle, be attributable to mental acts, such as intentions, decisions, choices and the like, the terms that would fall under the Stoic definition of assent. Human behavior determined by external antecedent causes both necessary and sufficient could not be considered as "ours" at all.

So, on the secondary assumption that principal causes are to be understood as sufficient (or more likely necessary and sufficient) conditions of human behavior, Chrysippus would be justified in concluding that if the antecedent conditions determining such things as the impulse to behavior in human beings were "perfect and principal causes" there would be no such thing as human autonomy. Chrysippus' distinction between types of causes thus undermines the damaging application to human actions of the doctrine of the necessity of fated events.

Cicero[205] explained the mechanism of the formation of assent in Stoic theory.[206] External sensory stimulus causes an internal presentation in the agent. The sensory presentations, however, according to the Stoic doctrine are not "attributable to us," i.e. they are not of human nature. They are merely necessary events or happenings internal to the agent.

---

205 Cicero, *De fato*, 39. In *On the Orator: Book 3. On Fate. Stoic Paradoxes. On the Divisions of Oratory: A. Rhetorical Treatises* (Loeb Classical Library No. 349). Translated by H. Rackham (Cambridge, MA: Hravrd University Press, 1942).
206 SVF 2.974, 1000.

Events that are attributable to human beings are not an automatic consequence of sensory presentations! To issue an impulse sensory presentations require the assent of the person experiencing them. Chrysippus maintains that although assent cannot occur unless it is stimulated by a presentation, the sensory stimulus is an auxiliary not a principal cause.

If it is correct to distinguish between an external sensory stimulus and an internal presentation of sense, then the latter is an internal auxiliary cause. If, like other antecedent causes, they were not only necessary but also sufficient to explain human behavior, such behavior could not be considered action. "In the same way therefore, he says, as a person who has pushed a cylinder forward has given it a beginning of motion, but has not given it the capacity to roll, so a sense presentation when it impinges will it is the impress and as it were seal, its appearance on the mind, but the act of assent will be in our power (*in nostra potestate*), and as we said in the case of the cylinder, though given a push from without, as to the rest will move by its own force and nature."

Thus, human behavior, like the motion of a cylinder, requires a stimulus without which it cannot take place, and Chrysippus located this antecedent cause in sensory presentations. But the behavior of human beings, like the motion of the cylinder, cannot be understood without looking beyond (external) antecedent causes to the respective "natures" of those things.

Human nature, unlike that of a cylinder or anything else in nature, is characterized by the faculty of intelligent assent, (the faculty of reason, *logos* distinguishes the assent and behavior of human beings from that of other animals),[207] so that the impulse to behavior that issues from assent in a human being will not be quite like that of any other part of Nature. It will be an impulse to behave that is distinctively human, the action by assent. Chrysippus believed that the act of assent is "attributable to us," i.e. it is in human nature. We may say that the faculty of assent gives human beings the capacity to act, as opposed to the capacity merely to move or perhaps to be moved as in the case of the cylinder. Intelligent assent therefore is a necessary feature of an action and distinguishes it from an event or happening. What a person

---

207   SVF 2.988, 992, 3.377, 3.175.

does will depend on which presentations he assents to, and the assent given to sensory presentations will be a function of his own individual "nature," his own personality and character. A human agent, by virtue of giving his assent, makes the event that follows *his* action. In this case the talk about cause and action is not particularly illuminating in the context of moral discourse where it is often important to establish responsibility for actions. Thus responsibility is a realm typically human and pertains to human actions only.

To say that virtue and vice are attributable to us as persons is to say, in effect, that certain events in Nature are properly regarded as our actions and to that extent they are events that fall into the domain of moral discourse—events for which we as agents may be held responsible. To determine responsibility we must look for an agent or doer, and that is not the same as looking for the customary causal explanation. There may be many causes of an occurrence, but if that occurrence is an action, none of these causal explanations can cancel the fact that it is the action of some person or persons. Clement of Alexandria[208] described it in similar way.[209] He says that many factors may combine to bring about a certain result, and although the end occurs because (*dia*) of all of them, not all are responsible for (*aitía*) what results. To be the *aitía*, the event of which something occurs must also be *poiethikon*, that is, productive of it. The notion of a cause as *poiethikon* comes very close to what we, in the case of persons, call an agent. Clement illustrated it with the case of Medea: Medea would not have killed her children if she had not been angry; she would not have been jealous had she not been in love; she would not have been in love if Jason had not sailed to Colchis, and so forth ... The end result of this chain, namely the slaughter of her children can be said to have occurred because of all these events but only Medea is *aitía*. The multiple reasons for the slaughter of Medea's children do not constitute competing explanations because they are not commensurate—they are different explanations answering different questions. We may ask: 1. Why did the event happen? 2. Who did it? (Whose action was it?) Only if there is an answer to question 2 we are likely to be dealing with an event that falls into the category of things attributable to us. The answer does not imply that the person in question may in fact be accountable but

208   Clement of Alexandria (Stromat. , VIII, 9, 27).
209   SVF 2.347.

merely that questions of responsibility may be legitimately raised. The category of things "attributable to us" does not establish responsibility but rather distinguishes a domain of events within which moral responsibility is possible. The Stoic view of human nature and action is further elaborated by Origen.[210, 211] His point is a focus on capacity for movement of things in Nature. The Stoics differentiated human beings from all other natural things by a particular kind of movement unique to them. What distinguished those things from others that are moved from without is that they have a certain kind of cause (*aitía*) of motion in themselves.

Things like plants and animals have internal cause of motion, "nature" and "soul"; inanimate objects must have an external agency to be moved along, they move by thrust of external force (*hupo exethen kinountos*). Plants and animals by virtue of having soul (and nature) are capable of self-movement. Origen adds that the Stoics also included in this group certain inanimate things—such as metals, fire, and perhaps streams which were held to move "out of themselves" (*hupo tinos metatithemena*), but these things are nevertheless contrasted with living things which move "from themselves" (*hupo tēs enupargchouses fuseos psuchēs kinoumena*). In the case of animals sensory stimulation is a necessary condition of the impulse to self-movement. Those lacking intelligence move according to a prescribed pattern (*tetagmenos*). Human beings do not move in a set fashion— because the faculty of reason (*logos*) enables them to judge (*krinō*) their sensory presentations— to reject or accept and to be guided. Origen calls this third kind of movement, self-movement of which only rational animals are capable, motion "through themselves" (*di'autou kineisthai*).[212] Origen's account of the difference in motion (between humans and other animals) gives rise to morality.

He says "our nature as human beings furnishes the souls for considering the noble and the base and for judging between them. Even though we have no control over the fact that something external causes in us a presentation of this or that sort—the decision (*krisis*) to

---

210 Origen, *De princ.* III, 1,2,3.
211 SVF 2.988.
212 SVF 2.989, 879.

use this occurrence in one way or another is the function of nothing other than the reason within us."[213]

We are deserving of praise when we choose the noble and avoid the base, but when we follow the opposite course we are blameworthy. Origen reasons: It is neither true nor reasonable to lay the blame on external things and release ourselves from the accusation making ourselves analogous to wood and stones inasmuch as they are drawn along by external things that move them; such is the argument of someone who wants to set up a counterfeit notion of autonomy (*autexousion*). For if we should ask him what autonomy is, he would say that it obtains "if there are no external causes, when I intend to do something in particular, that incite to the contrary."[214] The Stoics believed that human beings are capable of self-movement without actually initiating their own motion. The beginning of motion of external objects, and self-movement, consists in the response of a sentient creature to those external causes. Moreover, it is clear that the faculty of reason, which informs assent to sensory presentation, makes the self-movement of human beings different in kind from that of any other living being.

That difference is crucial to the Stoic position and can be captured by contrasting the notion of action with mere movement. Applying the distinction between motion (event) and actions to the Origen text, we may understand him to say that it is the faculty of intelligent (*logikos*) assent that gives persons the capacity to act (autonomously) rather than merely move, or be moved, as wood and stones are moved. The *logos* qualifies the self-movement of human beings as action.

For the Stoics it is the *logos* that defines the notion of autonomous action and which (unlike the idea of cause) has logical ties to the concept of responsibility. There will be many forms of movement behavior in living things which, in the Stoic view, will not qualify as action and for which the question of moral responsibility will not therefore arise. It is an appropriate matter of concern only within the domain of behavior of living things capable of giving rational assent. And it is worth noting that not even all human behavior must count as action, according to the

---

213   Cf. SVF 2.992.
214   SVF 2,990.

Stoic account. "A person can be moved against his will if he is pushed, for example, and he can move involuntarily if he falls, but he cannot act, cannot run without giving his intelligent assent. To misplace the responsibility for human actions on external events is to make ourselves analogous to wood and stones." It is a misconception of human nature to model it as an inanimate object, which is capable of nothing more than being moved. A similar argument against those who would deny that anything is attributable to us is also recorded by Origen.[215] Anyone who claims that nothing is attributable to us is foolishly committed to the view that we are neither animals nor rational. The famous dog simile[216] attributed to Zeno and Chrysippus, already mentioned illustrated the Stoic view of the relation between human action and fate. This example incorporates the Stoic view of human action and mental events attributable to us into the deterministic framework of their philosophy.

The special realm of human action is located by the Stoics within an all-encompassing Nature governed by causal laws. There is therefore an important sense in which our actions, the things we can do, are limited by Nature. We cannot change the laws of Nature including those of our own human nature (e.g. we cannot take actions to alter the course of the seasons). No sane person would attempt to accomplish the impossible. The madman, though he is "unwilling to follow," will be "compelled" by Nature in any case. But other limitations on what we can do are not so easy to discern. There are many actions that we can undertake which are nevertheless regulated by our own individual natures, and it is in this region that the above quotation is especially relevant. For human beings can set out to do things that are impossible in fact for them to achieve, given their individual temperaments, talents, and capabilities.

These sorts of limitations, though rarely plain to the understanding, were no less binding for the Stoics.[217] So by our self ignorance, we may show ourselves "unwilling to follow" and end by being "compelled" by the boundaries of our own natural capacities. The dog simile does not imply that our actions, whether undertaken out of wisdom or ignorance

---

215   SVF 2.989.
216   SVF 2.975.
217   DL. VII.89.

of Nature and the consequent success or failure of these undertakings, are not attributable to us.

The effort to bring ourselves into harmony with Nature, as well as the effort to resist, will result from mental acts that are attributable to us and so will qualify as actions for which we as agents may be held responsible.

Far from doing violence to such mental acts as choosing, deciding, deliberating and the like, the Stoic dog's simile actually reinforces the importance of these acts in determining responsibility. Nevertheless, any attempt to exceed the limitations that Nature has imposed on us, though preeminently our own and for which we are in principle responsible, will be defended by the necessities of nature compelling us, in spite of ourselves, to yield to its power.

The same subtle relation between fate and human responsibility is implicit in the hymn to Zeus of Cleanthes quoted already.[218]

The supreme importance that the Stoics placed on *logos* and the understanding of Nature can be most fully appreciated in this context. Understanding frees us from the compulsion of Nature. The person who understands the laws of external Nature as well as those of his own inner self will be able to approximate more closely the ideal human condition that the Stoics called freedom (*eleuthería*) and contrasted with slavery.

It is essential to recognize that although the concept of freedom is of singular importance in Stoic moral philosophy, it cannot be equated with their theory of responsibility. Both the ethical ideal of freedom as well as its opposed state of enslavement presuppose the concept of autonomous action. The Stoic ideal of freedom is often confused with the quite different concept of "freedom of the will." The early Stoics did not conflate the notion of what is attributable to us with that of freedom, but this distinction does become blurred later in the writings of Epictetus.[219]

---

218   SVF 1.527.
219   Epictetus *Enchiridion* Translated by George Long (Amherst NY: Prometheus Books, 1991) 1.

The man who is ignorant, and thus a slave to Nature and his passions, is no less an agent, a doer of actions, than the enlightened sage who is free. That part of our behavior that is "attributable to us" as persons, whether undertaken in a state of freedom or slavery, is just that part for which we are morally responsible.

The Stoics' claim that a person acts in accordance with his character is equally as bold as is their account of character formation. The kind of person he is or will be is a product of both his own individual nature, which is inherited, and the environment external to him—including the persons he encounters and with whom he associates, especially in early years.[220] These conditions are not in the sort of things to be within the range of choices that any individual can make. Human behavior is causally linked to many factors over which we as persons have little or no control.[221] Many critics followed Aristotle's assertion[222] claiming that if we are not responsible for the formation of our character we cannot justifiably be held responsible for actions determined by our character.

The Stoic account of human action and responsibility which differs markedly from the Aristotelian view, undermined this inference which considers a person's character as if it were a causal determinant in behavior, distinct from the person himself and operating independently of his purposes, wants, and desires.

Such a picture conjures up the image of an individual as prisoner of his character, itself fashioned independently of himself and his wishes by external forces to which he has fallen victim. There is nothing in the Stoic doctrine that would warrant such an extreme picture. What, then, can be made of the view, apparently held by the Stoics, that a person is responsible for his actions, but not for his character?

Character in their account is shaped by inherited nature and environment and not by choice, with the implication presumably that human beings cannot be held accountable for that to which they have not given their assent.

---

220 SVF 2.937, 951; 3.225.
221 Causes of wrong doing in painful childhood and corrupting environment SVF 3.228, 229.
222 Aristotle *Ethica Nicomachea* in Aristotle *The Basic Works*. Edited and with an introduction by Richard McKeon (New York: Random House, thirty fourth printing, originally published in 1941), chapt. III.

The position that we are responsible for what we do, and not for what we are, can be made intelligible on the supposition that character is something over and above the things an individual actually does—the actions he actually performs—perhaps a set of dispositions to behave in such and such ways conceived independently of the actions he does in fact perform on any given occasion. Such a position is compatible with Stoic materialism, according to which mental dispositions are identical with physical states of the human soul.

Given that view of character, it might be argued that even though a dishonest person (for example) is surely blameworthy, it is for his dishonest dealings that we blame him and not because he has become a person of the sort to be inclined to act in those ways. For that he may very well be disliked, disapproved of, shunned, and perhaps even pitied, but not held accountable or blamed.

The common practice of holding persons accountable only for their actions is not, on the face of it, unreasonable even in the Stoic view of character formation. It clearly does not follow, from the proposition that a person is not responsible for his character in the above (Stoic) sense, that he cannot legitimately be held responsible for his actions.

Conclusion and Impact of the Stoic Ethical Theory

Among philosophers who were affected most, one has to mention Immanuel Kant. His "categorical imperative," as something "conceived as good in itself and consequently as being necessarily the principle of a will which of itself is confirmed to reason"[223] corresponds to the Stoic "right reason."

The relation between the Stoics' subjective content of a moral action and the Kantian objective necessity or universal law is obvious. But for Kant, welfare or happiness is not a constituent of moral goodness, whereas Stoic virtue constitutes something which is in the interests of man *par excellence.*

Another philosopher who was affected by the Stoics is Baruch Spinoza. His proposition is more deterministic than that of the Stoics: "in the nature of things nothing contingent is granted but all things are

---

223 Kant *Ethics op. cit.,* 38.

determined by the necessity of divine nature for existing and working in a certain way."[224] Or "All ideas, in so far as they have reference to God [or nature] are true."[225] But Spinoza renounced the conventional meanings of virtue.

---

224 Spinoza *Ethics op. cit.*, pt I. XXIX.
225 Spinoza *Ethics op. cit.*, pt II. XXXII.

THE ETHICS OF PHILO OF ALEXANDRIA (20 B.C.E.-50 C.E.)[226]

Introduction

Philo of Alexandria (20 B.C.E.-50 C.E.), a Hellenized Jew, is a figure who spans two cultures, the Greek and the Hebrew. When Hebrew mythical thought met Greek philosophical thought in the first century B.C.E. it was only natural that someone would try to develop speculative and philosophical justification for Judaism in terms of Greek philosophy. Thus Philo produced a synthesis of both traditions developing concepts for future Hellenistic interpretation of messianic Hebrew thought, especially by Clement of Alexandria, Christian Apologists like Athenagoras, Theophilus, Justin Martyr, Tertullian, and by Origen. He may have influenced Paul, his contemporary, and perhaps the authors of the *Gospel of John* (C. H. Dodd) and the *Epistle to the Hebrews* (R. Williamson and H. W. Attridge and H. Koester).[227] In the process, he laid the foundations for the development of Christianity in the West and in the East, as we know it today.

Philo's primary importance is in the development of the philosophical and theological foundations of Christianity. The church preserved the Philonic writings because Eusebius of Caesarea[228] labeled the monastic ascetic group of Therapeutae and Therapeutrides, described in Philo's *The Contemplative Life,* as Christians, which is highly unlikely.[229] Eusebius also promoted the legend that Philo met Peter in Rome.

---

226 Part of an article published in Internet Encyclopedia of Philosophy: *Philo of Alexandria*.

227 C. H. Dodd, *The Interpretation of the Fourth Gospel* (Cambridge: Cambridge University Press, 1953). Ronald Williamson, *Philo and the Epistle to the Hebrews* (Leiden: E. J. Brill, 1970). Harold W. Attridge, Helmut Kester, Hebrews: *A Commentary on the Epistle to the Hebrews (Hermeneia: A Critical and Historical Commentary on the Bible)* (Augsburg Fortress Publishers, 1989).

228 Eusebius, *The History of the Church from Christ to Constantine.* Translated with introduction by G.A. Williamson (Harmondsworth: Penguin Books, 1984). 2.17.1.

229 The view that the Therapeutae were Christians survived until the Middle ages when the Protestants began to consider them to be Jews. Today opinions are divided, but all the evidence indicates that they were remnants of the Buddhist tradition (Theravadins) introduced by the missionaries sent by King Asoka in the third century B.C.E. to King Ptolemy II Philadelphos. (Elmar R. Gruber and Holger Kersten, *The Original Jesus. The Buddhist Sources of Christianity,* Shaftesbury: Elements, 1995, 176-186; Z. P. Thundy, *Buddha and Christ,* Leiden: E. J. Brill , 1993.) The name Therapeutae is of Buddhist origin. It is the Hellenized form of the Sanskrit/Pali term Theravadins who were members of the Buddhist missionary order Theravada (= Teachings of the Old Ones) founded during the reign of King Asoka (274-232 BCE) with the main center at Gandhara. The members of this order called themselves Theraputta ("Sons of the Old Ones"). They were also, according to Asoka's edict preserved on a rock inscription, to provide medical assistance which was a common occupation of the Buddhist monks (Buddha was

Jerome (345-420 C.E.) even lists him as a church Father.[230] Jewish tradition was uninterested in philosophical speculation and did not preserve Philo's thought. According to H. A. Wolfson,[231] Philo was a founder of religious philosophy, a new habit of practicing philosophy.

Philo was thoroughly educated in Greek philosophy and culture as can be seen from his superb knowledge of classical Greek literature. He had a deep reverence for Plato and referred to him as "the most holy Plato" (*Prob.* 13). Philo's philosophy represented contemporary Platonism which was its revised version incorporating Stoic doctrine and terminology via Antiochus of Ascalon (ca 90 B.C.E.) and Eudorus of Alexandria, as well as elements of Aristotelian logic and ethics and Pythagorean ideas. Clement of Alexandria even called Philo "the Pythagorean."[232] But it seems that Philo also picked up his ancestral tradition, though as an adult, and once having discovered it, he put forward the teachings of the Jewish prophet, Moses, as "the summit of philosophy" (*Op.* 8), and considered Moses the teacher of Pythagoras (b. ca 570 B.C.E.) and of all Greek philosophers and lawgivers (Hesiod, Heraclitus, Lycurgus, to mention a few). For Philo, Greek philosophy was a natural development of the revelatory teachings of Moses. He was no innovator in this matter because already before him Jewish scholars attempted the same. Artapanus in the second century B.C.E identified Moses with Musaeus and with Orpheus. According to Aristobulus of Paneas (first half of the second century B.C.E.), Homer and Hesiod drew from the books of Moses which were translated into Greek long before the Septuagint.[233]

Life

Very little is known about the life of Philo. He lived in Alexandria, which at that time counted, according to some estimates, about one million people and included largest Jewish community outside of Palestine. He came from a wealthy and the prominent family and

---

also extolled as the King of Medicine). Thus Philo linked the name of the sect with two Greek terms, therapeuo = I cure, I heal; I do service, and therapeia = service; medical attendance; worship, as "healers of souls." He also calls them "suppliants" and "beggars" which terms are connected with the Sanskrit name of the monks "bhikshu" (beggars).

230 Jerome Eusebius Hieronymus Stridensis Presbyter, *De viris illustribus* Ch. 11 in Migne PL Vol. XXIII.
231 H. A. Wolfson, *Philo* (Cambridge, Mass: Harvard University Press, 1947), Vols. 1-2.
232 Clement of Alexandria, *Stromateis*, I.15.
233 Eusebius, *Praeparatio evangelica*, 9.27; 13.11.

appears to be a leader in his community. Once he visited Jerusalem and the temple, as he himself stated in *Prov.* 2.64.

Philo's brother, Alexander, was a wealthy, prominent Roman government official, and a custom agent responsible for collecting dues on all goods imported into Egypt from the East. He donated money to plate the gates of the temple in Jerusalem with gold and silver. He also made a loan to Herod Agrippa I, grandson of Herod the Great. [234] Alexander's two sons, Marcus and Tiberius Julius Alexander were involved in Roman affairs. Marcus married Bernice,[235] the daughter of Herod Agrippa I, who is mentioned in Acts (25:13, 23; 26:30). The other son, Tiberius Julius Alexander, described by Josephus as "not remaining true to his ancestral practices" became procurator of the province of Judea (46-48 C.E.) and prefect of Egypt (66-70 C.E.).

Philo was involved in the affairs of his community which interrupted his contemplative life (*Spec. leg.* 3.1-6), especially during the crisis relating to the pogrom which was initiated in 38 C.E. by the prefect Flaccus, during the reign of emperor Gaius Caligula. He was elected to head the Jewish delegation, which apparently included his brother Alexander and nephew Tiberius Julius Alexander, and was sent to Rome in 39-40 B.C.E. to see the emperor. He reported the events in his writings *Against Flaccus* and *The Embassy to Gaius*.

Emphasis on the Contemplative Life and Philosophy

The key emphasis in Philo's philosophy is contrasting the spiritual life, understood as intellectual contemplation, with the mundane preoccupation with earthly concerns, either as an active life or as a search for pleasure. Philo disdained the material world and physical body (*Spec. leg.* 3.1-6). The body was for Philo as for Plato,[236] "an evil and a dead thing" (*LA* 3.72-74; *Gig.* 15), wicked by nature and a plotter against the soul (*LA* 3.69). But it was a necessary evil, hence Philo does not advocate a complete abnegation from life. On the contrary he advocates fulfilling first the practical obligations toward men and the use of mundane possessions for the accomplishment of praiseworthy works (*Fug.* 23-28; *Plant.* 167-168). Similarly he considers pleasure

---

234 Josephus, *Jewish Antiquities,* 18.159-160; *Jewish War* 5.205.
235 Josephus, *J. Antiq.* 19.276-277.
236 Plato, *Rep.* 585 B; *Timaeus* 86 B; *Soph.* 228.

indispensable and wealth useful, but for a virtuous man they are not a perfect good (*LA* 3.69-72).

He believed that men should steer themselves away from the physical aspect of things gradually. Some people, like philosophers, may succeed in focusing their minds on the eternal realities. Philo believed that man's final goal and ultimate bliss is in the "knowledge of the true and living God" (*Decal.* 81; *Abr.* 58; *Praem.* 14); "such knowledge is the boundary of happiness and blessedness" (*Det.* 86). To him, mystic vision allows our soul to see the Divine Logos (*Ebr.* 152) and achieve a union with God (Deut. 30:19-20; *Post.* 12). In a desire to validate the scripture as an inspired writing, he often compares it to prophetic ecstasy (*Her.* 69-70). His praise of the contemplative life of the monastic Therapeutae in Alexandria attests to his preference of *"bios theoreticos"* over *"bios practicos."* He adheres to the Platonic picture of the souls descending into the material realm and that only the souls of philosophers are able to come to the surface and return to their realm in heaven (*Gig.* 12-15). Philo adopted the Platonic concept of the soul with its tripartite division. The rational part of the soul, however, is breathed into man as a part of God's substance. Philo speaks figuratively "Now, when we are alive, we are so though our soul is dead and buried in our body, as if in a tomb. But if it were to die, then our soul would live according to its proper life being released from the evil and dead body to which it is bound" (*Op.* 67-69; *LA* 1.108).

Philosophy and Wisdom: a Path to Ethical Life

Philo differentiated between philosophy and wisdom.[237] To him philosophy is "the greatest good thing to men" (*Op.* 53-54), which they acquired because of a gift of reason from God (*Op.* 77). It is a devotion to wisdom, and a way to acquire the highest knowledge, "an attentive study of wisdom." Wisdom in turn is "the knowledge of all divine and human things, and of the respective causes of them" that is, according to Philo, contained in the Torah (*Congr.* 79). Hence it follows that Moses, as the author of the Torah, "had reached the very summit of philosophy" and "had learnt from the oracles of God the most numerous and important of the principles of nature" (*Op.* 8). Moses was also the interpreter of nature (*Her* 213). By saying this

---

237   Cicero, *Leg,* I.22; *SVF* II.36; Plutarch, *Epitome,* I.13.

Philo wanted to indicate that human wisdom has two origins: one is divine, the other is natural (*Her.* 182). Moreover, that Mosaic Law is not inconsistent with nature. A single law, the Logos of nature governs the entire world (*Jos,* 28-31) and its law is imprinted on the human mind (*Prob.* 46-47). Because of this we have a conscience that affects even wicked persons (*QG* 4.62).

Wisdom is a consummated philosophy and as such has to be in agreement with the principles of nature (*Mos.* 2.48; *Abr.* 16; *Op.* 143; *Spec. leg.* 2.13; 3.46-47, 112, 137; *Virt.* 18). The study of philosophy has as its end "life in accordance with nature" and following the "path of right reason" (*Mig.* 128). Philosophy prepares us to a moral life, i.e., "to live in conformity with nature" (*Prob.* 160). From this follows that life in accordance with nature hastens us towards virtues (*Mos.* 2. 181; *Abr.* 60, *Spec. leg.* 1.155), and an unjust man is the one "who transgresses the ordinances of nature" (*Spec. leg.* 4.204; Cf. *Decal.* 132; *Virt.* 131-132; *Plant.* 49; *Ebr.* 142; *Agr.* 66).

Thus Philo does not discount human reason, but contrasts only the true doctrine which is trust in God with uncertain, plausible, and unreliable reasoning (*LA* 3.228-229). Philo's ethical doctrine is Stoic in its essence and includes the active effort to achieve virtue, the model of a sage to be followed, and practical advice concerning the achievement of the proper right reason and a proper emotional state of rational emotions (*eupatheia*).

To Philo man is basically passive and it is God who sows noble qualities in the soul, thus we are instruments of God (*LA* 2.31-32; *Cher.* 127-128). Still man is the only creature endowed with freedom to act though his freedom is limited by the constitution of his mind. As such he is responsible for his action and "very properly receives blame for the offences which he designedly commits." This is so because he received a faculty of voluntary motion and is free from the dominion of necessity (*Deus* 47-48).

Philo advocates the practice of virtue in both the divine and the human spheres. Lovers only of God and lovers only of men are both incomplete in virtue. Philo advocates a middle harmonious way (Decal. 106-110; Spec.

leg. 4. 102). He differentiates four virtues: wisdom, self-control, courage, and justice (LA 1.63-64).

Human dispositions Philo divides into three groups – the best is given the vision of God, the next has a vision on the right i.e., the Beneficent or Creative Power whose name is God, and the third has a vision on the left, i.e., the Ruling Power called Lord (*Abr.* 119-130). Felicity is achieved in the culmination of three values: the spiritual, the corporeal, and the external (*QG* 3.16).

Philo adopts the Stoic wise man as a model for human behavior. Such a wise man should imitate God who was impassible (*apathes*) hence the sage should achieve a state of *apatheia*, i.e., he should be free of irrational emotions (passions), pleasure, desire, sorrow, and fear, and should replace them by rational or well-reasoned emotions (*eupatheia*), joy, will, compunction, and caution. In such a state of *eupatheia*, the sage achieves a serene, stable, and joyful disposition in which he is directed by reason in his decisions (*QG* 2.57; *Abr.* 201-204; *Fug.* 166-167; *Mig.* 67). But at the same time Philo claims that the needs of the body should not be neglected and rejects the other extreme, i.e., the practice of austerities. Everything should be governed by reason, self-control, and moderation. Joy and pleasure do not have intrinsic values, but are by-products of virtue and characterize the sage (*Fug.* 25-34; *Det.* 124-125; *LA* 80).

II. CHRISTIAN ETHICS

THE JUSTIFICATION OF MORALS
IN THE PHILOSOPHY OF THOMAS AQUINAS[238]

Thomas Aquinas[239] is considered by some a "rational" theologian *par excellence*. However, the term "rational" applied to Aquinas is misleading. More accurately, he rationalized and tried to give systematic explanations for the traditional religious assumptions of Christianity and of the institution - the Catholic Church. He tried to organize them in a legalistic system as a basis for an all-encompassing canon law. He was primarily a compiler and classifier of religious speculations, ideas, papal and ecclesiastical decrees. Thomas imitated the Greek philosopher Aristotle by interpreting him in light of the Neo-Platonic philosophy adopted by Christians. His system of philosophizing always takes as a point of departure the assumption of religious absolutes and then fits all aspects of human life and action into the mythological religious scheme common to many religions (the age of innocence, original sin, revelation, redemption, grace, second coming, salvation) by means of speculation. These religious absolutes, dogmas, are determined and imposed by the religious organization - the Catholic Church. Moreover, this organization claims a supernatural origin and its leader demands absolute obedience in all matters, including the intellectual processes of reasoning and inquiry, as a visible substitute for God on earth.

Metaphysics and Humanistic Philosophy

Aquinas represents a wide conception of the scope of philosophy. Philosophical reflection derives from a spontaneous tendency of the human mind to understand the data given by experience, to explain ourselves and the world in which we live, in the most complete possible way. Thus such an attempt leads to the exercise of the human mind we traditionally call philosophy and metaphysics. This desire requires an attempt to reach a unifying interpretation of reality as known to us, and to obtain a clarity about the general situation which makes all particular situations possible. This represents an imperative tendency of the human mind to reduce multiplicity to unity. It operates in all

---

238 Published in *and Humanism*, American Humanist Association, Houston, 1992, pp. 21-40.
239 The text of Aquinas's "Summa Theologiae" is that published in Latin-English version by Blackfriars in conjunction with McGraw-Hill Book Company, New York, and Eyre & Spottis-woode, London, 1963-1972.

intellectual endeavors. Aquinas as a metaphysician was concerned with the understanding of finite things and relating them to the meta-finite ultimate reality in which he believed. His finite view of nature itself was derived from the anthropocentric and analogous orientation. He, together with other medieval metaphysicians, believed that he was able to construct empirical hypotheses and attain final knowledge by means of metaphysical reflection[240].

The development of a particular science, however, has wrested from philosophy the field it regarded as its own. Cosmology is today part of physics, the philosophy of life is now scientific biology, and speculative psychology became scientific psychology. The sciences do not treat theological problems, or "ultimate" metaphysical questions, which are nothing but analogous anthropomorphic projections. Metaphysicians did not show that they have a method whereby these questions can be answered. They attempted to explain the world, but they do not have any recognizable way of verifying or testing their speculations.[241] We realize today that the only understanding of the world which we can attain is that provided by the sciences, interpreted in a very broad sense, as a factual, rational, and empirical approach to realities known to man. It does not mean that we should abandon an attempt at developing a unifying system of philosophy, a "new metaphysics". On the contrary, we observe in the modern world development of the Humanist philosophy, a new unifying system, a "new metaphysics" with wider generality than scientific constructs, which is, at least in some way, testable. Also, no appeal to the authority of the philosopher can be made. Thomas Aquinas himself considered such an argument the weakest.

Thomist Theory of Morals

Aquinas did not attempt to develop a moral philosophy outside Christian doctrines, since he considered that the knowledge of the purpose of human life, of the human supreme good, cannot be fully understood without revelation. To his credit it should be emphasized that he believed that such a system can exist and he had a great respect for Aristotle who epitomized this line of thought. His starting

---

240 F. C. Copleston "Aquinas", Harmondsworth: Penguin Books, 1961, p. 20.
241 Ibidem, p. 19.

point is the Aristotelian conception of happiness or moral well-being [*eudaimonia*][242] as the last end of human living.[243] He supplements this concept by the assumption of the religious doctrine, common to all mythological religions, of beatification in heaven: "If we speak of the ultimate end with respect to the thing itself, then human and all other beings share it together, for God is the ultimate end for all things without exception";[244] "There can be no complete and final happiness [*beatitudo*] for us save in the vision of God";[245]"the human mind's final perfection is by coming to union with God".[246] Obviously, Aquinas's artificial assumption, which he does not prove, poses a restriction on the value of his doctrine and leads to a peculiar speculation, namely, that the ultimate criterion for the moral value of human actions will be in relation to this hypothetical end. For Aquinas, reality is hierarchical, and human beings fit in above the physical objects because they have a double nature - spiritual and material. He shared with Aristotle the view that the possession of reason distinguishes man from the animals. Our actions as human actions are rational and voluntary, and depend on our choice.

Aquinas correctly states that only such free acts based on the will in view of an end and apprehended by reason can be classified as moral actions, good or bad ("acts are called human inasmuch as they proceed from deliberate will" and "moral acts and human acts are the same").[247] For a human act to be morally good, a number of factors have to be present. Absence of any one of them is sufficient to prevent calling it good. Moreover, an act is morally obligatory only when not to do it or to do something else would be morally bad. Aquinas differentiates between interior and exterior acts. But there cannot be an exterior act without an interior act of the will. He then develops a finalistic, teleological conception of the will striving to achieve an ultimate, presumed good of man. All particular ends or goods such as riches, honors, fame and glory, power, pleasure, or speculative knowledge are only a means to the attainment of this ultimate good.[248] Since he believed

---

242 English text of Aristotle's "Nichomachean Ethics, in "The basic Works of Aristotle", edited and with introduction by Richard McKeon, New York: Random House, 1941.
243 *S.T.* 1a 2ae, 1,7; *S.T.* 1a 2ae, 90,2.
244 *S.T.* 1a 2ae, 1,8
245 *S.T.* 1a 2ae, 3,8.
246 *S.T.* 1a 2ae, 3,8.
247 *S.T.* 1a 2ae, 1,3
248 *S.T.* 1a 2ae, 2,1-8.

in the creation by God of human nature with its innate tendencies, he presupposed a common supreme good, that is union with God, for all people. This is the fundamental flaw in Thomas's system of ethics. Note that it is not the moral behavior of human beings in relation to each other in a society that is the basis of morality, but the unspecified glorification of God. Though Thomas did not neglect personal morals, they became dependent on our relation to the institution, and were not measured by our relation to other human beings. Morality and moral justifications became a legalistic system based on the acceptance or not of the Church orthodoxy, the theoretical, unverifiable Church speculations about the supernatural, and whatever the Church ordered mankind to believe. Morals are put on a secondary and tertiary plane in the system of Aquinas's ethics. The primary precepts dealt with are the recognition of the cult, speculations about religious supernatural reality (that is, religious dogmas), ritual veneration of the sacred, and the unquestioned, submissive, servile, total subordination to the institution, the "party." This institution usurped its supernatural origin, supernatural power in ordaining what is good, and what is bad, what is wrong and what is right.

The power of the Church was formally extended to the domination over the secular state by Pope Boniface VIII in his bull "Unam Sanctam" (1302).[249] Using the then current metaphor the Pope declared that there are two "swords" (i.e., powers) under the control of the Church - the spiritual sword is wielded in the Church by the hand of the clergy, and the secular sword is employed for the Church by the hand of the civil authority, under the direction of the spiritual power. The Church has then the right to establish, to judge, and to dismiss the secular power. Whoever opposes its power, opposes the law of God. Moreover, every human being must be the subject of the authority of the Roman Pontiff: "Now, therefore, we declare, say, determine and pronounce that for every human creature it is necessary for salvation to be subject to the authority of the Roman Pontiff." The same was declared by the Fifth Council of Lateran in 1516 and this doctrine was eventually formulated by the theologians as the fundamental principle of Catholicism in a dogma "*Extra Ecclesiam nulla salus.*"

---

249 "The Catholic Encyclopedia", New York: The Encyclopedia Press, Inc., 1913, pp. 126-127.

Clearly, the Church usurps totalitarian domination over the entire world, over the mind, feelings, and morals of every individual. It is, needless to say, that it is the "moral" obligation according to such a doctrine to spread the faith (however faith may be defined by the Church) by force or any other means. In modern times the doctrine was upheld by Popes Gregory XVI and Pius IX,[250] by Leo XIII in his encyclical "*Immortale Dei*" (1885), and by Pius X in his "*Vehementer Nos*" (1906) in which he declared null and void the law of the French Republic separating Church and state. In 1911 the encyclical "*Jamdudum in Luisitania*" repeated the same stand for Portugal.[251]

Thomist Justification of Morals

Aquinas's entire theory of justification of morals is analogous, developed on the model of the positive human law and the legal system. It is basically a play on words in which morality is reduced to legality, but it was used since it fitted into the totalitarian doctrines of the Church. It is important to emphasize that, as in any legal system, one finds here also the legislator, the judge, and the executor, are all embodied in the institution of the Church. The intellectual paradigm that Aquinas develops may be summarized as follows: Since in reality there is a hierarchy of beings, there must be a hierarchy of laws governing it. At the top is the ETERNAL LAW - the deity Himself, the supreme

---

250 Freedom of conscience and worship was officially and explicitly condemned by Pope Gregory XVI in his encyclical "Mirari vos" of 1832. The Pope calls these principles "*deliramentum*" (insanity). The same was repeated by Pope Pius IX in his encyclical "Quanta Cura" of 1864. In addition he condemned the will of the people, manifested.... in the public opinion" as constituting "the supreme law". In the accompanying infamous "Syllabus" he condemns in the name of totalitarian domination of the ecclesiastical party over entire humanity, practically every rational, human and moral achievement of mankind, e.g.: "Human reason, without any reference whatsoever to God...;" that "Every man is free to embrace and profess that religion which, guided by the light of reason, he shall consider true;" that "Protestantism is nothing more than another form of the same true Christian religion, in which form it is given to please God equally as in the Catholic Church;" that "It appertains to the civil power to define what are the rights of the Church, and the limits within which she may exercise those right;" that "Roman pontiffs and ecumenical councils have wandered outside the limits of their powers, have usurped the rights of princes, and have even erred in defining matters of faith and morals;" that "The sacred ministers of the Church and the Roman pontiff are to be absolutely excluded from every charge and dominion over temporal affairs;" that "The immunity of the Church and of ecclesiastical persons derived from civil law;" that "The entire government of public schools in which the youth of a Christian state is educated, ... may and ought to appertain to the civil power, and belong to it so far that no other authority whatsoever shall be recognized as having any right to interfere....; that "Kings and princes are not only exempt from the jurisdiction of the Church, but are superior to the Church in deciding questions of jurisdiction;" that "The Church ought to be separated from the State, and the State from the Church;" that "By law of nature, the marriage ties not indissoluble, and in many cases divorce properly so called may be decreed by the civil authority;" that "In the present day it is no longer expedient that the Catholic religion should be held as the only religion of the state, to the exclusion of all other forms of worship;" that "Hence it has been wisely decided by law, in some Catholic countries, that persons coming to reside there in shall enjoy the public exercise of their own peculiar worship." In Anne Fromantle, ed., *The Papal Encyclicals in Their Historical Context. The Teachings of the Popes from Peter to John XXIII*, with introduction by Gustave Weigel, S.J., New York: A Mentor Omega Book, The New American Library, 1963; pp. 135 &ff.

251 Anson Phelps Stokes, *Church and State in the United States*, introduction Ralph Henry Gabriel, New York: Harper & Brothers Publishers, 1950, Vol. 1, pp. 340 & ff.

mind ("*suprema ratio in Deo existens*"), His mind and reason ("*ratio in mente divina existens*"). "Hence the Eternal Law is nothing else than the plan of the divine wisdom which is considered as directing all the acts and motions".[252] This concept is very old, having its roots in the Stoic and Platonist idea of the immanent reason in things or universal logos absolutized in God's Wisdom and personified in the Christian religion as the second person of the Trinity.[253] According to Aquinas, the Eternal Law is recognized by all ("*lex aeterna omnibus nota*"). It is the governing idea of the Supreme Sovereign from which all rules derive. Thomas used many anthropomorphic analogies in his explanations. Even failures in the natural causes fall under the rule of the Eternal Law. We do not have direct knowledge of this Eternal Law, but in some manner we have a notion of the Eternal Law, such as when we are prone to receive the virtues, or we have the fear of God.

In accordance with his religious belief in the sacred books, he then postulated, in a puerile and naïve way, the positive DIVINE LAW, which is two-fold: the Old Divine Law, imperfect, underdeveloped, of the Old Testament, and the New Divine Law, perfect, fully developed, of the New Testament. The common good was envisaged by the Old Law as material and earthly benefit (the promised land of Canaan). The spiritual and heavenly good is directed by the New Law in the promise of eternal life. The office of law is to lead men into keeping its commandments. The Old Law did it by fear and penalty, the New Law does it through love and the grace of Christ. The Old Law was given to the people who were still backward, whereas the New Law could come only after Christ's redemption as a condition for salvation. Both laws are for the guidance of human conduct and are required for four reasons:

1. Humans are destined to ends beyond their natural abilities and this requires a law to direct men to the actions matching what they are made for, namely toward eternal happiness.

2. Human judgment is not trustworthy, and different people can come to different decisions. Men must have divinely given law to know what

---

252 *S.T.* 1a 2ae, 93,1.
253 John Dillon "Logos and Trinity: Pattern of Platonist Influence on Early Christianity" in *The Philosophy in Christianity*, edited by Godfrey Vesey, Cambridge: Cambridge University Press, 1989, pp. 1-13.

should or should not be done. Also they need grace in order to know truth and to do good.

3. Men cannot make law on inward motion, only on outward and observable behavior.

4. Human law cannot forbid or punish all wrongdoing: therefore there is a need for a law that leaves no evil unforbidden and unpunished. So the distinction between a crime and a sin is that a crime is a punishable offense against the public order, while a sin is an offense against the ultimate common good. The Last Judgment will be a summing up of Justice.

There are many problems with the acceptance of the positive Divine Law of the Old and the New Testaments, even giving Aquinas the benefit for not knowing about the scripture what we know today. The so-called Divine Law was never formulated to any extent, and the term has rather phraseological usage. Aquinas accepted all natural phenomena, all events - historical, political, social, and miracles described in the Testaments as unquestionably true and factual. He also accepted all explanations given by the scriptures as true and factual. Moreover, speculations on the religious scheme developed and derived from these scriptures by the Church became the basic and obligatory tenets for everyone. These speculations are obviously arbitrary and tendentious. The scriptures are used to illustrate and justify certain positions, often to justify moral judgment by quoting convenient phrases. The Church owned the sacred scriptures and had the sole authority and right (as it believed) to develop these tenets.

The precepts we find in these scriptures are two-fold: related to the worship of God, and morals related to human behavior *vis-à-vis* other humans or God. Even Aquinas and the Church had tremendous problems in reconciling their presumed supernatural character and the reality of their contents. All religious ritual prescripts of worship found in the Old Testament were rejected. From the New Testament - some new rituals were speculatively derived and especially a theory of the supernatural origin of the Church institution, most fundamental for the Catholic faith, was invented. As to the moral precepts - these were formulated with various degrees of relevance, and regardless of whether we believe in their supernatural origin or not, they represent accumulated human experience not unique to the Greco-Judean tradition. However, even Aquinas had problems in accepting all the tenets except the very general moral imperatives. Simply, the moral sensitivities of his time were vastly different from those of people living in biblical times. For example, he goes to considerable pain to explain away adultery, so prominent in the Old Testament, as commanded by God! It did not matter to Aquinas that he contradicted the nature of God. Scriptures thus contain the sum total of the experience and information about the world and the history of a given group. As such they might contain certain elements of permanent value as the Greek scriptures ascribed to Homer or Hesiod. Aquinas needed them as a pretext and an element of his religious scheme for justification of the new religion and the religious institution.

Thomist Theory of the Natural Law

Aquinas develops next his theory of NATURAL LAW ("*lex naturalis*" or sometimes called "*lex naturae*"), the third universal law in his hierarchy of laws. It is analogous to the concept of positive law or HUMAN LAW (fourth law in Aquinas's hierarchy of laws). Human Law, defined by him as "an ordinance of reason for the common good made and promulgated by the authority who has care of the community",[254] is the outgrowth of Natural Law. The basis for Natural Law is the religious scheme of reality, of the human condition and of the governance of the world by God. Since all things are ruled and measured by Eternal Law, which is nothing else than God himself, it follows that all somehow share in it and their tendencies to their own proper acts and ends are from its impression. The participation of the rational creature in the Eternal Reason through which it has its own natural aptitude for its due activity and purpose Aquinas calls "NATURAL LAW." And the light of natural reason by which we discern what is good and what is evil is the impression of the divine light on us. He describes it further as the first principles of human moral activity that are self-evident, indemonstrable ("*sunt quaedam principia per se nota*"), known to all. The first command of law is "that good is to be sought and done, evil to be avoided"; on this command "are founded

---

254 *S.T.* 1a 2ae, 90,4.

all the other precepts of the law of nature".[255] The commandments of the Natural Law are recognized by the practical reason of itself as being human good (*"quae ratio practica naturaliter apprehendit esse bona humana"*). According to Aquinas the order of the natural commands corresponds to that of our natural tendencies:[256]

1. The inclination towards the good of nature has in common with all substances the tendency to preserve its own natural being.

2. The inclination towards things man's nature has in common with other animals, such as coupling of a male and a female, and bringing up the young.

3. The human inclination for the good of his nature of intelligent being proper to him, for example, that he should know the truth about God and living in society, that he should shun ignorance, that he should not offend others with whom he ought to live in civility.

All these inclinations fall under one single root, namely that of Natural Law. Next Aquinas argues that since our activity of reason and will derives from what we are by nature, and since all reasoning originates from the principles which we recognize naturally as well as the desire for objectives that are subordinate to ends derives from the natural desire for the ultimate end, therefore it is only proper that first our acts should be directed towards this ultimate end by Natural Law.[257] Aquinas assumes here that our nature depends on Eternal Reason, that there is an ultimate end that is God, for which we have a natural desire, and that the very first principles which we recognize are not reasoned out and our natural desire is not chosen. Therefore, natural here is what is preconscious, predetermined, and not reasoned out. At another place he seems to accept the definition of Ulpian that the natural is what we have in common with animals,[258] or what is instinctive or intuitive, according to the definition of Gratian.[259] Only later do we

---

255   *S.T.* 1a 2ae, 94,2.
256   *S.T.* 1a 2ae, 94,2.
257   *S.T.* 1a 2ae, 91,2.
258   *S.T.* 1a 2ae, 94,2.
259   Ulpian (murdered in 223 C.E.) and Gaius (ca 110 - ca 180) were Roman jurisconsults ("jurisperiti") who set in order Roman law. Roman law was systematized by Emperor Justinian in "Digest" ("Digesta", 533 C.E.), "*Institutes*" ("*Institutiones*", 533), and "*Justinian's Code*" ("*Codex Justinianus*", 528, 534). These were supplemented by additional decrees accumulated over the years as "*Novellae*" ("*Novels*"). Roman law was adapted to the politics of state and church. Ulpian and Gaius introduced the definition of "natural law" in terms of what we share in common with animals. Gratian published in 1141 a miscellany of texts related to legislation of the Western church

recognize these natural tendencies as laws, precisely because we are rational creatures. Even non-rational creatures participate in Eternal Reason in their own way: however, they cannot perceive it as a law. When referring to them we may use the word "law" only in a figurative manner. Because of the double nature of humans (rational and animal), some acts of virtue are done following Natural Law since they belong to it by the fact that our proper form is the soul. Therefore our natural tendency is to act according to virtue. Many virtues, however, do not belong to Natural Law, but are reasoned out before they are held to be helpful to the good life: for example, temperance modulates our natural desire for food, drink and sex. Sins, if they are against reason, are against nature. On the other hand, some special sins run against nature, such as homosexuality, which, as Thomas thought, is against the course natural to all animals.

Aquinas maintains further that the first common principles of theoretical or practical reason, "the law of nature," are the same as the truth or rightness for all and are equally recognized. With respect to the specific conclusions of theoretical reason, the truth is the same for all, though not all recognize it equally. With respect to the particular conclusions derived by practical reason, there is no general unanimity as to what is true or right, and even when there is agreement there is not the same degree of recognition. In a few cases the desire to do right or information may be wanting. He summarizes what is a natural right by quoting Gratian that natural right is that "by which everyone is commanded to do to others what he would have done to himself, and forbidden to do to others what he would not have done to himself."[260] And it is generally held that all human inclinations should be directed according to reason.

Thus, according to Aquinas, Natural Law is a spontaneous, intuitive, instinctive reflex of the tendency to seek what is good to preserve natural being, to preserve the species, and to learn about God and to venerate him. This "law" has supernatural origin being created

---

entitled "*Decretum*" which became the canon law of the church and the state. "*Decretum*" I, 1,7: "*Ius naturale est commune omnium nationum, eo quod ubique instinctu naturae, non constitutione aliqua habetur*". In "Corpus Iuris Canonici, editio Lipsiensis secunda post Aemilii Ludovici Richteri curas ad librorum manu scriptorum et editionis Romanae fidem recognouit et adnotatione critica instruxit" Aemilius Friedberg. Graz: Akademische Druck U. Verlagsanstalt, 1959.

260 Gratian "Decretum" I,1: "Ius naturae est, quod in lege et euangelio continetur, quo quis que iubetur alii facere, quod sibi uult fieri, et prohibetur alii inferre, quod sibi nolit fieri."

together with human nature and is self- evident. The practical reason next arrives at the common principles of this law which may differ in details and in specific conclusions. However, he postulates one most general principle of practical reason quoting it in Gratian's formulation. This principle is taken from the Judaic tradition into Christianity, but is found in all cultures.

Natural Law can be changed by Divine Law as well as by Human Law in the sense of being added. But as for change by subtraction, meaning that something that once was Natural Law ceases to be so, it is not possible. The first principles of the law of nature ("lex naturae") are altogether unalterable. But its secondary precepts, which are like particular conclusions close to first principles, though not alterable in the majority of cases where they are right as they stand, can nevertheless be changed on some particular and rare occasions.

Now expanding the scope of the Natural Law, Aquinas is using the notion of Natural Law in a double meaning - the one, narrow as the very first principle or principles we recognize unconsciously, and second, in the broader meaning including also particular conclusions presumably derived from it in society. This very special twist led to such monstrosities as justifying religious persecutions by Natural and Divine Laws. The persecution of the so-called heretics, apostates, and unbelievers was the greatest perversion of the most fundamental human tendencies, moral conscience, instituted by the Natural Law (if we accept the existence of such a law). This is a typical example of Thomas's rationality and moral precepts of the Catholic luminary. This sophistry served only one purpose: that of justifying ecclesiastical totalitarianism.

Justification of Celibacy

To deal with the sensual side of human nature Aquinas introduces the fifth law, namely the "law of sin" ("*lex peccati*"), the LAW OF "FOMES" or urge to sensuality. This is the most bizarre among the differentiated laws. The word "*fomes*" means kindling, tinder, touchwood and signifies the readiness of our sensual nature for passion. The term comes from Peter Lombard's "Sentences"[261] and was used by the Council

---

261 Peter Lombard (1100-1160) "Sentences" ("Libri Quatuor sententiarum") published and commented by Heinrich von Gorichem, Basel 1498, reproduced by Minerva, G.M.B.H., Frankfurt, 1967. Book II, XXX.

of Trent to describe the effects of original sin. The Church claimed that human sensuality is sinful and originated from divine punishment. Aquinas somehow had to explain this pathological Church view on the sexuality and sensual life of man. So he tries to explain that the urge of sensuality in non-rational animals has the character of a law; in men, however, it is rather a deviation from the rational law. Nevertheless it has the character of a law by being a penal consequence of divine justice and loss of the original dignity by men. Thomas here is at pains to explain that this law, when taken as a purely animal tendency, serves the common good, namely the conservation of species, and so it exists also in man when his sensuality is subordinate to reason. This "law" was designed to serve as a justification of celibacy and presenting it as a true, correct, original way of life, whereas non-celibacy is a sinful degeneration of human nature. Never mind the biological nonsense of this law - its purpose was to justify the psychological superiority of the clergy as a class.

The Church on Trial

In time Aquinas's system was adopted by the religious organization as its own ideology. Due to the domination of the theocratic societies by the Church, Aquinas's speculations were implemented in the form of canon law or positive state laws, with disastrous results. It is enough to mention the infamous immoral laws against the so-called "heretics" and apostates which found their formal expression in Aquinas's postulates. These questions of freedom of inquiry, and of freedom of conscience are basic for the defense of human dignity and fundamental principles of morality.[262]

Aquinas clearly stated: "Among unbelievers there are some who have never received the faith, such as gentiles and Jews. These are by no means to be compelled, for belief is voluntary. However, there are other unbelievers who at one time accepted and professed the faith, such as heretics and apostates of all sorts, and these are to be submitted to physical compulsion that they should hold to what they once received and fulfilled what they promised. Jews who have not accepted the faith should in no way be coerced into it. Those however who have accepted

---

262 Stanisław Zapaśnik "Tolerance and the Question of Rationality" in *Dialectics and Humanism*, Vol. XIV, No 1/1987, p. 147-158.

it should be compelled to keep it..."[263] And further, he writes: "With regard to heretics there are two points to be observed, one on their side, the other on the side of the Church. As for heretics their sin deserves banishment, not only from the Church by excommunication, but also from this world by death. To corrupt the faith, whereby the soul lives, is much graver than to counterfeit money, which supports temporal life." By persecuting the heretics, apostates and unbelievers (with all reservations alluded to by Aquinas, considered) the Church was persecuting anybody who dared to develop independent opinion, who dared to think differently from what was ordered by the pope and his institution, presumably only in the questions of faith. Even so however, history proves that everything from astronomy to the state laws, from customs to the scripture, was a matter of faith and was regulated by the Pope's authority (Decretum I,12).[264] Anyone who resisted the ruling or had his own opinion was defined by Thomas Aquinas as a heretic: "after they [points of the faith] have been defined by the authority of the universal Church, one who obstinately resisted the ruling would be counted a heretic."[265] Once faith is accepted (i.e., baptized) one should keep it as a matter of obligation.[266] Never mind that Catholic Church obligatorily baptized children in infancy, and later indoctrinated and brainwashed children unilaterally. At the same time any critical thought or doubt was declared to be sinful. The extermination of heretics and apostates by death Aquinas justified by Divine Law using the rule of analogy with state law: "Since forgers and other malefactors are summarily condemned to death by the civil authorities, with much more reason may heretics, as soon as they are convicted of heresy, be not only excommunicated, but also justly put to death."[267] Obviously this unjustified statement assumes that the Church has an absolute power over the members of a society and is superior to that of the civil power, that this power is imposed on the society and does not derive from the consent of the society itself. Aquinas himself contradicts (1) the most fundamental moral principles and moral sensitivity (or of the fundamental principles of Natural Law, which he defined himself) and

---

263 *S. T.* 2a 2ae, 10,8.
264 Decretum Gratiani in "Corpus Iuris Canonici, editio Lipsiensis secunda post Aemilii Ludovici Richteri curas ad librorum manu scriptorum et editionis Romanae fidem recognouit et adnotatione critica instruxit" Aemilius Friedberg. Graz: Akademische Druck U. Verlagsanstalt, 1959; I.12.
265 *S. T.* 2a 2ae, 11,2
266 *S. T.* 2a 2ae, 10,8
267 *S. T.* 2a 2ae, 11,3

(2) the fundamental principles of Christianity. According to Aquinas his law was dictated by God's command, the Divine Law, which he thought was given in the parable from the scripture: "Yet if heretic be altogether uprooted by death, this is not contrary to our Lord's command, which is to be understood of a case when the tares could not be weeded without uprooting the wheat."[268]

All Catholic opponents of the freedom of conscience claimed that it was against Divine Law. Since the biblical parable is the only justification given by Aquinas or anybody else for that matter, for the persecutions as a divine command, let us examine it closer. Matthew in his Gospel (13.24-30) writes: "He put before them another parable: 'The kingdom of heaven may be compared to someone who sowed good seed in his field, but while everybody was asleep, an enemy came and sowed weeds among the wheat, and then went away. So when the plants came up and bore grain, then the weeds appeared as well. And the slaves of the householder came and said to him; 'Master, did you not sow good seed in your field? Where, then, did these weeds come from? He answered, 'An enemy has done this.' The slaves said to him, 'Then do you want us to go and gather them?' But he replied, 'No; for in gathering the weeds you would uproot the wheat along with them. Let both of them grow together until the harvest; and at harvest time I will tell the reapers, collect the weeds first and bind them in bundles to be burned, but gather the wheat into my barn.'"[269] The parable is a literary, metaphoric expression of a certain idea. It uses an imagery taken from the reality well known in an agricultural setting. The author of the metaphor simply tries to convey the following message: 1. we may compare the kingdom of heaven to the field of wheat; 2. the plants producing grain are virtuous people deserving reward; 3. the weeds growing among the wheat plants represent the wicked deserving to be separated and punished; 4. judgment is done only at the end of time (in accordance with religious belief) and is explicitly forbidden before. So, the parable even taken literally, has nothing to do with doctrines, intellectual speculations, views, opinions etc. Moreover, there is no

---

268   S. T. 2a 2ae, 11,3.
269   Matthew's "Gospel", 13.24-30. In "The New Greek-English Interlinear New Testament." A new interlinear translation of the "Greek New Testament", United Biblical Societies, third, corrected edition. Translators Robert K. Brown, Philip W. Comfort, ed., J.D. Douglas. Wheaton, Illinois: Tyndale House Publishers, Inc., 1990.

indication of any power on earth authorized to pass judgment, the less so to have the power to exterminate people for ideas!

Only by an incredible sophistry, in which morals were perverted into an adherence or non-adherence to the orthodoxy of the organization, Aquinas could make such a statement! It is clear that the function of these moral laws was to maintain total and absolute dominion over the individual and society exerted by the organization, the "party." Even today the Church refuses to recognize that the unspeakable crimes it committed against humanity were a moral evil. Instead it claims that its acts were legally just.[270] In some cases especially in the Western European countries, the Church obviously imposed its immoral law on the society, but in Poland in XVIth and XVIIth centuries, it acted even against the law. The irony is that this justification was written in 1913, long before the Nazis claimed the same excuse -most of the Nazis did not write the evil laws, they simply followed the law! The international court at Nuremberg did not accept these excuses.

Though the present leaders of the Church cannot be held personally responsible for Church crimes of the past, it is the Church itself as an organization and its moral precepts that are on trial; its crime is more grievous because it is the Church itself that created these laws! So, at least those of Aquinas's concepts that were put into use in practice, turned out to be false, morally evil, or vastly inadequate. A great deal of what Aquinas wrote, however, could be of permanent value as a collection of definitions and concepts, especially his general outlook and conception of philosophy. Also there will remain the argumentation regardless whether the arguments are sound or not, and "whether the writer wished to arrive at the conclusion at which he did in fact arrive or whether he already believed in that conclusion on other grounds"[271], as a historical testimony to the ways in which human thoughts develop.

Conclusions

Aquinas, to a certain degree, is a realist and recognizes the conditions necessary for human actions to have moral value: They must be voluntary, they must be a rational choice, and they must depend

---

270   "The Catholic Encyclopedia", *op. cit.*, p. 763-773.
271   F. C. Copleston *op. cit.*, pp. 17-18.

on circumstances. As such these actions cannot be imposed by any absolute or human power.

Observation demonstrates that human moral behavior displays certain characteristics common to all people and that all people have the same very general sense of righteousness, i.e. habitual knowledge of the primary moral principles which Thomas calls "*synderesis.*" Acts of applying these moral principles to particular actions he calls "*conscientia.*"[272] Thomas explains this characteristic by assuming the existence of a Natural Law. He defines natural as that which is predetermined, instinctive, and not reasoned out, or as that which we have in common with animals. The concept is developed analogously from the positive Human Law and put artificially into a larger scheme of hierarchy of beings and religious metaphysics of Aquinas. This law is only one of a series of laws instituted by the supreme being. It is expressed in the natural commands (imperatives) that follow the order of human tendencies. The highest of these commands is that man should know the truth about God and living in society, that he should shun ignorance, that he should not offend others with whom he ought to live in civility.

Aquinas's precept about "Natural Law" as predetermined, preconscious impressions of Eternal Law does not have any justification. It is redundant and artificial. There are also many dangers in the Aquinas's paradigm. There is no logical connection between moral behavior and the metaphysically conceived happiness of man. Moreover, in Catholic doctrine the religious organization assumes an absolute authority to determine what is good or bad. That decision is based on three sources: an arbitrary interpretation of the scripture, which in itself is contradictory; the imaginary and theoretical end of glorifying God; and the speculation of a few individuals with the final goal of protecting the power and domination of the religious organization. These moral rules do not derive from the human experience and have nothing to do with the human sense of morality. The danger is that such a position leads to imposition of many laws which run against even "Natural Law" as postulated by Aquinas, in the name of the so-called glory of God. This allowed Aquinas to impose a prohibition on the human mind to search for the truth, forbid intellectual freedom, and persecute the so-

---

272   *S. T.* 1a 2ae, 79,12-13.

called heretics and apostates. Clearly the whole scheme was designed to enhance the domination of the powerful institution of the Church.

Humanism recognizes the existence of a "general moral sense" or "conscience" common to people that is recognized as the universal principles of moral behavior. Its essence is the behavior of human beings toward each other and the surrounding world. Our human experience indicates that the origin of our moral sense or conscience is rational from our common living in a society.[273] The first precepts of human behavior can be summarized in the words of *Leviticus* 19:18, *Ecclesiasticus*, and *Tobit* 4:16: "Do to no-one what you would not want done to you." These precepts were popularized in the Western world via the Judean culture, but in the East they were recorded by Confucius and Buddha. All other models of ethics are simply variations on the same theme depending on the philosophical and metaphysical orientation of the author. A XXth century Polish philosopher, Tadeusz Kotarbiński, for example, has postulated a normative secular ethic independent of religion, independent of the worldview, and independent of the social system.[274] He started with the observation that people constantly need advice and guidance about how to live better and more happily. They also evaluate each other in the ethical categories of good and evil. Kotarbiński stated that a normative ethic is possible only because there exist in human societies certain immanent and common values, which are absolute and objective. Such an ethic is not easy and requires a reflective attitude in order to recognize these values. As a model for ethical behavior Kotarbiński postulated a realistic and practical ideal of a "dependable protector," which he contrasted with the impractical and artificial ideal of "neighborly love" postulated by traditional religious ethic.

Acknowledgment.

The author expresses his thanks and gratitude to Mrs Claire S. Allen for reading the manuscript and her comments.

---

273 Władysław Tatarkiewicz, *Pogadanki Obyczajowe*, (Warsaw: Państwowe Wydawnictwo Naukowe, 1957), p. 11, p. 21.
274 Małgorzata B. Jakubiak, *Tadeusz Kotarbiński, filozof, nauczyciel, poeta*, (Warsaw: Krajowa Agencja Wydawnicza, 1987).

III. CRITIQUE OF CHRISTIAN ETHICS

FRIEDRICH NIETZSCHE: SOCIAL ORIGIN OF MORALS, CHRISTIAN ETHICS, AND IMPLICATIONS FOR ATHEISM IN HIS *THE GENEALOGY OF MORALS* [275]

Friedrich Nietzsche (1844-1900) belongs among the most misunderstood or most enigmatic writers of philosophy. Nietzsche was educated in Leipzig where he was under influence of Schopenhauer's *The World as Will and Representation*. He was appointed professor of classical philology in Basel in 1869. He remained there until 1879 when he resigned from his post for health reasons. His philosophical production was not very abundant (e.g. *Human, All Too Human,* 1878) before his retirement. After his retirement he became more involved in philosophical studies and published several works: *Daybreak* (1881), *The Gay Science* (1882), *Thus Spoke Zarathustra* (1883-1885), *Beyond Good and Evil* (1886), *On the Genealogy of Morals* (1887), *Twilight of the Idols* (1889), *The Antichrist* (1895), and *Ecce Homo* (published posthumously in 1908). His works represent trends and anxieties of his epoch which was rich in new approaches: development of new studies in science such as the discovery made by Darwin and the publication of his two most influential books, *On the Origin of Species* (1859) and *The Descent of Man* (1872), a critical analysis of the evils of capitalism, new studies in comparative religions, and new studies in literary biblical criticism. Such intellectual enterprise gave rise to critical attitudes and abandonment of traditional ways of thinking and created a void which was succinctly formulated by Nietzsche in his famous expression, the "death of god." Undoubtedly, Nietzsche, influenced by the pessimism of Schopenhauer, searched for new ways to overcome it, to fill the created void and find an affirmation of life. He was often characterized as a "nihilist" because he described the void produced by the collapse of the traditional system of values and worldview. But, on the contrary, by formulating the "death of god" which meant the abandonment of everything that related to the god-hypothesis, Nietzsche postulated a rethinking of the human existence, knowledge, morality, and elaborating

---

275 Published in the Essays in the Philosophy of Humanism, Vol. 16 (1) Spring-Summer 2008. American Humanist Association, Washington, DC, pp. 59-84.

a new account based on naturalistic analysis and affirmation of life. This program was the only tenable alternative to nihilism. His writing, however, is not organized in a form of systematic treatises, rather, it is a collection of observations, comments and loosely connected thoughts.

Among the major trends of Nietzsche's philosophy we may list the following:

1. Nietzsche considered that human thought has basically an evaluative and interpretative character and called for a new assessment of all previous interpretations including a reevaluation of previous values and an analysis of their genealogy, hence the title of one of his works.

2. It seems that under the influence of developing science, he recognized the temporality of all human knowledge which offered nevertheless a certain perspective on the relationship between things and the ideas.

3. In his search for truth and knowledge Nietzsche postulated the use of naturalistic epistemology in place of the traditional religious and metaphysical. He advocated abandonment of the god-hypothesis as an "unworthy belief," a product of "naïveté, error, all too-human need and ulterior motivation." He rejected as well the notion of substantial soul and "self-contained things." He considered such notions linguistic shorthand representing the natural processes.

4. Nietzsche certainly read the works of Charles Darwin and was impressed by them. He considered the world as undergoing constant organization and reorganization in an evolutionary process. He described this process as "will to power" which produces new relationships, perhaps, by analogy to the idea of Lamarck who postulated a certain "élan vital" as a driving motor for the evolutionary process. "This world is the will to power – and nothing besides, and you yourselves are also this will to power – and nothing besides."

5. Nietzsche visualized the world as being without a beginning and end, and formulated this idea in an aphorism of an "eternal return" which meant that things happen repeatedly in a linear fashion.

6. He considered human nature and societies in naturalistic terms emphasizing the importance of social structures and interactions. The

characteristic feature of his sociology was the possibility of humans developing with a special creativity whom he called "higher men," or "supermen." They would be responsible for the enrichment of humanity with cultural life. This attainment of life would be an expression at the highest level permitted by creativity and the transformation of human existence from nihilism to integrating the human condition with the world. The First Life Essay. "Good and Evil", "Good and Bad" and the Critique of Christian Ethics

The topic of *The Genealogy of Morals* is "the provenance of our moral prejudices," as Nietzsche himself states, and he considers the present work as a continuation of the theme begun in his *Human, All Too Human*. This topic was of interest to philosophers and theologians, but Darwin was among the first who in modern times posed this question in the context of natural sciences. The answer was not possible in the nineteenth century – only today the development of neuroscience and psychology allows us to approach it from a scientific perspective (e.g., work of Marc D. Hauser). Nevertheless, Nietzsche proposed this topic for prizes for essays on the evaluation of moral ideas: "All sciences are now under an obligation to prepare the ground for the future task of the philosopher, which is to solve the problem of value, to determine the true hierarchy of values."

Nietzsche from an early age was interested in the provenance of morals and ethics. The question of evil in the world was of primary importance and Nietzsche resolved it by separating it from theological inquiry to the question "Under what conditions did man construct the value judgments *good* and *evil*"? And, what was their effect on human lives? This implied that we humans are responsible for the creation of our value systems through our own doings.

His own thoughts were opposed to the ideas which were developed on the origin of morals by the English writer Paul Rée. Nietzsche also opposed the ideas of Schopenhauer who transcendentalized as absolute values such things as "non-egotistical instincts, the instincts of compassion, self-denial, and self-sacrifice." He was especially concerned with the "overestimation of pity" which he considered a debilitating and sinister symptom of European civilization. And it was held in the lowest esteem by most philosophers. He suggests a re-evaluation of moral values and search for the conditions from which they developed as a consequence and also the results it produced. We assume that the "good" man represents a higher value than the "evil" one, but what if the "good" man represented a "narcotic" preventing the development of the future? Here Nietzsche injects his vision of the future development of man into a superior being, the *Übermensch*.

The book is divided into three essays of which the first, entitled *"Good and Evil," "Good and Bad,"* is the subject of our essay. The only psychologists who posed the question of the origin of morals were the English writers who, however, derived for example, e.g., altruism from praise for their actions by their beneficiaries which later became a habit. Nietzsche is criticizing here the utilitarian explanation of ethics that altruistic deeds were originally committed for their usefulness and later their usefulness was forgotten.

The other theory which is equally untenable is that of Herbert Spencer who claimed that the concept *good* was the same as the concepts *useful* and *practical.*

Nietzsche argues that the notion of *good* did not derive from those who benefited from the good, but it was the good themselves who declared themselves and their actions to be good. The source of the distinction between *good* and *bad* being in the aristocratic class contrasted with the lower classes. There was no need to associate altruistic deeds with the word good, since it was the temper of the dominant ruling class. That differentiation came about when aristocratic values began to decline and the people became aware of the dichotomy egotism-altruism. Nietzsche next explains the derivation of the concept *good* from the concept *noble* in the hierarchical, class sense, and the concept *bad* from the notions *common, plebeian, base.* He gives as an example the etymology of the word *schlecht* (bad) which was used for a long time until the Thirty Years War interchangeably with the word *schlicht* (simple) to designate the commoner as distinct from the nobleman. Only later it acquired a contemptuous connotation. Further support for his hypothesis Nietzsche derives from the words which were used by the ruling classes to describe themselves – arya (= rich, possessor also truthful, in the Iranian and Slavic languages); the words *esthlos* (= having true reality, later truthful in Greek) and *agathos* describing aristocracy was contrasted with *kakos* and *deilos* for plebeians; similarly in Latin *malus* (or *melas*) might designate a dark-haired commoner or pre-Aryan settler of the Indian soil; the Latin *bonus* (good) which he interprets as meaning a warrior, Nietzsche derives from *bellum* (war). Also the priestly class would be classified by Nietzsche as the *pure* and contrasted with the *impure* originally in the physical sense as the one who washed himself and avoided certain foods that entailed skin disease. From such neurasthenia and morbidity of the priestly class derived dietary restrictions, fasting, and sexual continence. What is interesting is that Nietzsche recognizes that among that priestly class the human mind was able to develop profound as well as evil thoughts. These two classes, the aristocracy and priests, developed with time opposite systems of valuations. The priestly class is generally characterized by Nietzsche as "the most evil enemies" one could have, precisely, because they are the greatest haters in history but also the most intelligent.

Now referring in general terms to Christian ethics, the ethics of love, Nietzsche characterizes it as the ethics of slaves which is a result of the vengeance and hatred exerted by the Jewish race. It was a "debilitating narcotic power the symbol of the 'holy cross,' the ghastly paradox of a crucified god, the unspeakably cruel mystery of God's self-crucifixion for the benefit of mankind." In this way everything became Judaized or Christianized, and the ethics of the common man triumphed in the world. This gave birth to values. In a truly aristocratic society morality grows out of triumphant self-affirmation of the sort, "We nobles, good, beautiful, happy ones." It goes necessarily with action and leads to an active life stance. The aristocratic valuation can go amiss too and do violence, but only to those aspects of life they do not know. As an example of such a noble representing this type of ethics Nietzsche gives Mirabeau "who lacked all memory for insults and meanness done to him, and who was unable to forgive because he had forgotten." The noble man respects his enemies and that respect allows him to speak of "loving one's enemy." But Nietzsche does not spare the critique of the noble races: "For these same men ... when once they step outside their circle become little better than uncaged beasts of prey." And he gives a short historical survey of how various tribes and nations behaved in the past. Though he does not condone this behavior he prefers it to the "current state of affairs" characterized by "leveling and retribution." Perhaps he refers to the Marxist and socialist movements of his epoch.

The slave ethics derives, on the other hand, from the rancorous reaction to the "outside;" it requires an outside sphere different and hostile. Happiness in this ethical system is passive and derives from tranquility, emotional slackness: "the rancorous person is neither truthful nor ingenuous nor honest and forthright with himself. His soul squints; his mind loves hide-outs, secret paths, and back doors; everything that is hidden seems to him his own world, his security, his comfort; he is expert in silence, in long memory, in waiting, in provisional self-depreciation, and in self-humiliation." Such a person requires an enemy who is a true product of his conception as an "evil enemy" and he contrasts him with himself as the "good one."

Nietzsche complains that this ethics dominates: "The leveling and diminution of European man is our greatest danger: because the sight of him makes us despondent. ... We no longer see anything these days that aspires to grow greater; instead, we have a suspicion that things will continue to go downhill, becoming ever thinner, more placid, smarter, cosier, more ordinary, more indifferent, more Chinese, more Christian – without doubt man is getting "better" all the time. ... This is Europe's true predicament: together with the fear of man we have also lost the love of man, reverence for man, confidence in man, indeed the *will* to *man*." And he defines this situation as *nihilism*.

Nietzsche summarizes his views on the origins of ethics by giving an example of the lambs and the birds of prey: "There is nothing very odd about lambs disliking birds of prey, but this is no reason for holding it against large birds of prey that they carry off lambs." And "These birds of prey are evil, and does not this give us a right to say that whatever is the opposite of a bird of prey must be good?" Such ethics reduces us to doing no violence, no retaliation, leaving vengeance to God, shunning evil, being patient and humble. It requires a complicity of impotence and belief that a free subject chooses a meritorious act. It translates weakness into merit and forgiveness, impotence into kindness, pusillanimity into humility, submission before those one hates into obedience to god. No doubt, Nietzsche criticizes Christian ethics here. His most important point is that in spite of such ideals it ends up with hatred and vengeance against all those who are not on their side:

"Now I can make out what they seem to have been saying all along; 'We, the good ones, are also the just ones.' They call the things they seek not retribution but the triumph of justice; the thing they hate is not their enemy, by no means – they hate injustice, ungodliness; the thing they hope for and believe in is not vengeance, the sweet exultation of vengeance ... but 'the triumph of God, who is just, over the godless'; what remains to them to love on this earth is not their brothers in hatred, but what they call their 'brothers in love' – all who are good and just. And what do they call that which comforts them in all their sufferings – their phantasmagoria of future bliss? ... They call it Judgment Day, the coming of their kingdom, the 'Kingdom of God.'"

And what is it that Christians hope for, have faith for and love? Nietzsche gives as an answer the gruesome description of the joy to Christians offered by the spectacle of the Day of Judgment which can be found in Tertullian's *De spectaculis*. On this day all the generations of unbelievers will be consumed by fire.

"What sight shall wake my wonder, what laughter, my joy and exultation as I see all those kings, those great kings, welcomed (we are told) in heaven, along with Jove, along with those who told of their ascent, groaning in the depth of darkness! And the magistrates who persecuted the name of Jesus, liquefying in fiercer flames than they kindled in their rage against the Christians! Those sages, too, those philosophers blushing before their disciples as they blaze together, the disciples whom they taught that God was concerned with nothing, that men have no souls at all, or that what souls they have shall never return to their former bodies!" And he calls the *Book of Revelation* the "most rabid outburst of vindictiveness in all recorded history."

The Second Essay: *"'Guilt,' 'Bad Conscience' and Related Matters."*

In the second Essay of the *Genealogy of Morals*, Nietzsche attempts to describe the origin in the human psyche of "guilt" or "bad conscience" as an expression of moral rule, the evolution of punishment and its purpose and draws a far reaching conclusion about the consequences of these feelings.

The feeling of guilt derives, according to Nietzsche, from the faculty in humans which is to make promises but at the same time we have a defense mechanism, an oblivion which operates by keeping clean our mental functions and clear and quiet our consciousness. Without it happiness or serenity may not be possible. This power, however, can be superseded by another which is remembering. The operation of remembering requires, however, learning to "calculate" by which Nietzsche understands making moral judgments.

And this is the generation of the faculty of responsibility. That is, the final step in the moral analysis or moral development of man. These two things are not clearly differentiated, nevertheless by achieving this man becomes an autonomous agent leaving behind the "straight jacket" of moral customs. Man then, according to Nietzsche, acquires freedom, a sense of power, and is burdened with a sense of responsibility. At the same time he inspires trust, fear, and reverence among his peers. The awareness of his responsibility man will call his conscience. Such a conclusion reminds us of the autonomous categorical imperative of Kant (1724- 1804) by virtue of which humans become moral lawgivers and subject to their own law.

Now Nietzsche speculates on the mechanism of the development of this conscience. It has a long history of transformation. He links it with memory in the early stages of human development, with that that is painful: "A thing is branded on the memory to make it stay there; only what goes on hurting will stick." Thus it was developed because of the experience of torture, sacrifice, and bloodshed, cruel religious rituals (which have their origin in the instinct that pain is the strongest factor to produce memory). Their purpose was moral teaching. Germany was not an exception in this past; nevertheless he places Germany as "one European nation among whom is still to be found a maximum of trust, seriousness, insipidity, and matter-of-factness, which should entitle us to breed a mandarin caste for all of Europe."

In search for the origin of guilt or bad conscience, Nietzsche advises us to discard the approach done by other philosophers as useless, because they did not have a historical perspective. Just as previously he derived the concept of good and evil from the linguistic analysis, so now he refers to the moral term *Schuld* (guilt) as derived from the commercial term *Schulden* (= to be indebted). The feeling of guilt is thus a product of the oldest relationship between humans, that of "buyer and seller, creditor and debtor." With this origin is linked the concept of punishment as compensation for the contractual relation between debtor and creditor. Damage produced by not keeping a contract results in a rage and for every damage some equivalent for compensation may be found, even in inflicting pain.

In older civilizations drastic pledges were made by the debtor in order to guarantee fulfillment of the promise. These compensations were in the form of inflicting bodily harm through which the creditor, in place of material compensation such as land or money, was receiving pleasure. Later this punitive authority was passed on to the legal authority and the creditor then enjoyed seeing the debtor despised and mistreated.

Thus through such a process of contracts and legal obligations these moral concepts were developed: guilt, conscience, duty. And Nietzsche ponders that even not long ago the pain was brought to a level of apotheosis characterizing the whole history of higher culture, for example public celebrations associated with executions, tortures, *autos da fé*.

Now Nietzsche draws awkward conclusions that during the old times when inflicting pain was considered a pleasure, life was more enjoyable than today since people were not ashamed of their cruelty; today life is pessimistic. Moreover he suggests that then pain was not as hurtful as is today. He makes an assumption that even today pleasure exists in suffering in a sublimated form in imaginative or psychological terms. In the old days it was a spectacle which was not senseless neither is it today. It is interesting that Nietzsche links with this ancient spectacle the invention of the gods – they would witness any unseen suffering, a spectacle edifying to the gods (e.g., the Trojan War and similar atrocities; or the heroism of Heracles and other Greek heroes). Here Nietzsche is quite on target in anticipating modern psychological studies where the invention of gods is necessary for natural moral instincts (e.g., the study of Pascal Boyer). However, he stops short of taking this step and that constitutes a limitation of his take on the origin of morals.

He insists on the origin of morals as deriving from this "oldest and most primitive relationship between human beings, that of buyer and seller, creditor and debtor." This is the basis of the social context of humans which is the essence of moral behavior. "Here, for the first time, the individual stood and measured himself against individual." And Nietzsche summarizes his conclusions: "Here we find the oldest variety of human acuteness, as well as the first indication of human pride, of superiority over other animals … man saw himself as the being that measures values, the 'assaying' animal. Purchase and sale, together with their psychological trappings, antedate even the rudiments of social organization and covenants. From its rudimentary manifestation of interpersonal law, the incipient sense of barter, contract, guilt, right, obligation, and compensation was projected onto the crudest communal complexes (and their relations to such complexes) together with the habit of measuring power against power." The other direction led humans through grand generalizations to postulation of "the oldest and naïvest moral canons of justice, of all 'fair play,' 'good will,' and 'objectivity.'"

In the next parts of his essay Nietzsche now tackles the problem of how punishment evolved in society. In the early society, a debtor who lived in a group enjoyed the privileges associated with this membership. When he broke the contract, he at the same time broke his pledge to the group and forfeited all the benefits and amenities of the community. His infraction produced the rage of the creditor, rejection from the community and thus every kind of hostility could be applied to him. The punishment mimicked the attitude toward a conquered and hated enemy. When the societies grew in wealth and power, the situation changed – the offender no longer represented a danger and his treatment became more lenient, rules were introduced which led to the development of the penal code, justice, and its self-canceling mechanism called *mercy*.

Other philosophers attempted to trace the source of justice to other sources. Nietzsche strongly opposes the view of E. K. Dühring

(1883-1921) who proposed as the source of justice reactive emotions. "The doctrine of vengeance is the red thread that runs through my entire investigation of justice." On the contrary, says Nietzsche, the just man remains just even under the stress of harm done to him and will not seek vengeance. And he supports his point by a historical argument. Laws were developed just in order to regulate the senseless rage of rancor. Only with the establishment of laws can one talk of "right" and "wrong." He maintains that from the biological point of view a legal system is an exceptional condition, since it limits the natural life-will acting in the direction of power, but which must serve, in the final analysis, the collective purpose. Thus it is only an instrument which regulates the struggle for power complexes in the society of individuals. In this statement, Nietzsche also rejects the notion of Dühring which he considered a communist cliché that "every will must regard every other will as its equal" as demoralization.

Another problem associated with punishment is the origin of the purpose of punishment. Nietzsche takes quite a Darwinian perspective in denying any purpose or goal in the cultural or biological evolution of "a thing, custom, an organ." He postulates instead that "it is a sequence of more or less profound, more or less independent processes of appropriation, including the resistances used in each instance, the attempted translocations for purposes of defense or reaction, as well as the results of successful counterattacks." In the final analysis Nietzsche clings to his concept of progression in the form of the will tending toward "greater power" and at the expense of "lesser powers." It does not seem, however, that he advocates the Spencerian view of society rather, he expresses the role of a psychic trait, *activity* in contrast to mere reactivity which is a passive trait which he labels as *adaptation*.

The meaning and purpose of punishment underwent various changes in history and in various societies. Nietzsche gives a long list of such meanings emphasizing their utilitarian purpose: punishment as "rendering the offender harmless and preventing his doing further damage;" as "the payment of damages to the injured party;" as "isolating of a desequilibrating agent;" as "a means of inspiring fear;" as "the elimination of a degenerate element;" as "a means of creating memory;" as "a 'triumph,' that is, the violating and deriding of an enemy finally subdued;" as "a compromise with a traditional vendetta;" as "a declaration of war." In popular minds punishment is supposed to create "remorse' or "pangs of conscience." He strongly opposes this use of punishment. On the contrary, All conscientious observers agree that "punishment hardens and freezes; it concentrates; it sharpens the sense of alienation; it strengthens resistance." Moreover, as Nietzsche brilliantly observed, those who are victims of the punitive authority are prevented from regarding their own deeds as intrinsically evil when they see that "the very same actions performed in the service of justice with a perfectly clear conscience and general approbation: spying, setting traps, outsmarting, bribing, the whole tricky, cunning system which chiefs of police, prosecutors, and informers have developed among themselves; not to mention the cold-blooded legal practices of despoiling, insulting, torturing, and murdering the victims." In the final analysis Nietzsche postulates that man can be *tamed* by punishment, but not *improved*.

As to the origin of "bad conscience" Nietzsche suggests the transformation in human psyche when he developed a "polity." With time and due to this transformation man became a sociable and pacific creature. Nietzsche emphasizes that this transformation was so profound and pregnant with possibility that it required "a divine audience"- whether it be called Zeus or Chance – to justify it. Man, therefore, invented divinity. Here Nietzsche brilliantly anticipates modern psychological and anthropological studies which demonstrate that one source of religion is the natural moral faculty of man. This transformation was not a gradual or voluntary process; it was an act of violence by which a race of conquerors organized for war organized others and fiercely dominated them. Then old instincts adapted to wilderness, war, and free roaming were not allowed free play and turned inward, becoming internalized. With it also punishment was developed as a means of protection of the "polity" against ancient instincts of freedom. Man turned against himself those tendencies to "hostility, cruelty, the delight in persecution, raids, excitement, and destruction." This led to the invention of "bad conscience" which Nietzsche describes as "a disastrous malady," "man's sickness of himself," and "the declaration of war against old instincts." And he says "In its earliest phase a bad conscience is nothing other than the instinct of freedom forced to become latent, driven underground, and forced to vent its energy upon itself." This phenomenon of formation of the "bad conscience," though ugly and painful, created "beauty," "selflessness, self-denial, self-sacrifice." "A bad conscience, the desire for self-motivation, is the wellspring of all altruistic values."

The relationship between debtor and creditor was projected into another context, namely into the relationship between living and the forebears. This obligation felt toward the forebears seems to be a juridical one instead of an emotional one which is rather a new acquisition. Early societies felt that they could survive only because of the sacrifices of the earlier generations, so they had to repay the debt by burnt offerings, rituals, shrines, and obedience to them. But the doubt about the repayment grew with the success of the tribe leading eventually to the necessity of a grand act of repayment (redemption) in the sacrifice of the first-born or other form of human blood. Ancestors slowly became so powerful that they were turned into divinities – "all gods have arisen out of fear." And this is the second source of religion anticipated by Nietzsche. This sense of indebtedness to gods and desire to make final restitution grew through the centuries with an evolution of the concepts about the deity. And when combined with despotism it led to a form of monotheism. It ended up in Christianity with a paradoxical and ghastly sacrifice – "god's sacrifice of himself for humanity;" "the creditor offers himself as a sacrifice for his debtor out of sheer love (can you believe it?), out of love for his debtor …" The invention of religion serves to exacerbate man's self-torment, the projection of his denials of self as embodiment, as true reality, as god, as transcendence, endless guilt and punishment. And Nietzsche calls it "sickness, the most terrible sickness that has wasted man thus far." And he contrasts this image of deity with the image of Greek divinities. Homeric Zeus spoke thus of humans: "How strange that the mortals complain so loudly of us gods! They claim that we are responsible for all their evils. But they are the ones who create their own misery, by their folly, even in the teeth of fate." To explain the foolishness of one of their members, Greeks would explain: "Well, he must have been deluded by a god." It resonates like Dawkins's "Religion is the source of all evil." Nowadays there is a steady decline in the belief in a Christian god in the western world – does it mean that the growth of atheism will lead to a decline in man's guilt consciousness? - asks Nietzsche. Perhaps breaking of an altar requires raising another one.

The Third Essay: *"What Do Ascetic Ideals Mean?"*

The third essay in the book, the longest one, is the most interesting of the three and attempts to dispel the myth of asceticism. Nietzsche's analysis also has far fetched implication for the modern world, not only for his time, but especially for our own. It can be divided into several sections: the ascetic ideal in art; the philosopher's ascetic ideal; the priest and his ascetic ideal; the human condition and the function of the ascetic priests; the mechanisms of alleviating depression and the corruption of the mental health; and finally what does the ascetic ideal signify?

It may be instructive to begin this essay by reporting the end of the book in which Nietzsche summarizes the rise and disappearance of the ascetic ideal. The whole concept is intricately linked with the notion of the will as the driving motor of human activity, intellectual and practical. Man began his existence as an aimless animal. He suffered because he could not answer questions about his existence, how to justify, explain, affirm himself. He invented the ascetic ideal to give meaning to his existence, the best he could invent. New suffering arose through new interpretations and the notion of guilt. Yet he was able now to will something …

Nietzsche begins this essay with a short introduction trying to review the various meanings of ascetic ideal for different people: for women – an angelic look of a pretty "animal;" for men who are physiologically maladjusted – an attempt to see themselves as too good for this world; for priests – the main instrument of their power; for saints – an excuse to hibernate or repose in nothingness; for scholars and philosophers – a condition favorable for intellectual distinction.

This ideal which means so many different things to different people Nietzsche explains in general terms as a *psychological fear of the void*. One can conclude from this that Nietzsche assumes that our will, which is evidently a major element of our consciousness, requires a purpose or aim. We fill it with a variety of desires or aims. Nietzsche shows here that he is an acute observer and a good psychologist. Indeed, humans need a certain motivation for carrying on their everyday lives.

The Ascetic Ideal in Art

Next Nietzsche proceeds with a few remarks concerning why Wagner (1813-1883) in his later years paid homage to chastity. For in his earlier years (in 1867) he wrote a piece of wedding music inspired by Martin Luther's marriage entitled *Die Meistersinger von Nürnberg (The Mastersingers of Nuremberg)*. Nietzsche was part of Wagner's inner circle during the early 1870s, and his first published work *The Birth of Tragedy* proposed Wagner's music as the Dionysian rebirth of European culture in opposition to Apollonian rationalist decadence. He broke with Wagner following the first Bayreuth Festival (1876). He believed that Wagner preached conversion to Christian medieval pieties and surrender to the new demagogic German Reich. The views of Wagner on religion are well described by his son in law, Houston Stewart Chamberlain (1855-1927), who stated that Wagner, even during the years 1848-1852, in which he was hostile to Christianity, would talk about religion as the foundation of "human dignity" or the "source of all art." The churches, however, and the formulation of the revelation in dogmas, though in general are treated by Wagner with great respect, seem to be alien to him in such a way that by reading his writings one is not able to guess to which Christian confession he belongs, and to which formal Christian doctrine he subscribes.[276]

Though Nietzsche realizes that there need be no conflict between the sexual urge and chastity, even a balance between these two can provide an enticement for life. The other side of the coin is that those who fail in their sensuality may turn around and begin to worship chastity. This episode leads to another question: What did Parsifal mean to Wagner? Parsifal was a character of his last opera written under the same title by Wagner in 1877. Wagner, as usual, wrote his own librettos for his operas. *Parsifal* is an opera based on a thirteenth century epic poem by Wolfram von Eschenbach (1170-1220), *Parzival*, the Arthurian knight (Percival) and his quest for the Holy Grail. The Parsifal of the story was

---

276   Houston Stewart Chamberlain, *Richard Wagner*, (Library Reprints, 2001). Houston Stewart Chamberlain was a British-born naturalized German natural scientist, and author of popular scientific and political philosophy books on Richard Wagner, Immanuel Kant, and Johann Wolfgang Goethe and a proponent of a nationalist and pan-Germanic antisemitism. His book, *The Foundations of the Nineteenth Century* (1899), became one of the references for Teutonic supremacy and pan-Germanic movement of the early 20th century.

in the end converted to Catholicism. Was this end an expression of Wagner's turnabout and a conversion to medievalism from the follower of Feuerbach (1804-1872)[277] who advocated "healthy sensuality."?

Analyzing Wagner's change, Nietzsche speculates about the effect Arthur Schopenhauer[278] exerted on him and his notion on the role of music. Wagner changed his view of music as a means to see music as a sovereign manifestation of one's being; the musician now became now an oracle, more like a priest and consequently a "mouth-piece" of God, thus appropriating the ideals of asceticism. Next Nietzsche deals with Kant (1724-1804) and his view of art. He complains that Kant, like all other philosophers, approached art from the side of the spectator and not from the side of the artist. Hence beauty becomes that which provides us with "a disinterested pleasure." And he contrasts this definition with that of Stendhal (1783-1842) who postulated beauty as "a promise of happiness." For Stendhal the moment of aesthetic contemplation is a moment of excitement of the will, of "interest." Nietzsche makes fun of the estheticians who, in support of Kant's view, claim that we may view even nudes disinterestedly. Schopenhauer according to him was much closer to the art when he claimed that aesthetic contemplation counteracts sexual interest. It delivers us from the "urgency of the will" and it acts as "a sedative of the will." In the final analysis both these attitudes, that of Stendhal and Schopenhauer, derive from the interested personal motive. Nietzsche's own view is that

---

277 Ludwig Andreas Feuerbach was a German philosopher, anthropologist, and critic of religion who influenced Marx and Engels.

278 Arthur Schopenhauer (1788-1860), was a German philosopher who developed his philosophy as a reaction against the post-Kantian metaphysics of his contemporaries and is indebted to Kant and Spinoza as well as to oriental philosophy especially Buddhism and Hinduism. His main work is *Die Welt als Wille und Vorstellung* (*The World as Will and Representation*). Schopenhauer's starting point was Kant's division of the universe into the phenomenal and noumenal. Some commentators suggest that Schopenhauer claimed that the noumenon was the same as that in us which we call will. The will was the inner content and driving force of the world. This is parallel to *purushartha* or goals of life in the Hindu and Buddhist thought. He maintained that philosophy and logic cannot alleviate the fundamental problems of life produced by desire; more effective are art, certain charitable practices such as "loving kindness," and certain forms of religious discipline. Since humans live in the realm of desires, they are tormented by them – point similar to the Hindu tradition. The other imprtant aspects of Schopenhauer's metaphysics is the role of aesthetics. The aesthetic viewpoint is for him more objective than scientific because it separates in the form of art the intellect from the will. Art is a spontaneous act not linked either to the body or to the will. Intellect allows humans to suffer because it brings suffering into a more vivid coinsciousness. Whereas aesthetic contemplation objectifies the will. But it cannot be completely satisfied, therefore making existence futile and this want of satisfaction he calls happiness. So Schopenhauer is basically characterized as a pessimist and contrasted with the rest of his contemporaries such as Goethe, Hegel or Schelling. Art for him was a spontaneous pre-determined idea in the artist's mind. Thus it is above science and nature, beyond the realm of reason. Moreover, philosophy is not necessarily a pursuit of wisdom but rather, it is a means for interpreting experience of one's own life. This powerful drive to reproduce caused suffering and pain in the world and art provided for Schopenhauer one way to escape them. Art provided also a means to meditate on the unity of human nature. The highest place in art he gave to tragedy and music. Music, especially, is a medium able to represent the universal.

"the aesthetic condition does not suspend sensuality, as Schopenhauer believed, but merely transmutes it in such a way that it is no longer experienced as a sexual incentive."

The Philosopher's Ascetic Ideal

Returning to the original question "What does it mean when a philosopher pays homage to the ascetic ideal?" Nietzsche gives a first answer: the philosopher "craves release from torture." He proceeds to muse over this term in a somewhat convoluted way. He discusses Schopenhauer as an example of philosophers who are characterized by a special resentment against sensuality. Schopenhauer treated sexuality as a personal enemy on an equal basis with his intellectual enemies and would have become a pessimist without them. Philosophers, on the positive side, have a prejudice in favor of the ascetic ideal. What is the meaning of these two dispositions? It is related to the natural instinct to strive for the optimum conditions for releasing one's powers. And Nietzsche emphasizes that this is not the path to happiness, but to power. On the contrary, it leads in most cases to unhappiness. The philosopher, according to Nietzsche, abhors marriage and this can be exemplified by such figures as Heraclitus, Plato, Descartes, Spinoza, Leibniz, Kant, and Schopenhauer. An exception was Socrates; Buddha left his house in search of freedom: "Close and oppressive is life in a house, a place of impurity; to leave the house is freedom." It becomes clear that the ascetic ideal for the philosopher is a bridge to independence, it allows him the exercise of his intelligence, but at the same time it affirms his existence as in saying; *"pereat mundus, fiat philosophia, fiat philosophus, fiam!"*

Thus the philosophers are prejudiced against the value of the ascetic ideal which encompasses these three elements to some degree: poverty, humility, and chastity. They are not "virtues," but conditions for their optimum existence. Philosophers withdraw from busy everyday life, from noise, adulation, accolades. They need peace above all. Their motto is: "We are owned by the things we own." They hate disturbance, they use big words sparingly, even the word "truth" As to "chastity," the philosopher's immortality comes through other means and really has nothing to do with chastity understood in the sense of ascetic scruple, hatred of the flesh, but is the mandate of his dominant instinct. In contrast, the pseudo-intellectuals seek "fame, princes and women."

This specific asceticism, the lofty continence, was always treated preferentially by philosophers. Moreover, says Nietzsche, philosophy took its first steps with the help of this ideal which supports the virtues of the philosopher: "bent toward skepticism, toward negation, toward suspension of judgment, toward analysis, toward neutrality and objectivity." These tendencies were "forbidden ground" for accepted ethics, even *reason* which was characterized by Luther as "Madame Sophistry, the clever whore." And he goes further explaining that all good things which constitute pride in man look like impiety and *hubris* and things contrary to them "had conscience on their side and God for their guardian." *Hubris* is our attitude toward nature in which Nietzsche sees also bad aspects saying that we violate it with the help of machines and "heedless ingenuity of technicians and engineers" *Hubris* is our attitude toward God whom we characterize as "some putative spider weaving purposes and ethics behind the web of causation," our attitude toward ourselves when we analyze our "souls" and no longer care for "salvation." These are good things which at one time were considered evil. Among other things Nietzsche lists marriage which for long time was "looked upon as an infraction of the right of the community," an expression of "the gentle, benevolent, compassionate feelings," a submission to the law. The progress mankind made had many martyrs. In his book *Daybreak* Nietzsche wrote: "Nothing was ever bought more dearly than the small portion of human reason and freedom that is now our pride. And it is that pride which make it almost impossible for us today to imagine the vast tracts of ritual ethics which, as the truly determining history, precede our world history; those times when suffering, cruelty, dissimulation, vengeance, irrationality were all seen as virtues; well being, intellectual curiosity, peace, and compassion as danger; to be pitied and to labor as disgrace; madness something divine, and change as immoral and a herald of disaster."

From the historical perspective a philosopher had to assert himself as an accepted type of sage and usually as a priest, soothsayer, or similar figure. And he had to do this under the guise of the ascetic ideal. As a model of such development for the most ancient and most modern philosopher he quotes the case of the King Vishvamitra,[279] hence derives the austere attitude of philosophers which persists until today. The question which Nietzsche now poses is whether the things changed enough so that there is enough *freedom of the will* to make philosophy possible?

The Priest and His Ascetic Ideal

After discussion of the role of the ascetic ideal for a philosopher and its origin as a priest or similar figure, Nietzsche is ready to handle the problem of the ascetic priest. The priest derives his asceticism from his ideal, his faith, his determination, his power and, his interest. He stands or falls with this ideal, so there is no surprise that he will defend it to the bitter end against those who attempt to oppose it.

The important point is what value the ascetic priest places on existence. He views life as a bridge to transcendence, and that we must retrace in this life our steps to the point at which we entered, and he insists that we conduct our lives according to his ideal. What is appalling is that this is the longest and the broadest tradition. "An observer from an outer planet could be persuaded that we are a race of proud repulsive creatures unable to rid-ourselves of self-loathing, hatred of the earth and of all living things, who inflict as much pain as possible on ourselves, solely out of pleasure in giving pain – perhaps the only kind of pleasure we know." The priest does not propagate himself by biological means, he looks malevolently on all biological growth, beauty and joy, and finds delight in everything that is misshapen, in pain, disastrous, ugly. He finds joy in gratuitous sacrifice and self-castigation. He has an insatiable power-drive to dominate life itself. When he begins to philosophize he will declare an error where normal life will consider truth most authoritatively. Just like the Indian Vedas[280]

---

279   The King Vishvamitra is a character in many old Indian Sanskrit epics. The most recent one is *Srimad Valmiki Ramayama* considered from about the second century B.C.E. This *Ramayana* is arranged into six books. The first book Bala Kanda (*Book of Youth*) tells the legend of the King Vishvamitra who was born a Kshatriya (belonging to the warrior caste), but by intense austerities he raised himself to the Brahmin caste, and became one of the seven great Rishis (sages). In Nietzsche's time the Western world was fascinated by the recently "discovered" wealth of Eastern literature and wisdom.

280   The name *Vedas* refers to the four Sanscrit texts which constitute the basis of an extensive system of sacred scriptures of Hinduism. The word *veda* in Sanscrit literally means "know." These *vedic* texts were developed within the so-called *vedic* culture which is based on the differentiation of people into castes (*varna* = color) and the stages of life (*asramas*). Virender Kumar Arya and Malcolm Day, *The Book of the Vedas: Timeless Wisdom from Indian Tradition*, (Fair Winds Press, 2003). William Dwight Whitney, *The Translation of the Veda*, (1868). *Hymns from the Rig-Veda*, translated by Jean Lee Mee, (Jain Publishing Co., 2004).

he will consider the physical objects, their multiplicity, an illusion and deny their reality.

He reaches his triumph when reason itself declares that that is a realm of truth not accessible to it. We find traces of it in the Kantian concept of the "noumenal" character of things, that is that aspect of things we can never comprehend. Nietzsche urges philosophers to be on guard against such hallowed myths of "pure reason," "absolute knowledge," or "absolute intelligence" for they presuppose that the human "eye" cannot have active and interpretative power. Moreover, he insist that our "seeing" is perspective, that we should allow more emotions and will to be expressed in order to be more objective. In such an attitude Nietzsche again expresses his naturalistic epistemological stance.

Next Nietzsche proceeds to explain how the ascetic ideal arose. Its source is the protective instinct of life, in defense of itself. Thus the situation is contrary to what the worshipers of asceticism believe it to be. The ubiquitous existence of asceticism confirms the persistent morbidity of civilized man and his persistent struggle against death. The ascetic priest becomes an incarnation of this wish to be different, but at the same time he is the instrument of bettering the human condition. He is able to maintain in life his flock of self-tormentors, affirming life. And this is so because man becomes most anxious to live when he wounds himself most. Though the human race is the most inventive and the most daring and defiant among the creatures, it is the most unsatisfied and unrealized; certainly humans are the most precarious and the sickest of all animals.

The Human Condition and the Function of Ascetic Priests

Next Nietzsche analyzes the human condition from his perspective of a strong man. Such a strong man is an ideal man for Nietzsche, and the weak ones are those who visit disaster upon themselves. The real danger for humanity comes from loathing and pitying man. Those who are failures and victims, poison life and the social structure; they complain "If only I could be someone else." "How could I get rid of myself?" Here is the vindictiveness, conspiracy of the sufferers against the successful one. They parade their innocence; with a pharisaic gesture they simulate noble indignation. As an example Nietzsche cites Eugen Dühring[281] and his anti-Semitism. Their aim is to implant their own misery, to make the happy ones acknowledge happiness as a disgrace and doubt their happiness by saying "There is too much misery in the world!" Clearly, Nietzsche despises such people and claims that they mime only the virtues such as justice, love, wisdom, superiority. But at the same time he is asking "how [the healthy and strong] should be able to do what they alone can do, and simultaneously act the part of physicians, comforters, saviors of the sick?"

Nietzsche advises us first of all to stay away from loathing and pitying man, and that the ones who should be the "physicians" of the sick should be the sick themselves, that is, the ascetic priests. For if the priest has dominion over the sick, he is sick himself and understands them, yet he must be strong enough and master over himself with intact will to power, to be their overlord, disciplinarian, tyrant, god. He must defend them against the healthy, and also against their envy of the healthy. The priest is a new species of animal which conducts a war of cunning using his calculated superiority. But before he starts curing he must first create his patients. He carries balms too, but as he alleviates pain, he pours poison into the wounds of his patients.

---

281 Eugen Karl Dühring (1833-1921), German philosopher and economist who was a strong critic of Marxism. His major works are: *Kapital und Arbeit* (1865); *Der Wert des Lebens* (1865); *Naturliche Dialektik* (1865); *Kritische Geschichte der Philosophie* (1869); *Kritische Geschichte der allgemeinen Principien der Mechanik* (1872), *Kursus der National und Sozialekonomie* (1873); *Kursus der Philosophie* (1875), *Wirklichkeitsphilosophie*; *Logik und Wissenschaftstheorie* (1878); and *Der Ersatz der Religion durch Vollkommeneres* (1883). His philosophy was a naturalistic philosophy of reality. He repudiates Kant's separation of phenomenon from noumenon, and affirms that our intellect is capable of grasping the whole reality. This is due to the fact that the universe contains only one reality, i.e. matter. But matter is to be understood with a deeper sense as the substratum of all conscious and physical existence. Thus the laws of being are identified with the laws of thought. His system of thought has a teleological aspect, namely, he considers as the end of nature the production of a race of conscious beings. He explains the enigma of pain claiming that it exists to throw pleasure into conscious relief. In ethics Dühring follows Auguste Comte (1797-1857) in making sympathy the foundation of morality. Comte coined the word "altruism" to refer to what he believed to be a moral obligation of individuals to serve others and place their interests above one's own. He opposed the idea of individual rights, maintaining that they were not consistent with this supposed ethical obligation. In political philosophy Dühring teaches an ethical communism, and attacks the Darwinian principle of struggle for existence. In economics he advocates, just as American writer H. Carey, an ultimate harmony of interests of the capitalist and laborer. He was a German patriot but denounced Jews, Greeks, and the cosmopolitan Goethe. He denounced theistic religion and substitutes for it a doctrine simular to that of Auguste Comte and Feuerbach. Comte attempted to found a new religion which would be in harmony with the fundamental principles of positivism. As his philosophy denies the existence of any divinity or spirit, he admits only humanity as the object of the new cult. He published in 1848 *Discourse on the Totality of Positivism* in which he claimed that the new religion was a necessary addition to his philosophy. In the next year he published an important work, *The Positivistic Calendar, the Systematic Cult of Humanity or the General System of Public Commemoration*. In this work he proposed a cult of adoration of humanity for itself represented by the great men of all epochs, twelve of whom he considered deserving to represent the twelve months of the year, others the weeks, still others would preside over the days of the week. In 1852 he published *Positivistic Catechism* or a summary exposition of his universal religion. He even practiced this religion and considered himself a pontiff.

The priest thus accomplishes two things, he defends his flock against themselves and all the troubles that arise among them, and, at the same time, causes accumulation of resentment and aggression and redirects it against a new object. According to Nietzsche this release of aggression alleviates the pain through emotional excitation. This is a physiological mechanism by which a strong, violent emotion dulls the pain. But it is consciously expressed by the type of reasoning; "Somebody must be responsible for my discomfort." "I suffer, it must be somebody's fault." And the ascetic priest says to his flock: "You are quite right, my sheep, somebody must be at fault, but that somebody is yourself."

According to Nietzsche these healing instincts are through the agency of the priests dominated by such concepts as *sin, perdition, damnation.* Their goal is to render the sick harmless and to make the incurable to destroy themselves, and to introvert the resentment of the less severely inflicted. Their goal is not the rehabilitation of the personality but to create a chasm between the sick, that is between the church, and the healthy. Nietzsche emphasizes that sinfulness is not a basic human condition, but the ethico-religious interpretation of physiological distemper. If a person feels "sinful" or "guilty" it does not mean that this person is so. Similarly if a person feels healthy, it does not mean that he is so. As an example Nietzsche cites the witch trials. In those times the judges and the "witches" themselves had no doubt about their guilt. Yet there was no guilt! For, Nietzsche states, psychological pain is not a fact but a causal interpretation of a set of facts. If one cannot get rid of a psychological pain, the fault lies in his physiology and not in his psyche.

Mechanisms of Alleviating Depression and Corruption of Mental Health

So the priest is not really a physician though he likes to see himself as a savior. He only alleviates the discomfort of the sufferer, at least temporarily. But the priest and Christianity have been an inexhaustible source of a variety of nostrums, restoratives, palliatives, narcotics. Nietzsche observes quite acutely that large masses of humans periodically suffer from some physiological anxiety which is not understood and then religion steps in and provides psychological and moral remedies. He quotes a variety of reasons for this anxiety: crossing the barriers between classes and races which could be interpreted in today's terminology as social and racial conflicts, senescence of population, faulty diet, alcoholism, and various diseases.

People were combating this anxiety in a variety of ways. One of them was the philosopher's approach which is too abstruse and too remote from practical life to have any effect. The philosopher tries to prove that pain is an error and once recognized as such should disappear. However, this does not happen. Among other means used, the first is the reduction of vital energy which involves "no willing, no wishing," "no love, no hate, equanimity, no retaliation, no acquisition of riches, no work, mendicancy, and preferably, no woman." This is the situation described in psychological and moral terms as self-abrogation, sanctification. In physiological terms Nietzsche describes it as hypnosis or hibernation, starving one's body and emotions. Scornfully the adepts of this method are called by Nietzsche "sportsmen of sanctity" who undoubtedly were successful in combating their physiological depression. Yet they cannot be considered mad as it was suggested by freethinkers, though these methods may lead to much mental disorder such as mystical and ethereal experiences (Hesychasts on Mount Athos,[282] visual and auditory hallucinations, the voluptuous inundation of ecstasies of St. Teresa). The explanation of these phenomena given by them is extravagantly false. Redemption is given as the highest mystery in all cases, expressed as a "deliverance from illusions," as a state between "good and evil" (Buddhist and Vedic expression). All three religions admit openly that such a state cannot be achieved by moral improvement, only through the deep sleep can the souls be united with the Supreme Being: "In profound sleep the soul is lifted out of the body, enters the highest sphere of light, and thus puts on its true identity. It becomes the Supreme Spirit, who walks about, dallies, plays and muses himself, whether with women, or chariots, or friends. The soul no longer thinks of its appendage, the body, to which the prāna (the breath of life) is harnessed like a draught animal to a cart."

282　Hesychasts (from Greek *hesychastes* = quietist) were Greek and Eastern Orthodox hermits who claimed that it is possible by a system of asceticism, withdrawal from the world, submission to a master, prayer, and perfect repose of body and will, to see a mystic light, which is the *uncreated light* of God. The contemplation of this light is the highest end of man on earth and through this a man is intimately united with God. This light is the same as appeared at Christ's transfiguration.

The same approach, says Nietzsche, we find even in the cool Epicurus. In all pessimistic religions this "nothingness" is called God.

Other means, much more common, for combating depression, is mechanical activity labeled as "the blessing of labor." Relief here is accomplished by turning attention away from suffering. All that the priest has to do in dealing with the lower classes, or slaves and prisoners, or women who are both, is to change the name – dissatisfaction is changed into blessing. Still another means is ministering the curative pleasures in the form of "giving pleasure" e.g., charity, comfort, praise, friendly advice. In prescribing love, such as loving one's neighbor, the priest prescribes excitation of the strongest urge, that is, the "will to power." This is the "minimum superiority" which is the best help if is well administered. Primitive Christian societies were dominated by the "will to mutual aid." This movement developed later the "will to power" and organizations, the *masses*. The will to power was *promoted* by the priest, and it is, according to Nietzsche, an expression of instinctive longing and a desire to get rid of a feeling of weakness. For the weak find consolation in aggregation, whereas for the strong it is natural to disaggregate. If they join the group it is done for some aggressive action or gratification of the will to power. History demonstrated that every oligarchy concealed a desire to tyranny by the individuals.

These measures are rather harmless remedies. Now Nietzsche proposes to discuss more deleterious "drugs" which are characterized by "extravagance of feeling" rampant in modern society. By this Nietzsche means the moralistic hypocrisy of educated modern men. They are not able to distinguish between the true and false in themselves. "The 'good' of today are, to a man, determined to treat every issue in a spirit of profound hypocrisy – innocent, straightforward, true-blue hypocrisy." He gives a few examples such as Lord Byron, Thomas Moore, Schopenhauer, and the biographer of Beethoven. The simplistic but innocuous account of the Reformation by a Catholic priest, Cornelius Jansenius the Elder, aroused an outcry in Protestant Germany.[283] What if a psychologist decided to give a true account of Luther with intrepidity and not in the spirit of connivance?

---

283 Cornelius Jansenius Gandaviensis or Cornelius Jansen the Elder (1510-1576), bishop of Ghent, must be differentiated from his homonym, Cornelius Jansenius Yprensis, bishop of Ypres (1585-1638) who initiated the movement of Jansenism. Cornelius Jansenius Gandaviensis was one of the most distinguished exegetes of the sixteenth century, and his work *"Concordia Evangelica"* was epoch-making in the history of the Catholic exegesis. He insisted on the literal interpretation of the scripture against the mystical and emphasized the importance of the text in the original languages.

Next Nietzsche complains that psychologists are too infected by this moralistic taste, though they feel contempt for such a taste, that prevents them to be honest with themselves. They should, according to Nietzsche, say "let us distrust our first reactions, they are invariably much too favorable." The main issue is the use of the ascetic ideal as a safety valve for emotions which pile up and need to be released. The ascetic priest does it, at least temporarily, by all these techniques discussed earlier – "rage, fear, lust, vengeance, hope, triumph, despair, cruelty" – and under some religious justification. These remedies, though unacceptable today, did not cure but only provided a temporary relief, and often produced a mental disturbance. They have been employed in good faith, and often the priest himself was shuttered by the misery he had to inflict. Now it becomes clear why the priest had to use the concept of guilt to achieve his goal. Man, searching for the cause of his anxiety, was given an answer by the priest – to look into himself, into his past and to view his suffering as a penance, exaggerated by his "sadistic conscience." From now on he will be trapped in the circle of "sin" and "sinfulness," in a deliberate misinterpretation of suffering as guilt, terror and punishment, crying for redemption. Nietzsche writes: "No doubt such a system of procedures, once instituted, made short work of ancient depression and tedium. Life again became a highly interesting business. Initiated into these mysteries, the sinner became wide-awake, eternally wide-awake, aglow yet burned out, exhausted yet far from weary. The ascetic priest, that grand old magician and warrior against depression, had conquered at last; his kingdom had come. People no longer complained of pain but were insatiable for it."

Now Nietzsche asks the question: What was the "benefit" of all of this "medication"? The "benefit" means here only to "make worse"-it made depressed people sicker. And he reviews briefly results of this treatment in collective epileptic epidemics, the change of temperament in entire cities like Geneva and Basel, witch craze, mass somnambulism, and a mass delirious cry for death. He calls this religious neurosis a form of evil! "This ascetic ideal, with its sublime moral cult, with its brilliant and irresponsible use of emotions for holy purposes, has etched itself on the memory of mankind terribly and unforgettably. I can think of no development that has had a more pernicious effect upon the health of the race, and especially the European race, than this. It may be called, without exaggeration, the supreme disaster in the history of European man's health."[284] The present day sorry condition of some parts of our modern world and some sections of our society show how true are these words of Nietzsche and how perspicacious was his psychological analysis.

Next Nietzsche expresses his contempt for the New Testament – "this most esteemed, over-esteemed, document" with which the priest has corrupted man's esthetic taste. But he has the highest respect for the book of the Old Testament in which he finds real passion of a people who tried to attract the attention of the "Great Demiurge," though he does not accept the veracity of its content. He has no good word to say about Martin Luther, "the most eloquent and presumptuous of German peasants," who produced "turbulence" against the church etiquette. Nietzsche sarcastically speaks of Luther as the one who wanted to speak directly and without mediation of the hierarchy with God, though Nietzsche does not have any respect for the Pope, either.

What Does the Ascetic Ideal Signify? Its Implications for Atheism

It is the last topic concerning the ascetic ideal which Nietzsche particularly wants to discuss. He is concerned with the meaning of this power and why people yielded to it and did not resist. According to Nietzsche, the ascetic ideal is an expression of the will, its goal is universal, and it orients epochs, nations, and individuals, has absolute superiority and claims that it gives meaning and value to human existence. It has no antithesis and the modern scholarship that "gets along without God, transcendence and restrictive virtues" is not the opposite but the noblest and latest form of this ideal. There are many scholars who labor in many fields, especially in the field of science and the humanities, and proclaim that everyone should be content with what one is doing. But it does not prove that learning today has an ideal, a passionate belief. On the contrary, says Nietzsche, learning today is "a hiding place for all manner of maladjustment, lukewarmness, self-depreciation, guilty conscience" and the scholars are sufferers "unwilling to admit their suffering... mortally afraid of regaining consciousness."

---

284   In my book *The Case of Michael Servetus (1511-1553): The Turning Point in the Struggle for Freedom of Conscience*, (Lewiston, Lampeter, Oxford: The Edwin Mellen Press, 1997), I reviewed the entire history of Christianity and the results if its domination over the fifteen centuries.

Now Nietzsche expands further his discussion of the scholars, philosophers, and scientists, all these atheists, skeptics, and agnostics, asking whether they are really free from the ascetic ideal? And his answer is that it is they, precisely, who today represent this ascetic ideal because they believe in truth. They are tied to their belief in truth and do not have the true freedom and detachment epitomized for Nietzsche by the eastern order of the Society of Assassins[285] whose slogan for the highest ranks was "Nothing is true; everything is permitted." For real freedom means disposing of the notion of truth. The absolute "will to truth" which is so typical of those scholars is an unconscious belief in the ascetic ideal in its most radical form. Even science is not free of assumptions and a philosophy is always needed to give science a direction. "The faith on which our belief in science rests is still a metaphysical faith." In the past and even today, according to Nietzsche, those who are atheists and anti-metaphysicians look up to the Christian faith for truth that was divine. But if the divine turns out to be an error and lies, and God the longest lie, our inquiry still needs a justification, and the new problem arises of the value of truth.

Where do we find this ideal antithetical to the ascetic ideal? Science, according to Nietzsche, requires normative value outside itself; learning and inquiry are not antagonistic to the ascetic ideal, rather, it is their driving force, they oppose its temporary dogmatism; art is more opposed to an ascetic ideal than science, as epitomized by a contrast between Homer and Plato. Throughout history, inquiry was only able to "raze the wall of fortifications" around the ascetic ideal, that is to explain things such as "theological astronomy," but it did not abolish the need for a transcendental solution to questions concerning life. The destruction of man's special status in the hierarchy of beings by scientific discovery and his self-contempt constitute his serious claim to respect and did nothing to the ascetic ideal. Kant, though he destroyed the conceptual apparatus of dogmatic theology, opened the way for transcendentalists. Similarly for agnostics the question mark became a new god. Nietzsche does not have good words for historians either. He divides them into two groups – those who do not prove anything, who do not want to be judges, only describe (Tolstoy, Dühring), and

---

285 The Assassins was a shadowy group located in remote stateless areas, practicing a radical brand of Islam. They promised their followers a reward in the hereafter if they died in battle. They fought fiercely the invading Christian crusaders in the Middle Ages. There are obvious parallels with the modern groups.

the others who are engaged in the praise of contemplation (Ernest Renan). He is outraged at the anti-Semites who, using the cheapest of the propaganda tricks, a moral attitude, try to stir the lowest elements in the nation. And this is done through spreading "counterfeit ideals," "fake idealism, fake heroism, and fake eloquence."

Nietzsche promises to treat more extensively the issue of the significance of the ascetic ideal in another book *The Will to Power: a Study in the Transvaluation of All values*. Here he limits himself to stating that in places where the strict and scrupulous spirit survives, idealism seems to have vanished. Such places are where *atheism* is practiced and where the "will to truth" constitutes an ideal itself in its most sublimated form. Honest atheism is not opposed to asceticism, but is "one of the last evolutionary phases of that idea, one of its natural and logical consequences." Atheism now prohibits the lie of the monotheistic religion that lasted for two millennia.[286] A similar process happened in India where the identical ideal was converted into Sankhya philosophy and codified by Buddha into a religion. "Christianity as dogma perished by its own ethics, and in the same way Christianity as ethics must perish; we are standing on the threshold of this event." Christianity will now, according to Nietzsche, draw its own conclusion by which it shall do away with itself. And he ends his book by claiming that "It is by this dawning of self-consciousness of the will to truth that ethics must now perish." Of course, he does not mean that we will behave unethically, but we may speculate that he postulates an optimistic and utopian vision of the future where the ideal humans will no longer need the restrictive, and normative rules, they will know only "good."

Bibliography

Friedrich Nietzsche, *The Birth of Tragedy and The Genealogy of Morals*, translated by Francis Golfing, Anchor Books, New York, 1956.

Peter Singer, ed., *A Companion to Ethics*, Blackwell, Oxford, UK, 1993.

---

286 Nietzsche seems here to anticipate the modern philosopher of religion, StanisławCieniawa, who postulates as the final stage of the process of the evolution of religion the development of an authentic "religion" of the Highest Values. Traditional theistic religions he classifies as "confessions" in opposition to the natural and moralistic lifestance based on reason, science and moral principles. Stanisław Cieniawa, "The Plurality of Confessions and One religion," in *Essays in the Philosophy of Humanism*, Vol, 11, pp. 13-20, 2003. Stanisław Cieniawa, "Let's Learn Religion from ... Flowers," in *Essays in the Philosophy of Humanism*, Vol, 14, pp. 69-78, 2006.

Immanuel Kant, *Foundations of the Metaphysics of Morals*, translated with an introduction by Lewis White Beck, Macmillan Publishing Company, New York, 1988.

Marc D. Hauser, *Moral Minds. How Nature Designed Our Universal Sense of Right and Wrong*, HarperCollins, New York, 2006.

Pascal Boyer, *Religion Explained. The Evolutionary Origins of Religious Thought,* Basic Books, New York, 2001.

Eugen Karl Dühring, *The Value of Existence, A course in Philosophy, (Der Werth des Lebens; eine Denkerbetrachtung im sinne heroischer Lebensauffassung)*, O.R. Reisland, Leipzig, 1922.

IV. DISCURSIVE ETHICS

JÜRGEN HABERMAS: A PRACTICAL SENSE SOCIOLOGIST AND A KANTIAN MORALIST IN A NUTSHELL[287]

Introduction

Post World War II Germany was facing enormous problems caused by its immediate past: psychological, economical, social, political, moral. In addition it had to deal with an awkward situation of the country being split artificially into two diametrically different republics. It had to cope with its heritage and recent past and find a way out of the impasse to be able to function in the modern and increasingly integrated world. Habermas's intellectual career reflects these problems, political climate, and tensions; his own views are a testimony to how people can seek various solutions to intricate issues. In fact he became an intellectual conscience of Germany. He wrote prolifically on almost every aspect of public life and inspired the democratic movement.

Habermas was born in 1929 in Düsserldorf in a German family that uncritically accepted the Nazi reality without actively participating in the political process. He joined in 1945, as many other German youths, the *Hitler jugend*, the Nazi youth movement. After the war he became completely disillusioned with the Nazi past when he learned the extent of moral catastrophe perpetrated by the Nazis, especially by their attempt at eliminating ethnic and social groups they considered undesirable. Habermas studied philosophy in Göttingen, Zurich, and Bonn and obtained his doctoral degree in 1954 for his studies on the German idealist philosopher Friedrich Schelling. He joined the Institute for Social Research at Frankfurt where he became a research assistant to Theodore W. Adorno (1903-1969). He was influenced by Adorno and by Max Horkheimer (1895-1973), both of whom were of Jewish origin.[288] In such a context Habermas discovered his own

---

287 Published in Houston Freethought Alliance Newsletter, Vol. 111-117, 2009.

288 Max Horkheimer was the director of the Frankfurt Institute for Social Research and author of the philosophical trend labeled "critical theory." It was based primarily on Marx and Hegel's dialectical philosophy augmented by the insights from developing new sciences, psychology and anthropology. This multidisciplinary approach was characterized as self- reflective, dialectical and critical. It was contrasted with the so-called traditional theory which claimed that the approach of the natural sciences was the only valid empirical approach. Moreover in the traditional theory the facts were independent of the theory. The critical theory also encompassed a practical

identity as belonging to German tradition viewed, however, from a critical distance. He was, for example enthusiastic about Martin Heidegger, but quickly turned away from him as well as from Konrad Adenauer's regime which, according to him, did not acknowledge the break with the German immediate past. Habermas developed a certain sympathetic attitude toward Marx and the Marxist movement and because of it he was forced to leave the Frankfurt Institute and move to the University of Marburg where he received his habilitation in 1961. Since 1964 he worked as a professor of philosophy and sociology at the University of Frankfurt until his retirement in 1994 with a break between 1971 and 1983 when he became a director of the Max Planck Institute in Stanberg.

Habermas was always responding to the pressing current issues of society. In the 1960's he initially supported the student movement, but quickly became disappointed by their radical policies. After the fall of the Berlin Wall in 1989 and the reunification of Germany he criticized the way the process was done. In the 1990's he studied American democracy and American liberal constitutional traditions and valued the appropriation of the Western democratic traditions by Germany, though he remains in his methodological approach a strong critic of both capitalism and liberalism. On the political level he advocated a "constitutional patriotism" as a form of identification with one's now traditions:

> The political culture of a country crystallizes around its constitution. Each national culture develops a distinctive interpretation of those constitutional principles... such as popular sovereignty and human rights – in the light of its own national history. A "constitutional patriotism" based on

---

normative aspect leading to the transformation of the society. The Frankfurt School relocated during the war to the US where its theorists became exposed to the American consumer, industrialized capitalistic society which they characterized as manipulative leading to a false sense of freedom and happiness. After the return to Frankfurt, Adorno and Horkheimer became pessimistic about the possibility of realizing the goal of a critical theory – to transform society. In their further analysis, they came to the conclusion that the modern bureaucratized world is shaped by rationalization which involves mathematization, objectification of nature, and the demise of mythical and religious worldviews. Through the increased role of science and technology, the modern vision of the world becomes more and more institutionalized and instrumentalized. Thus the Enlightenment instead of liberating men from nature leads to man's imprisonment in the new system of administrative and economic control. It leads to misery, poverty, moral regression, violence, intolerance and intellectual *aporia* (perplexity, or in the extended meaning, impossibility of change).

these interpretations can take the place originally occupied by nationalism.[289]

Habermas belongs to the second generation of the Frankfurt School of theorists and follows the pragmatic American tradition of Charles Sanders Peirce (1839-1914)[290] and John Dewey (1859-1952).[291]

1. Methodological pragmatism of Habermas

Habermas developed his critical theory by responding to the pessimistic aporia of the first generation of Frankfurt thinkers. His methodological approach starts with a *critical analysis of language and its meaning,* not unlike Ludwig Wittgenstein's.[292] He calls it a "linguistic turn" and contrasts it with "the paradigm of the philosophy of consciousness" which was based on certain basic assumptions: Cartesian subjectivity – subject or self is an internal mind as the locus of ideas; Cartesian metaphysical dualism of body and mind; subject-object metaphysics – the world is a totality of objects and a totality of acting subjects;[293] the grounding of knowledge on sense data or a class of primitive sentences;[294] the requirement of the "first philosophy" which would provide a demonstration of the validity of scientific inquiry. This "philosophy of consciousness," according to Habermas, establishes

---

289 Jürgen Habermas, *The Inclusion of the Other,* transacted by C. Cronin and P. De Greiff, (Cambridge: Polity Press, 1996). p. 118.

290 Charles Sanders Peirce (1839-1914) was an American logician, mathematicians and philosopher. His formal education was in the field of chemistry. Because of his contribution to logic and the founding of pragmatism, he is appreciated as one of the most original and versatile American philosophers. Bertrand Russell evaluated him as "Beyond doubt [...] he was one of the most original minds of the later nineteenth century, and certainly the greatest American thinker ever." He obtained his BA and MA degrees from Harvard University and in 1863 M.Sc. in chemistry from the Lawrence Scientific School. Between 1859 and 1891, Peirce was intermittently employed in various scientific capacities by the United States Coast Survey and in 1879, he was appointed lecturer in logic at the new Johns Hopkins University. His works were published in the eight volumes of the *Collected Papers of Charles Sanders Peirce,* published between 1931 and 1958. A selection of Peirce's philosophical writings was published in *Selected Writings. Values in a Universe if Chance,* edited by Philip Wiener, (Dover Publications, Inc., New York, 1966) and in two volumes *The Essential Peirce* (Vol. 1, edited by Houser and Kloesel; Vol. 2, edited by the Peirce Edition Project, Indiana University Press, Bloomington, 1992 and 1998).

291 John Dewey (1859-1952) was an American philosopher and psychologist but is primarily known as an educational reformer. He is considered, together with Charles Peirce and William James, as one of the founders of pragmatism. He advocated democracy which should comprise two important elements - schools and civil society. In the construction of society, full democracy was to be obtained not only by extending voting rights but also by ensuring that there exists a fully-formed public opinion accomplished by communication among citizens and politicians.

292 Ludwig Wittgenstein (1889-1951) was an Austrian born philosopher who contributed to the field of logic and philosophy of language. He was an inspiring force to the Vienna Circle and to the Oxford philosophers. His most important works are *Tractatus Logico-Philosophicus* translated by D. F. Pears and B. F. McGuinness with an introduction by Bertrand Russell, (London: Routledge & Kegan Paul, 1961) and *Philosophical Investigations,* edited by James C. Klagge and Alfred Nordmann, (Indianapolis and Cambridge: Hackett, 1993).

293 G. W. F. Hegel (1770-1831) postulated a single self-knowing subject spirit which formed the world.

294 This was the epistemological doctrine of the Vienna Circle and is a basis for much of modern philosophy.

criteria for correct knowledge[295]; social atomism – the community is constituted by individuals remaining in relation with each other while the individual subjects are not constituted by relationship among themselves or with society as a whole. Society simply serves the pre-existing needs and desires of the subjects; society is a kind of collective person, macrosubject.

Habermas rejects all the premises of the "philosophy of consciousness." He sees society as a medium in which we live. Society in his view is not an aggregate of individuals or a unity. It is, rather, a complex, multifarious, intersubjective structure with many different overlapping spheres. Moreover philosophy does not have priority over natural sciences. It may, however, fill gaps in the natural sciences and provide hypotheses which would require empirical confirmation.

1. Theory of Meaning.

In the standard theory of meaning, the meaning of a sentence consists of a truth proposition, that is to know what would make it true or false. This is propositional meaning and it makes sense for some descriptive sentences, e.g., "snow is white." But it does not fit into sentences such as "how do you do?" Thus Habermas develops a view that language has a pragmatic or performative function to establish intersubjective consensus for understanding what the utterance conveys.[296]

> One simply would not know what it is to understand the meaning of a linguistic expression if one did not know how one could make use of it in order to reach an understanding with someone about something.[297]

The meaning of utterances rests on reasons, and their relation with the consensus Habermas denotes as validity.[298] "We understand the meaning of a speech or act, when we know what would make it acceptable." Moreover, the meaning of utterances and actions is public

---

295 As proponents of such a view on philosophy one may list here René Descartes (1596-1650) and Immanuel Kant (1724-1804).

296 Habermas's view of language is an elaboration of the studies on the language use done by Karl Bühler (1879-1963) who differentiated three functions of the language depending on the three elements involved in communication: objects or facts – cognitive function, speaker – expressive function, and hearer – appeal function.

297 Jürgen Habermas, *On the Pragmatics of Communication*, translated and edited by Maeve Cooke, (Cambridge, MA: MIT Press, 2000), p. 228.

298 It is not the meaning of the term used in logic. In logic validity is understood as a "truth- preserving inferential relation between well-formed sentences."

or shared because the reasons are public or shared. Habermas treats meaning and understanding as one aspect of speech because they relate to interaction between interlocutors. Thus they are intersubjective.

Any act of communication by the speaker by necessity is characterized by three postulates to its validity which represent the same three types of meaning:

- to truth, i.e., epistemic, that there are good reasons for believing the statement, its content and its utterance;

- to rightness, i.e., normative, that the speaker claims the rightness of the underlying moral norm because there are reasons justifying it;

- to truthfulness, i.e., expressive.

And there are four factors involved in understanding the meaning of an utterance:

- recognition of its literal meaning

- evaluation of the intentions of the speaker or hearer

- knowledge of the reasons which would be adduced for justification of the statement

- acceptance of those reasons

This Habermas theory may be flawed, however, because it depends on his handling of meaning and understanding. For simple understanding of what others mean, shared understandings and shared meanings do not guarantee that they will adhere to the same social and moral rules. Rather, social order rests on intersubjective agreement. Moreover, normal language may combine in one utterance all the types of validity or meaning differentiated by Habermas.

B. Theory of Communication.

Based on his theory of meaning Habermas now builds his theory of communication or how agents in society develop consensus. The speaker must convince the interlocutor to accept his utterance. The general pattern would be like this: the meaning of the utterance depends on its validity which is conditioned by the reasons which the speaker could adduce to convince the hearer. Most often the reasons are tacitly recognized and accepted.

In the case wherein the hearer asks the speaker for explanations and reasons, we have discourse which can be defined as a reflective or critical form of speech between the listener and speaker, a two-way method of dialoguing and aiming at reaching a consensus. If they reach consensus, critical discourse leads to a rational agreement which Habermas labels as communicative action since the communication may lead to an action. Interpersonal discourse is an everyday form of communication in modern societies. And Habermas classifies it into three groups just as there are three types of meanings and validities (truth, rightness, truthfulness):

- theoretical discourse (truth statements in a very broad meaning)

- moral-practical discourse

- aesthetic discourse

What is important here is that each participant is obligated to reflect on his/her own discourse and correct it or modify it as the need arises. In the discourse the position of the interlocutor is assumed in order to point out its untruth or truth, whatever it may be. This is essentially the Socratic method of discourse adopted by many philosophers. There are certain rules which must be fulfilled to achieve a rational agreement:

1. The first level rules must fulfill the logical and semantic principles

2. The second level rules involve the principle of sincerity and the principle of accountability (participant will justify upon request what he/she asserts or provide reasons for not doing this)

3. The third level rules protect the discourse against coercion, repression and inequality such as:

- No one's participation can be refused;

- The discourse does not allow any dogma to be accepted, all participants must try to be open-minded;

- All participants are allowed to introduce any assertion;All participants are allowed to express their views, attitudes, desires.

The formation of many public institutions in the eighteenth century was probably paradigmatic for recognizing a public sphere in the discourse and formulating an ideology. Habermas's innovation was that he recognized this public sphere as open and universally accessible. In the nineteenth and twentieth centuries these public spheres became subject to manipulation by social structures, nevertheless he believes that they still can achieve their goal through, e.g., political parties or other social organizations. He wanted to identify those public institutions that foster autonomy and resist the negative effects of capitalism and state administration. In this point Habermas differed from Adorno[299] who aimed at the emancipation of the individual who should refuse to adjust to the current social reality and reach the Kantian level of autonomy. This communicative action represents discursive rationality and in turn is a point of convergence for various cultures and societies which is based on the role played by universal concepts such as truth, rationality, justification, and consensus found in every community. They form a "grammar" for the discourse by analogy to Chomsky's universal language grammar:

> We may assume that the know-how informing argumentative practices represents a point of convergence where participants, however diverse their backgrounds, can at least intuitively meet in their efforts to reach an understanding. In all languages and in every language community, such concepts as truth, rationality, justification, and consensus, even if interpreted differently and applied according to different criteria, play *the same grammatical role*.[300]

Though the norms of equality and universality of participation are part of language discourse, there is no perfect communicative action.

---

299 Adorno's aim for his critical theory was to equip people with the capacities to resist integration into the institutions of capitalistic society and the most important part of it was to use one's reason in order to think for oneself.

300 Jürgen Habermas, *Between Facts and Norms*, translated by William Rehg, (Cambridge, MA: MIT Press, 1998), p. 311.

It can be considered an ideal and various biases can be brought to light during the process. Nevertheless through such a procedure which is self-reflective, interpersonal, non-dogmatic, and inclusive, we may arrive at a universalized knowledge.

Habermas's approach became centered on the normative structures and development of moral consciousness as opposed to the views of the Vienna Circle which maintained that the knowledge of the social structures must conform to the rules of the natural sciences. He divided all knowledge into three categories:

a. Theoretical knowledge is concerned with the technical control over non- human nature;

b. Practical and moral knowledge is concerned with human interests and each other;

c. Critical knowledge of social interactions and psychoanalysis is concerned with emancipation of individuals, their freedom from illusions and realization of the good life.

The major difference between paradigms of the social sciences and the natural sciences is that the theories of the latter follow in a historical succession replacing one the other, whereas the theories of the former compete with each other undergoing continuous modifications and transformations.

This method now is applied to various realms of society: social structure, cohesion, secularization, and cultural pluralism; interpersonal relations; democracy, human rights. Thus Habermas develops several theories concerning society, morality, and politics. The scheme illustrates Habermas's reasoning which from a critical analysis of language leads to postulating theories concerning all aspects of social life:

critical analysis of the meaning of language

↓ communicative action

↕   ↕   ↕

social theory ↔ moral theory ↔ political theory

II. Structure and Function of Society

A. Social Theory

In his early years Habermas was engaged in the critique of Marxism contesting the Marxist tenets that the basic human relations are those of labor and forces of production. Hence it followed that freedom could be achieved by emancipation of the forces of production and transformation of the relations of production.

Habermas took a critical stand vis-à-vis Marxist theory and found inspiration for his own evaluation in two sources. One was the view of Simone Weil (1909-1943)[301] who argued that the relations of labor and work are instrumental relations of subject and object, whereas human relations are relations between subjects and are noninstrumental. The other was American pragmatism and German hermeneutic tradition which claimed that philosophical theories and ideas must find implementation in everyday life to be effective in changing lives of people.[302]

The starting point of Habermas's thinking was the analysis of the meaning of human action. The standard approach would consider that the meaning of human action depends on grasping the reasons for the action and knowing the circumstances of the action both of which must be accessible to the interpreter as well. Though Habermas accepts this procedure he points to the flaws in it, namely it assumes that each individual has his/her needs and desires independent of their social context, thus the public meanings would depend on private, individual meaning. Moreover, the standard approach is based on an assumption that people behave rationally. Habermas avoids this issue by postulating that people are streamlined by economic and administrative structures into instrumentally (directed by others rather than by themselves) rational patterns of behavior.[303] This reasoning is Habermas's basis for

---

301   Simone Weil (1909-1943) was a French philosopher, Christian mystic, and social activist. Weil was a precocious at school and studied philosophy at the École Normale Supérieure, receiving her aggrégation in 1931. Weil taught philosophy at a secondary school for girls in Le Puy. She had a broad interest in religions and tried to understand all religious traditions. She wrote extensively about political movements and about spiritual mysticism. Most of her works were published posthumously.

302   Among pragmatists one has to list William James (1842-1910), John Dewey (1859-1952), George Herbert Mead (1863-1931), and Charles Sanders Peirce (1839-1914). German hermeneutic tradition is represented by Wilhelm Dilthey (1833-1911) and Hans-Georg Gadamer (1900-2002).

303   With it is related the issue why the masses go along with the institutions or laws that oppress them as at the time of Marx (1818-1883), or still support the church and religious institutions today. The answer given by Marx was that they held false beliefs about what their true interests are. He used for such false beliefs the term "ideologies." And the problem was that it was not enough to make them aware of the false beliefs. One had to identify and alter ideology- generating mechanisms.

his theory of rationality, as well as for his social, moral, political, and legal theories.

From this general approach Habermas now speculates how the social order may develop. People commit themselves to actions by justifying them using language from good reasons which constitute their rational validation. This validation has practical function because it guides the action of the social agents. Commitments have moral status on the ground that they are universally applicable, are unavoidable, and produce obligations by others. Social agents now become accustomed to this pattern, develop mutual recognition of good reasons and, as a result, a social order and stability develops without the threat of punishment, religious traditions or previous moral values.[304]

Habermas is essentially a social scientist and his concern about society refers to the problem of how a social order and integrity can be maintained. His response is that in modern democratic and secular society this is possible through the communicative action and discourse which have a conceptual role and the instrumental or strategic action which is practical result of reasoning how to select the best means to a given end.

So Habermas differentiates between two types of practical action: instrumental and strategic. Instrumental action (which can be discussed together with the strategic action) occurs when the agent does something in order to bring about a desired end. Strategic action involves getting other people to do things as a means of realizing one's own ends. They are characterized by two criteria: 1. action is determined antecedently and independently of the means of its realization; 2. is realized by causative action in the objective world. Communicative action, on the other hand, does not meet these criteria. These two types of action are basic and irreducible to other types. Habermas wants to show by his distinctions that an adequate explanation of a society must involve first, the concept of communicative action, and that all successful action in the world depends on reaching a consensus. And he bases his analysis on the language analysis produced by J. L. Austin

---

304   This view of social order contrasts with the one held by Thomas Hobbes (1588-1679) (*Leviathan or the Matter, Forme and Power of a Commonwealth Ecclesiastical and Civil*, Macmillan Publishing Company, Collier Books, 1962. Originally published in 1651) who speculated how a social order could derive from a large number of individuals who do not know each other and are not able to coordinate their actions in an explicit agreement. Thus he postulated that the social order is created by the laws and authority of a ruler who is supported by the use of force and punishment

(1911-1960) who differentiated *illocutionary* and *perlocutionary* effects. An illocutionary effect of speech-act is to reach rationally motivated consensus; to make someone accept voluntarily an argument as valid or reasonable and comply with it. A perlocutionary effect is the effect of speech-act apart from eliciting understanding; it is a warning or alarm. It can be good, bad, or neither. Both these effects are parasitic on communicative action which alone is free-standing.

Habermas argues in this way against the instrumental and atomistic view of society which cannot account for the phenomenon of communication between agents and its integrative effect. Ancient, anthropological and modern views of society (inspired by Hobbesian or rational choice theory) neglect the role of communication and discourse in forming bonds between agents. This standard view assumes that society is an aggregate of lone individual reasoners essentially self-interested. And then the meaning of actions depends on truth conditions of propositional attitudes attributed to lone individuals on the basis of their behavior and the logical deductions performed inside their heads. According to Habermas, this is the wrong theory of meaning and false rationality,

B. Theory of Social Ontology

The theory of social ontology distinguishes between lifeworld and system both of which are the site of communicative and instrumental action and the latter depends on the first.

Lifeworld is the term used first by Edmund Husserl (1859-1938)[305] to contrast the pre-theoretical attitude of people to the world with that of the objectifying and mathematicizing perspective of natural science. In Habermas's perspective the lifeworld is the word for unmarketized and informal domains of social life: family, household, culture, political life outside organized parties, mass media, voluntary organizations, etc. This is a background for communicative action constituting a certain

---

305 Edmund Gustav Albrecht Husserl (1859-1938) was a philosopher who is credited with the foundation of phenomenology. He was born into a Jewish family in Moravia and was baptized a Lutheran in 1887. He studied mathematics and obtained his Ph.D. in philosophy under Franz Brentano and Carl Stumpf. He taught philosophy at Halle and became professor at Gottingen (9101) and at Freiburg im Breisgau (1928). His teachings influenced many philosophers and thinkers of the modern era: Jean Paul Sartre, Emmanuel Levinas, Rudolf Carnap, Paul Ricoeur, Jacques Derrida, Roman Ingarden. Major selections of his work: Dallas Willard, translator, *Early Writings in the Philosophy of Logic and Mathematics*, (Dordrecht: Kluwer, 1994); D. Welton, editor, *The Essential Husserl*, (Bloomington: Indiana University Press, 1999).

unity but not totality of vision. The contents of lifeworld can be revised and changed just like Otto Neurath (1882- 1945)[306] visualized it for the language situation. And this is done through communicative action and discourse.

Lifeworld has several functions: it provides the contents for action – i.e., shared assumptions and background knowledge, shared reasons to reach consensus; it is a force for social integration, a platform for agreement, and provides a condition for the possibility of critical reflection and possible disagreement. It is the medium for the symbolic and cultural reproduction of society and transmission of all kinds of knowledge. It provides 'social integration.'

System is the term referring to the structures and established patterns of instrumental action. It operates on the basis of resources of meaning coming from the lifeworld. It is subdivided into two subsystems: money and power which are the means by which it imposes external aims on agents. It is a 'steering media,' of the capitalist economy and the state administration and related institutions (including political parties). Agents fall here into pre-established patterns of instrumental behavior and action, which are determined antecedently and independently of reaching consensus. The chief function of the two sub-systems is the material reproduction of society, i.e., its goods and services. But they have also a coordinating and integrating effect of their own – 'system integration.'

In this view of social ontology Habermas differs from Horkheimer and Adorno. There are dangers in the structure of the system: systems promote situations where agents conceal their aims and do not reflect on the ends of actions, moreover the ultimate aims of agents are not up to them. There are other dangers of this arrangement: money and power become uncoupled from the lifeworld, capitalistic economy and administration become detached from family and culture, from public sphere such as mass media and slowly absorb lifeworld and its functions. Habermas list the following pathologies which may result from this 'colonization' of the lifeworld:

---

306 Otto Neurath (1882-1945) was an Austrian philosopher of science, sociologist and political economist. He was forced to flee Austria to Great Britain. He was a leading member of the Vienna Circle of philosophers. He was the major author behind the Vienna Circle Manifesto. *Philosophical Papers 1913-1946: With a Bibliography of Neurath in English (Vienna Circle Collection, Volume 16)* by Otto Neurath, Robert S. Cohen, and Marie Neurath, (D. Reidel Publishing Company, 1983).

1. decrease in shared meaning and mutual understanding (anomie);

2. social disintegration;

3. increase in the alienation of people – feelings of hopelessness and a lack of belonging;

4. An unwillingness to take responsibility (demoralization);

5. social instability and crisis. Thus this colonization produces malfunction of society and at the same time morally flawed individuals.

Theory of modernity

Habermas's social theory is a diagnosis and critique of modern forms of social life and his discourse ethics is a justification and elucidation of modern morality. They are developed on a background of his views on modernity which he discusses in two perspectives. One is a historical narrative of the development of Western society from the medieval period to the late twentieth century and the other the emergence of secular morality from a Christian religious tradition.

A. The Historical Account

From the seventeenth century there was a massive increase in knowledge, particularly in the natural sciences. It started in the Middle Ages from the Aristotelian principles of observation but it led to precise mathematical formulations, testing predictive hypotheses, and an increase in practical technical knowledge. As a result, this process led to the separation of the three major spheres of values: 1. scientifictechnical; 2. legal-moral; 3. aesthetic-expressive – all within the realm of lifeworld. This separation is associated with the transfer of epistemic and practical authority from religious traditions to validity of which Habermas differentiates three types: 1. truth; 2. rightness; 3. truthfulness. They, in turn, correlate with the three types of discourse: 1. theoretical; 2. moral; and aesthetic. Habermas considers that religious views collapse in the wake of rationalization and increase in our knowledge, however, this leads to an increasing gap between what we know and how we live.

Since Habermas considers modernity in historical development, it is an unfinished project. He sees it as a cultural movement that responds to particular problems arising from an increase in specialized knowledge and the need to connect it with common sense and everyday life. The discrepancy between the growth of technical knowledge and the worthwhile forms of social life (addressed already by Horkheiemer and Adorno) calls for a "post-metaphysical philosophy" which could produce a new interpretation and provide guidance. The process, however, cannot be stopped or reversed, and alternatives as suggested by Alasdair MacIntyre (b. 1929),[307] a return to the Thomist tradition of moral virtues or by Martin Heidegger (1889-1976),[308] a return to a more rural way of life, which together with post-modernism do not provide, according to Habermas, reasonable solutions. He recognizes the benefits of economic, cultural, technological, and social achievements. However, he warns against the corrosive effects of capitalistic system. He does not see at present any force to prevent these effects.

B. The Emergence of Secular Morality

Since Habermas considers modernity as a process in which subjects liberate themselves from traditional roles and values, and create a new social order through communication and discourse, it follows that they create new "normativity" out of their own discourses. And he understands "normativity" as new meanings and understandings which are shared and rational i.e., based on mutual recognition of validity claims. The issue here is the emergence of secular morality from the Judeo-Christian tradition, namely the question of how to live one's life. Habermas contends that gradually an ethics based on religious tradition was replaced by competing conceptions of the good and

---

307 Alasdair Chalmers MacIntyre (born in 1929 in Glasgow, Scotland) is a moral and political philosopher and works as a Senior Research Professor of Philosophy at the University of Notre Dame. He argues for one moral tradition which he considers "the best theory so far," namely, the tradition of Thomistic Aristotelianism. Alasdair MacIntyre, *Whose Justice? Which Rationality?* (Notre Dame: University of Notre Dame Press, 1988).

308 Heidegger was raised a Roman Catholic and first studied theology at the University of Freiburg then switched to philosophy and obtained his doctoral degree in 1916. He served as a soldier during the WW I and after the war as a senior assistant to Edmund Husserl at the University of Freiburg, then as a professor of philosophy at the University of Marburg until his retirement in 1928. In 1933 he became rector of the University and joined the Nazi party. After one year he resigned from this position and from the party in 1945. He regained his privileges as a former professor in 1951 and taught regularly until 1967 as professor emeritus. His best known work is *Being and Time* (1927) which is considered to be one of the most important philosophical works of the 20th century. *Being and Time,* translated by John Macquarrie and Edward Robinson (London: SCM Press, 1962); re-translated by Joan Stambaugh (Albany: State University of New York Press, 1996). Heidegger believed all investigations of being since Plato have been focused on particular entities and their properties or substance. The correct analysis of being should be focused on "that on the basis of which beings are already understood." Heidegger suggested that philosophical inquiry should be conducted in a new way, through a process of retracing the steps of the history of philosophy.

transformed from a set of commands to a system of principles and valid norms which are universal and unconditional. Though they are a legacy of the religious tradition, they function in a new social order. This consideration would refer to the existing morality in practice.

Similarly, one could consider the history of moral theory, and Habermas emphasizes that Kant was the first among the moral philosophers who pointed to modern conception of morality, namely, the "formula of universal law," maxims which are incorporated into the will:

Act only on that maxim by which you can at the same time will it to be a universal law.[309]

In Kant's ethics, moral actions are expressions of a free act, and based on establishing the validity of moral norms by each individual. Habermas, as a sociologist, criticizes Kant for this individualistic twist and considers morality a collective process of reaching a consensus:

The emphasis shifts from what each can will without contradiction to be a general law, to what all can will in agreement to be a universal law.[310]

Habermas develops Kantian ethics into a discourse of social consensus.

C. Theory of Social Evolution

Habermas develops also a theory of social progress by analogy to the theory of development of individuals and a learning process developed by Lawrence Kohlberg (1927-1987).[311] Though Kohlberg claimed that his theory has empirical support, nevertheless utilitarians and feminists objected to it pointing to some limitations that restrict

---

309 Immanuel Kant, *Foundations of the Metaphysics of Mortals, and What is Enlightenment?* translated with an introduction by Lewis White Beck, (New York : Macmillan Publishing Company, 1988), p. 39.

310 Jürgen Habermas, *Moral Consciousness and Communicative Action*, translated by Christian Lenhardt and Shierry Weber Nicholsen, (Cambridge, MA : The MIT Press, 1990), p. 67.

311 Lawrence Kohlberg developed a theory, based on the philosophical intuition of Cicero, of the moral development of children through three levels – the pre-conventional, conventional, and post-conventional, each subdivided into two stages: level 1: stage 1 – morality is understood as obedience and punishment and avoidance of harm to others; stage 2 – morality is understood as satisfying one's own interests and letting others do the same; level 2: stage 3 – morality is understood as playing the role of being a good person, i.e., meeting expectations, following the rules, and being concerned about others; stage 4 – morality is understood as doing one's duty, maintaining the social order and the welfare of the society. Level 3: stage 5 – morality is understood as basic rights, values, and legal contracts of a society. Laws and duties are calculated on overall utility (utilitarian morality); stage 6 – morality is understood as an accord with universal, self-chosen principles (e.g., justice, equality and respect for the dignity of all human beings) which confer validity to maxims and actions (Kantian morality).

the importance of their own theories. Habermas accepts this theory but replaces Kant's objective principles with his moral discourse theory. He equates the development of society as analogical to the development of moral consciousness achieved through the learning process. So he differentiates pre-conventional, conventional, and post-conventional societies. In conventional societies morality is bound to religious and tribal authorities; modern societies are those which are bound by universalistic morality and legitimate law. There is a problem, however, with such a differentiation and classification of societies. For one thing, the historical development of societies does not confirm their moral progression analogical to the individual behavior. Moreover in collective society there is no controlling consciousness analogical to individual consciousness. And he rejects Hegelian teleological concept of society as a form of self-developing spirit. We should see rather a development of societies as a fragile balance between pathologies associated with modernization and positive aspects linked to practical, economic and cognitive gains.

IV. Habermas and Traditional Religion

Habermas acknowledges the emergence of secular morality but he treats it as a consequence of the modern form of consciousness like abstract law, modern science, and art which could have developed only through the participation of Hellenistic Christianity and the Roman church in the process. He claims that through the concept of one God the Western world was able to achieve objectification of an external nature and a community of morally regulated agents in a society. Thus all modern achievements, egalitarian society, ideas of freedom, autonomous conduct of life, emancipation of individuals, the individual morality of conscience, human rights, and democracy are direct heirs of the Judaic ethics of justice and of the Christian ethics of love. Buddhism gained similar achievement through its concept of interpersonal consciousness. Globalization in the modern world is only a new infrastructure and not a new form of consciousness.

But modernity and globalization in turn affect religious consciousness and theology leading to ecumenism without paternalism, global inclusive Christian ethics and pluralism in worldviews. Each religious confession must now adopt a relationship with the competing messages of other religions and the objections of science and secularized common sense. Religions must become reflexive and call for reasonableness, restrain from violence and implement religious tolerance. In terms of globalization – human rights should become the universal language regulating global relations and not the Christian civilizing tradition. Confronting other cultures we should not see them as alien but recognize their distinctive character with their religion at the core. With respect to human freedom, we should recognize: (1) an intersubjective constitution of autonomy, that is that no one is free unless recognized by at least one other subject, and (2). the self-binding of the individual will to unconditionally valid norms, that is, the unconditional character of the moral "ought." These are the essential principles of Kantian ethical theory.

In pre-modern societies religious ideas are the glue for solidarity and are excluded from rational critique. In modern societies traditional worldviews are not immune to critical discourse: "when one enters into full communicative action, it is difficult to retain one's pre-modern, conventional, parochial view of the world." Traditional cohesion is threatened, group members must "agree to disagree," mythical traditions undergo destruction. Traditional groups may view it as a threat to their identity. But demythologizing of a culture is a necessary process for producing rational morality:

> To consolidate into a rational conduct of life … the cultural tradition must permit a reflective relation to itself … stripped of its dogmatism.[312]

But it is not Eurocentric intellectual colonization, because rational agreement via propositional language is already the *telos* of communication in all cultures.

Habermas maintains that religions will survive, at least for a long time, because neither science, art, the economy nor governmental bureaucracy can provide solidarity once generated by traditional religious beliefs. Only moral norms produced via communicative action have the potential to produce such solidarity. Only moral norms

---

312   Jürgen Habermas, *The Theory of Communicative Action,* translated by Thomas McCarthy, Vols. 1-2, (Cambridge UK: Polity Press, 1981). 1, p. 71.

have an emotional sense of religious power to produce strong moral obligations:

> The [traditional] binding force of moral agreement grounded in the sacred can be replaced only by moral agreement that expresses in rational form what was always intended in the symbolism of the holy: the generality of the underlying interest.[313]

> Something of the penetrating power of primordial sacred powers still attaches to morality; it permeates . . . culture, society, and personality in a way that is unique in modern societies.[314]

> The authority of moral norms rests on the fact that they embody a general interest, and the unity of the collective is at stake in protecting this interest. . . . The 'ought' quality of moral norms implicitly invokes the danger that any harm to the social bond means for all the members of a collectivity— the danger of anomie, of group identity breaking down, of the members' common life-contexts disintegrating.[315]

There is no other answer to the question, Why be moral?

When asked: "But can it be extended beyond the dimension of the nation to create global solidarity?" He answers: " 'Rationalization' does not plug the wellspring of solidarity; rather, it discovers new ones as the old ones run dry."

As for philosophy replacing the values of religious traditions, Habermas is pessimistic claiming that philosophy has not yet reworked all the values of religious traditions into secular language. Until that time the language of religion will continue to have a legitimate place in society. Philosophical translations of religious insight lose the "performative meaning" of faith:

> Philosophy, even in its postmetaphysical form, will be able neither to replace nor to repress religion as long as religious

---

313 Jürgen Habermas, *The Theory of Communicative Action*, translated by Thomas McCarthy, Vols. 1-2, (Cambridge UK: Polity Press, 1981). 2, p. 81.
314 Ibidem, 2, p. 92.
315 Ibidem, 2, 93.

language is the bearer of a semantic content that is inspiring and even indispensable, for this content eludes (for the time being?) the explanatory force of philosophical language and continues to resist translation into reasoning discours.es.[316]

Indispensable semantic potentials are preserved in religious language, potentials that philosophy has not yet fully exhausted by translating them into the language of public reasons, that is, reasons assumed to be capable of commanding general agreement. Taking the example of the concept of the individual person, ... I attempted to point out this deficit, or at least the clumsiness of philosophical attempts at translation. In my view, the basic concepts of philosophical ethics, as they have been developed up to this point, do not even come close to capturing all the intuitions which have already found nuanced expression in the language of the Bible and which we learn only through a halfway religious socialization. Mindful of this deficiency, discourse ethics attempts to translate the categorical imperative into a language that enables us to do justice to another intuition, I mean the feeling of "solidarity," the bond of a member of a community to her fellow members.[317]

When asked whether it is the goal of philosophy to assimilate, to translate, to rework and to "sublate" all religious contents worth preserving or whether he thinks that religion will indefinitely resist all such attempted interventions, and that it will therefore remain forever unassimilatable and inaccessible, and to a certain extent also autonomous and indispensable, he answers : "I don't know that will transpire when philosophy conducts its work on its religious heritage with more sensitivity than heretofore."

And more:

In the ethics of Christian love the imitation of Christ enjoins an active sacrifice of one's hard-won legitimate interests. But on earth there is no absolute power that may impose

---

316 Jürgen Habermas, "A Conversation about God and the World." In Jürgen Habermas, *Time of Transitions*, edited and translated by Ciaran Cronin and Max Pensky, (Polity Press, Cambridge, UK: 2006), p. 163.
317 Ibidem, p. 164.

a sacrifice upon an autonomous individual for supposedly higher ends. This is why the Enlightenment wanted to abolish sacrifice. Today, this same skepticism is directed against the death penalty and against the legitimacy of obligatory military service. This is the reason for the cautiously resigned restriction to a morality of justice.[318]

But I does not diminish our admiration for the case of selfless sacrifices, e.g., by mothers and women.

At the same time Habermas differentiates between religion and theology stating that theology has a certain "parasitic or derivative status." "It can never exhaust the performative meaning of lived faith." "It is all the more true for philosophy." "Philosophy can never more or less appropriate the forms of experience preserved in religious language along the 'path of translation.'" Moreover,

> Theology cannot provide a substitute for religion, for the latter's truth is nourished by the revealed Word, which inherently manifests itself in religious and not in learned form. But philosophy has an entirely different relation to religion. It seeks to express what it can learn from religion in a discourse that is marked precisely by its independence from revealed truth. Thus, every philosophical translation forfeits performative meaning of lived faith. A philosophy that makes itself dependent on, or takes solace from, 'destinies' is no longer philosophy. The goal of philosophy's 'translation program' is, if you like it, to rescue at most the profane meaning of interpersonal and existential experiences that have thus far only been adequately articulated in religious language. In contemporary terms, I am thinking of response to extreme situations of helplessness, of the loss of self, or of the threat of annihilation, which leave us 'at a loss for words.'[319]

V. The Pragmatic Discourse Theory of Morality

Habermas's moral theory is in the center of his social program and is a continuation of the Frankfurt School evaluation of modern

---

318 Ibidem, p. 166.
319 Ibidem, p. 165.

ethics represented by Adorno.[320] Adorno, however, was pessimistic about the possibility of living after Auschwitz and Hiroshima with a clear conscience. One can only resist the depredation brought about by mass culture. For Habermas the "new moral imperative" has a role in preventing the occurrence of another Auschwitz and organizing society in such a way that the individual could act on the basis of valid norms and answer to himself how should he act. Thus his moral theory is pragmatic and his norms are behavioral rules. He assumes that modern societies are at stage 6 of Kohlberg's developmental scheme corresponding to Kantian "categorical imperative" and the agents act on principles they can justify. Actual disputes are resolved through discourse and by establishing norms that the involved parties accept. Habermas's ethics is deontological with a small modification of the Kantian paradigm by introducing a social group factor in selecting the norm instead of a single autonomic agent acting through logical reasoning. There are two parts in the process of resolving a moral conflict: elucidation and justification.

A. Elucidation.

It starts with the assumption that there are valid moral norms recognized intuitively and contingently true. These moral norms are based, according to Habermas, on two principles: a. discourse principle and b. moral principle.

The discourse principle is a dialogical process because it always involves more than one person: "Only those action norms are valid to which all possibly affected persons could agree as participants in rational discourse." The action norms may include both legal and moral norms, and are based on the agent's moral intuition.

The discourse principle refers to discourses about norms but not all discourse involves norms (e.g., aesthetic discourse). This principle can function only in a negative way because the validity of a norm is not decided by a consensus. The meaning of the principle is that if a norm is valid then all persons involved can possibly reach a consensus. This principle may require a large number of people involved and even those who are not yet born. Thus its application is very limited.

---

320   Theodor W. Adorno, *Negative Dialectics*, (New York: Continuum International Publishing Group, 1983).

b. The moral principle or principle of universalizability is formulated thus "A norm is valid if and only if the foreseeable consequences and side effects of its general observance for the interests and value-orientation of each individual could be freely and jointly accepted by all affected." This principle is designed to test the "universalization" of the moral argument[321] but is not by itself a moral norm. Habermas argues that certain norms preserved from the Judeo-Christian tradition, e.g., "Thou shalt not kill," passed the test of time. However, Habermas neglects to mention other traditions which are even older than the Judeo-Hellenistic Christian tradition and devoid of the supernaturalistic element. This principle means that the norm is valid if the consequences of its application are universally acceptable, moreover the interests of each person must be accepted. Thus it represents another modification of the Kantian categorical deontological ethics where consequences of the action do not have any role. In Kant's system, universalization is a logical property of a maxim. The maxim does not explain why there is a moral obligation to follow it, though modern science gives an indication for its origin.[322] In the Habermas system, as in Nietzsche's,[323] it comes from the process of socialization where an individual is integrated into a social order. In this process an individual is modifying his own interests by taking into consideration the interests of others involved in the society. There are several detailed postulates associated with this principle of universalization:

1. The individuals involved, however, cannot take a position of third persons isolating themselves from the situation. They are not observers but participants in the social process.

2. The second issue involved here is that an actual discourse must take place even if it should include non-existent people.

3. This discourse has to be dialogical and cannot be only monological as in Kant's imperative.

---

321 Habermas adopted this concept of "universalization" from George Herbert Mead, an American pragmatic philosopher who considered universalization as dependent on our behavior in a social context. (*Mind, Self, and Society from the Standpoint of a Social Behaviorist*, edited by Charles W. Morris, Chicago: University of Chicago Press, 1967 [1934]).

322 Marc D. Hauser, *Moral Minds. How Nature Designed Our Universal sense of Right and Wrong*, (New York: HarperCollins Publishers, 2006).

323 Friedrich Nietzsche, *The Birth of Tragedy and The Genealogy of Morals*, translated by Francis Golfing, (Anchor Books, New York, 1956).

4. By the process of discourse individuals integrate themselves into the society, become part of it and serve the common good. Individual interests must be considered also from the perspective of other members of the society.

B. Justification of the Moral Discourse Principle

In the previous procedure of elucidation of the moral discourse principle, it is assumed that the moral principle exists and constitutes a premise for action. Next Habermas attempted to derive the moral principle from non-moral premises. Otherwise it would be only an expression of cultural and historical sets of values. Habermas, however, failed to do it. He refers us to the rules of discourse and its normative justification (universalization). But from these rules one cannot logically infer that if a norm leads to a consensus, that at the same time one must infer that such a norm must be valid.

Habermas's moral system can be objected to on the ground that there are very few universally accepted moral norms therefore, the discourse mechanism for their selection loses much of its import for solving social conflicts, and moral norms cannot be the vehicle for holding the society together. On the other hand, human rights discourse, when the rights of individuals are asserted, puts others under obligation. People do not readily assume their own obligations towards others, thus the rights discourse may serve as a mechanism for colonization. Another objection concerns the problem of a dialogical versus a monological concept of morality. In practice the number of participants in the moral discourse may be very small, but it would affect a huge number of people. Consensus in that case may not confer validity and to indicate that each person individually judged the norm.

A final objection is that the derivation of the discourse moral principle leads to circularity. This is due to the fact that his ethics assumes a need of justification on non-moral premises. But his rules of discourse have already moral significance.

C. Discourse Ethics in Political Context

The term ethics derives from the Greek term *ethos*, which refers to the customs of a city-state and to the morals or habits of its citizens. Until the time of Hegel, the terms were used interchangeably to designate both, ethics, a moral theory and morality, a pattern of behavior. Hegel differentiated ethics as a way of life of the community, with its values, practices, institutions, and laws. Habermas, following Hegel, in order to accommodate the political aspect of the moral issues, differentiated three types of discourses:

1. The so-called ethical discourse which concerns the choice of ends evaluating what is good for an individual or collective life of the society. It deals with values which are germane to a specific cultural tradition or group and are absorbed by an individual belonging to it. Thus they concern the self- understanding of an individual or a group. They are also subject to interpretation and to gradual change. They have relative validity, are prudential and teleological. They cannot, however, outweigh the moral considerations.

The questions arise now, relative to membership in cultural groups: the group must have a common character and be large enough; the members must mutually recognize their membership; the identity of the group must be recognized by others; belonging to the group is not a matter of administrative adherence but a result of a process, e.g. upbringing and birth. It is obvious that Habermas does not include among those cultural group associations with a specific agenda or program, e.g., interest groups or lobbying groups, but, e.g., traditional cultural ethnic groups of immigrants. These ethical discourses cannot be resolved and are the source of conflict which should be resolved through moral discourse which is concerned with universally shared interests. Ethical discourse, however, involving all parties concerned may lead to clarification and compromise and thus lead to the resolution of the conflict.

2. Moral discourse, in contrast to values, concerns norms which are absolute and are either unconditionally valid or non valid and hold across competing cultural traditions. They are evaluated as either right or wrong, just or unjust, and are deontological and their validity is unconditional. In many situations it is difficult to separate these two discourses, Habermas nevertheless insists on the priority of moral discourse and moral norms which always trump the ethical values. This is due to the fact that in this discourse values are cut

from the justification process; moral norms are not cultural values but are communicative ideals of universal validity; moral discourse is not rooted in any particular cultural tradition but belongs to the post-conventional level of understanding morality. Table 1 presents comparison of these two discourses.

3. Pragmatic discourse, deals with the means to achieve a given end. It is a form of dialogical and instrumental discourse especially applicable to a political situation. Habermas was influenced here by the ideas of John Rawls (1921-2002), an American political philosopher, who set the priority of the right over the good. Rawls observed that modern societies are no longer culturally homogeneous; they comprise a plurality of worldviews. Therefore a legal and constitutional framework cannot depend on the presumed truth or on any particular worldview. It follows that the concept of right in a legal system must not be metaphysical but political. In this view moral and religious values are eliminated from the political process of justification.

Political justifications appeal to ideas and values which are widespread and command assent across cultures. Rawls terms this situation "overlapping consensus" which means that they are accepted regardless of the tradition, because everyone has a reason to accept them. One such idea is view of the society as a system of co-operation between free and equal citizens. And Rawls classifies it among the universal moral ideas.

Table 1

Classification of ethical and moral discourse

	Ethics	Morality
Basic concepts	good/bad	right/wrongjust/unjust
Basic unit	values	norms
Basic questions	What is good for meor for us?	What ought I to do, and why?
Validity	relative and conditional	absolute and unconditional
Type of theory	prudential, teleological	deontological
Aims	advice; judgment preference ranking	establishing valid norms; discoveringduties

The concept of right or justice entails setting a political framework within which each individual is free to pursue his conception of the good provided it is compatible with everyone else's freedom to do the same. Thus various conceptions of the good can coexist but justice provides the limit. At the same time "right" has pragmatic priority over the good, i.e. moral considerations.

Habermas and Rawls agree on many aspects of the social theory: both accept pluralism of the society; they agree on the difference between morality and the right; they agree on the functional priority of the right. The differences concern Habermas's emphasis on the preference of secular morality in modern societies. He also rejects Rawls's interpretation of the principles of justice as being justified because they are accepted by all whether or not they deserve to be. Habermas insists on the acceptance of norms on the ground that they must be demonstrably universalizable (Habermas's moral discourse). Thus moral rightness is treated as analogous to truth. Rawls argues that this insistence on secular morality is another metaphysics.

The major critique of the Habermas discourse ethics concerns his distinction between norms and values. Such a distinction is fuzzy because norms already presuppose values which are culturally differentiated. Thus, in a social situation, resolution of conflicts must be done on a different basis than moral, preferably political and legal.

VI The Political Theory of Democracy

Describing modern society Habermas had in mind a model developed in the Western world, that is in Europe and United States. Such a model has limited application, nevertheless, judging from the direction China and India take it will be adopted in other parts of the world. It is based on a few general phenomena: 1. modern society does not have a controlling center; 2. it is not held together by a single overarching tradition or rules; 3. it is multicultural and multiethnic; 4. individuals in such a society are autonomous moral agents who conduct their lives according to general principles; 5. individual identities persist in spite of changes in and places of residence, nationality or career; 6. these identities and subjectivity are, however, under constant pressure of discourse, especially moral discourse which, according to Habermas, was to provide the main mechanism for integration in the society. But Habermas realized that moral discourse alone was too narrow to provide a unifying function. And this is due to the fact that there are very few valid moral norms and they may be loaded with controversial values; also because humans do not act always as reliable rational moral agents (as it also was postulated by Kant). Therefore, he introduced the concept of ethical discourse which takes into consideration political institutions and laws which are additional elements holding together modern society.

In his political views Habermas differentiated informal civil society which is comprised of voluntary organizations, political associations, and the media. They do not make formal political decisions but form public opinion on matters of general concern. They are contrasted with formal political organizations such as a parliament, cabinets, elected assemblies, political administrations which make formal decisions, pass laws, formulate and implement policies and comprise the formal medium of power. Such a political system may operate well in a democracy if input from the informal spheres is large enough to influence the formulation of policies and laws. Moreover, input based only on moral considerations may be too narrow. In political discourse, ethical and pragmatic considerations come into play and they seek rational consensus. Citizens participate in the political community and secure in this way their rights and freedom which is expressed in opportunities.

The state should be neutral with regard to the values of the citizens recognizing human rights. It is not possible, however, that the state be neutral with regard to values that are inconsistent with the idea of liberty for all. Thus it seems reasonable to insist that the laws should not be justified on the basis of controversial values. Law is legitimate only if there are appreciable reasons to obey it. It is a necessary condition for its being valid. The other two conditions are that it must be imposed by a recognized authority, and it must be coercible. Habermas especially emphasizes the legitimacy of law. It is essential because legitimate laws elicit rational compliance. And in modern societies lawful behavior must arise in most cases from recognition of the legitimacy of laws. From such a consideration Habernas derives his democratic principle: "Only those laws count as legitimate to which all members of the legal community can assent in a discursive process of legislation that has in turn been legally constituted." This principle implies that legitimate laws must be assented by all members of the legal community and not that they must be actually agreed to by all. Moreover, laws must be in tune with moral norms and ethical values, and directed toward the common good.

Habermas's political system combines the ideal of liberal democracy based on the idea of human rights and the ideal of republicanism based on the idea of popular sovereignty. He subscribes to the view that rights should be acquired only through socialization and that the state should be inclusive and tolerant of different cultures and world views. Thus at the same time he rejects some basic assumptions:

assumption of liberalism:
rights belonging to pre-political individuals,
membership in the political community is merely a means to safeguard individual freedom,
neutrality of the state as avoiding appeal to values and ethical considerations;
assumption of republicanism:

state embracing the values of the political community,
realization of these values is participation in the community,
derivation of the subjective rights from the ethical self-understanding
of the community.

Habermas's theorizing represents an ideal and utopian situation,
not the actual one achievable in the society. He argues for the right
interaction between civil society and the formal medium of power
(system in Habermas's terminology). Too much input from below
would lead to anarchy and instability. It is not clear to what extent
his theory is a normative ideal for a discursive democracy and to what
extent it is an empirical descriptive exercise. Habermas's theory does
not explain how the administrative power can be prevented from
destruction of the integrity of the moral and ethical discourse in the
sphere of lifeworld.

Habermas's legal and democratic theory appears to arise from the
critical analysis of the Western societies. The danger they are facing
is that, if their legislative bodies may be influenced by powerful
interest groups, political decisions may then lead to certain ideological
distortions. Some groups may feel marginalized and alienated.
Moreover, if the governments are delegating decision-making to
informed elites, experts and interest groups, they are eliminating the
discourse process entirely.

Bibliography

Jürgen Habermas, *The Inclusion of the Other*, translated by C. Cronin
and P. de Greiff, Cambridge: Polity Press, 1998 [1996]).

Jeffrey Tate, "Habermas for Humanists," in *Essays in the Philosophy of
Humanism*, Vol. 15, pp. 59-76, 2007.

Jürgen Habermas, *Structural Transformation of the Public Sphere: An
Inquiry into a Category of Bourgeois Society*, translated by T. Burger
and F. Lawrence, (Cambridge, MA : The MIT Press, 1962).

Jürgen Habermas, *The Theory of Communicative Action,* translated by Thomas McCarthy, Vols. 1-2, (Cambridge UK: Polity Press, 1981).

Jürgen Habermas, *Moral Consciousness and Communicative Action,* translated by Christian Lenhardt and Shierry Weber Nicholsen, (Cambridge, Mass: The MIT Press, 1990).

Maeve Cooke, ed., *On the Pragmatics of Communication,* (Cambridge, MA : The MIT Press, 2000).

Jürgen Habermas, *The Philosophical Discourse of Modernity: Twelve Lectures,* translated by F. Lawrence, (Cambridge: Polity Press, 1987).

Jürgen Habermas, *Justification and Application: Remarks on Discourse Ethics,* translated by Ciaran P. Cronin, (Cambridge, MA: The MIT Press, 1994).

Jürgen Habermas, "A Conversation about God and the World." In Jürgen Habermas, *Time of Transitions,* edited and translated by Ciaran Cronin and Max Pensky, (Polity Press, Cambridge, UK: 2006), pp. 147-169.

Jürgen Habermas, Joseph Ratzinger, *Dialectics of Secularization. On Reason and Religion,* edited with a Foreword by Florian Schuller, translated by Brian McNeil, (San Francisco: Ignatius Press, 2005).

Jürgen Habermas, *Between Facts and Norms,* translated by William Rehg, (Cambridge: Polity Press, 1996).

Craig Calhoun, ed., *Habermas and the Public Sphere,* (Cambridge, MA: the MIT Press, 1995).

Lawrence Kohlberg, *Essays on Moral Development,* (San Francisco: Harper & Row, 1981, 1984), Vols. 1, 2.

John Rawls, *A Theory of Justice,* revised edition, (Cambridge, MA: Harvard University Press, 1971).

James Gordon Finlayson, *Habermas. A Very Short Introduction*, (Oxford: Oxford University Press, 2005).

Henry Le Roy Finch, *Wittgenstein,* (Rockport: Element Books, 1995).

V. ETHICS AND EVOLUTION

WHAT DOES MODERN SCIENCE SAY ABOUT THE ORIGIN OF CO-OPERATION? SCIENCE CONFIRMS PHILOSOPHY[324]

Philosophical Intuition

Investigation of the phenomenon of co-operation has a long history. Perhaps the most eloquent expression of this phenomenon was given by the Stoic, Marcus Aurelius (121-180 C.E.), Roman Emperor during the years 161-180 C.E. Aurelius followed the principles of the Stoic moral philosophy which emphasized the well-being of the community and the naturalistic basis of human behavior:

Men exist for the sake of one another.

We ought to do good to others as simply as a horse runs, or a bee makes honey, or a vine bears grapes season after season without thinking of the grapes it has borne.[325]

Aurelius wrote his *Meditations* during his campaign between 170-180 C.E. for his own guidance for he was a priest at the temple in Rome. His book was first published in print in 1558 in Zurich from a manuscript that is lost today. However, there exists another manuscript that survived to our times now located in the Vatican library. His book was read throughout the centuries for moral and spiritual edification by rulers, politicians, philosophers and writers.

Another Stoic philosopher, Cicero (106-43 B.C.E.), claimed that the pattern of human behavior changes from purely animal-like and instinctive to fully rational and involves five stages. They represent the development of human nature, but only a few people will reach the highest stages, because the process is not independent of a man's own effort. The "function" or goal of man in this process is attainment of the perfection of his nature. The term used by Cicero is *officium* (corresponding to the English office, duty or task, as the office of an official charged with certain duties) and the Greek term is *kathekon*.

---

324 Published in *Essays in the Philosophy of Humanism*, Vol. 18 (2), pp. 43-52, 2010.
325 Marcus Aurelius, *Meditations,* translated with an introduction by Maxwell Staniforth (Harmondsworth, UK: Penguin Books, 1964).

One could not talk about the "duty" of an animal or of an infant, but rather of their natural function. The term duty becomes appropriate in stages three to five in human development as the changes in behavior become the functions of a rational being.[326] Thus the Stoics recognized a natural biological basis for human behavior from which reason draws conclusions, develops rules and constructs a moral philosophy.[327]

Even Immanuel Kant (1724-1804) wondered about the origin of the moral principle that humans display and which he called "goodwill":

Duty! Thou sublime and mighty name that dost embrace nothing charming or insinuating but requirest submission and yet seekest not to move the will by threatening aught that would arouse natural aversion or terror, but only holdest forth a law which of itself finds entrance into the mind and yet gains reluctant reverence (though not always obedience) – a law before which all inclinations are mute even though secretly work against it: what origin is worthy of thee, and where is the root of thy noble descent which proudly rejects all kinship with the inclinations and from which to be descended is the indispensable condition of the only worth which men alone can give themselves?[328]

This classification of the behavioral levels derives from the Stoic intuitive philosophical doctrine[329] and corresponds to the stages of moral development of man through which community life and virtue are recognized as pre-eminently "things belonging to man" in their terminology and are related to the autonomous behavioral level (categorical imperative of Kant). In modern times such a Stoic view of the moral development of man in the Kantian modification was wholly confirmed by modern psychology and philosophy. Lawrence Kohlberg (1927- 1987) suggested six stages of the moral development

---

326 Cicero, *On the Good Life*, translated with an introduction by Michael Grant (Harmondsworth, UK: Penguin Books, 1986). Marian Hillar, "Natural development, Rationality, and Responsibility in Stoic Ethics," in *Essays in the Philosophy of Humanism*, Robert D. Finch, M. Hillar, F. Prahl, eds., Vol. 6, pp. 44-78. American Humanist Association, Houston, 1998.

327 Marian Hillar, "Natural Development, Rationlity, and Responsibility in Stoic Ethics," published in the *Essays in the Philosophy of Humanism*, Robert D. Finch, M. Hillar, F. Prahl, eds., Vol. 6, pp. 44-78. American Humanist Association, Houston, 1998.

328 Immanuel Kant, *Critique of Practical Reason*, edited and translated with notes and introduction by Lewis White Beck, third edition, (New York: Macmillan Publishing Company, 1993), p. 90.

329 *Stoicorum Veterum Fragmenta* Collegit Ioannes Ab Arnim (Stutgardiae: In Aedibus B.G. Teubneri MCMLXIV). Vol 1-4. (abbreviated as SVF). SVF 1.197.

of children through three levels – the pre-conventional, conventional, and post-conventional, each subdivided into two stages. The first two levels correspond to the heteronomous behavioral level of Kant.[330]

Evolutionary Biology and Co-operation

Looking at the principles of evolutionary theory it seems at first that the existence of co-operation should be contradictory to the evolutionary process. This difficulty was noticed already by Darwin when he discussed the origin of social moral faculties in "the primeval man." Darwin admitted that such traits as courage and fidelity could increase in competition between tribes: "A tribe rich in the above qualities would spread and be victorious over other tribes."[331] But asking how within the same tribe could a large number of members become endowed with these social and moral qualities, Darwin answered himself:

> He who was ready to sacrifice his life, as many a savage has been, rather than betray his comrades, would often leave no offspring to inherit his noble nature. ... Therefore it hardly seems probable, that the number of men gifted with such virtues, or that the standard of their excellence could be increased through natural selection, that is by the survival of the fittest; for we are not speaking here of one tribe being victorious over another.[332]

Then Darwin postulated that though the high standard of morality may give a slight advantage to each individual in a tribe, yet an increase in the number of well-endowed men and an advancement in the standard of morality will certainly give an immense advantage to one tribe over another. A tribe including many members who, from possessing in a high degree the spirit of patriotism, fidelity obedience, courage, and sympathy, were always ready to aid one another, and to sacrifice themselves for the common good, would be victorious over most tribes, and this would be natural selection."[333] Evolutionary

---

330   Lawrence Kohlberg, *Essays on Moral Development,* (San Francisco: Harper & Row, 1981, 1984), Vols. 1, 2. Marian Hillar, "Foundation of Kant's Moral Philosophy and its Reinterpretation. A Quintessential Humanistic Doctrine," in *Essays in the Philosophy of Humanism,* Vol. 17 (1), 2009, pp. 71-90.
331   Quote from Darwin's The Descent of Man. Charles Darwin, *The Origin of Species* and *The Descent of Man and Selection in Relation to Sex,* (Toronto: Modern Library, reprint of the second edition of 1860, no date). p. 498.
332   Ibid. p. 499.
333   Ibid. p. 500.

scientists classify such a selection as a "between-group selection." Moreover, co-operative and altruistic behavior, understood not in the everyday sense of conscious act, but as a behavior which benefits other organism at a cost to the donor, is widely common throughout the animal kingdom. It seems from the studies of many biologists that entire organisms like multi-cellular organisms with specialized cells could also be considered as organisms made of co-operating cells and entire colonies of social organisms depend on co-operation and often altruistic sacrifice of some individuals for the sake of the group.[334] Thus Martin A. Nowak in building mathematical models for evolution considers co-operation the third fundamental process for evolution after mutations and natural selection.[335] The problem puzzled many biologists, economists and mathematicians. Darwin suggested that natural selection favored families whose members were cooperative and answered Kant's question about the origin of moral rule:[336]

> The following proposition seems to me in a high degree probable – namely, that any animal whatever endowed with well-marked social instincts, the parental and filial affection being here included, would inevitably acquire a moral sense or conscience as soon as its intellectual powers have become as weal, or nearly as well developed in man.

This prediction by Darwin is confirmed today by scientific investigations postulating the existence of the "moral faculty."[337] The concept of the "moral faculty" goes back to antiquity when the ancients had a premonition of innate moral principles (moral sentiment, sense of justice, common moral thought) which were working subconsciously. It is the basis for the moral rules which like rules of logic or of natural sciences are objective truths, outcomes of rational choice. These rules were developed and formulated in various cultures with varying degree of success and today they are at the foundation of humanistic ethics. John Rawls (1921-2002) in his well known treatise *A Theory of Justice*

334 James H. Hunt, *The Evolution of Social Wasps* (Oxford: Oxford University Press, 2007). Bert Hölldobler and E. O. Wilson, *The Superorganism: The Beauty, Elegance, and Strangeness of Insect Societies* (NEW York: W. W. Norton & Company, 2008).

335 Martin A. Nowak, *Evolutionary Dynamics: Exploring the Equations of Life* (Cambridge, MA: Belknap Press of Harvard University Press, 2006).

336 Charles Darwin, *The Descent of Man and Selection in Relation to Sex, op. cit.* p. 471- 472.

337 Marc D. Hauser, *Moral Minds. How Nature Designed Our Universal Sense of Right and Wrong,* (New York: HarperCollins Publishers, 2006).

(1971) suggested that these innate moral principles can be analogized to the "sense of grammaticality" (a "faculty of grammar") described by Noam Chomsky.[338]

Hamilton Model of Inclusive Fitness: "Kin Selection"

The process of group selection postulated by Darwin was at first in early days of neo-Darwinism discredited as a weak evolutionary force.[339] Still the phenomenon of natural co-operative, altruistic behavior needed an explanation.

The advent of modern genetic science could attempt to explain and expand the intuitive speculations of philosophers and explain the observations of Darwin by providing insight into how biological mechanisms operate. Thus our focus is now on the genetic conditioning for co-operation. William Hamilton developed a model based on genetic studies of social insects. It is based on the observation that the offspring of relatives count toward individual fitness by helping to spread shared genes. Such a situation exists in colonies of social insects composed of related individuals. The closer the degree of relatedness, the stronger the cooperation one may expect among individuals. This theory seems to be an explanation of Darwin's dilemma and was already vaguely suggested by John Burdon Haldane (1892-1964) in the 1930s.[340] The Hamilton model can be illustrated by behavior as when a parent or a close relative jumps into the water to save one's own or closely related child. Such behavior contributes to the survival of one's own genes. The degree of relationship is an important parameter in predicting how selection will operate and the behavior which appears to be altruistic may, knowing the genetic relatedness of the organisms involved, be explained in terms of natural selection. The genes which are selected for this behavior contribute to their own perpetuation regardless of the individual in which the genes appear.[341]

---

338   Noam Chomsky, *Aspects of the Theory of Syntax* (Cambridge, MA: Harvard University Press, 1965), pp. 3-9.

339   G. C. Williams, *Adaptation and Natural Selection* (Princeton: Princeton University Press, 1966). Maynard Smith J., "Group Selection and Kin Selection," *Nature*, 201, 1145-1147, 1964. R. Dawkins, *The Selfish Gene* (Oxford: Oxford University Press, 1976).

340   Robert L. Trivers and Hope Hare, "Haplodiploidy and the Evolution of the Social Insects," in *Robert Trivers, Natural Selection and Social Theory. Selected papers of Robert Trivers* (Oxford: Oxford University Press, 2002), pp. 164-206. John Burdon Haldane, *The Causes of Evolution* (Princeton: Princeton University Press, 1990, first published in 1932). John Burdon Haldane, *What I Require from Life: Writings on Science and Life from J. B. S. Haldane*, edited by Krishna Dronamvain (Oxford: Oxford University Press, 2009).

341   Hamilton W. "The Genetical Evolution of Social Behavior," *J. Theor. Biol.*, 7:1-52, 1964.

Trivers' Model of "Reciprocal Altruism"

The model of kinship co-operation, i.e., the kin selection model of Hamilton, however, cannot explain all co-operation. Humans, for example, belong to a species that developed a high degree of co-operation among genetically unrelated individuals. Such co-operation between genetically unrelated individuals is defined as altruistic behavior or as reciprocally altruistic. It can be selected even when the recipient is so distantly related to the organism performing the altruistic act that kin selection can be ruled out. Such co-operation will represent behavior between members of different species. It is a behavior that benefits another organism not closely related while being apparently detrimental to the organism performing the behavior. Here benefit and detriment are defined in terms of contribution to inclusive fitness. Natural selection favors these altruistic behaviors because, in the long run, they benefit the organism performing them.

Robert Trivers in the 1970s developed this idea of "reciprocal altruism" as a model for explaining co-operation between genetically unrelated strangers based on naturalistic observations.[342] One of them involves symbiosis. There are innumerable examples of fish of one species hosting of another to the host. It seems that this symbiosis evolved many times being favored by natural selection. In this symbiosis the hosts of the cleaning organisms, in turn perform several kinds of altruistic behavior such as not eating their cleaners and warning them about approaching predators. The host benefits from quickly and repeatedly returning to the same cleaner. Another example of this behavior is that of some birds which emit special calls warning other birds when spotting an approaching predator.

Human reciprocal altruism takes place in a number of situations and in all known cultures and is represented by such kinds of behavior as: helping in time of danger; sharing food; helping the sick, the wounded, or the very young and old; sharing tools and knowledge. This altruistic behavior meets the criterion of small cost to the giver and great benefit to the receiver. It seems that human altruistic behavior comes directly from reciprocity and not indirectly through

---

342   Robert L. Trivers, "The Evolution of Reciprocal Altruism," in Robert Trivers, *Natural Selection and Social Theory. Selected papers of Robert Trivers, op. cit.*, pp. 18-51.

nonaltruistic group benefits. Some social scientists and philosophers tended to explain human altruistic behavior in terms of benefits of living in a group without differentiating between nonaltruistic benefits and reciprocal benefits.[343]

Trivers' model explains the psychological mechanisms of emotions such as friendship, dislike, moralistic oppression, gratitude, sympathy, trust, suspicion, trustworthiness, aspects of guilt, forms of dishonesty, hypocrisy and moralistic aggression as adaptations to regulate the altruistic reactions. Anthropologists analyzed these human behaviors in terms of group survival, but Trivers model is more basic. Nietzsche is an example of a philosopher who, from an early age, was interested in the provenance of morals and ethics.[344] The question of evil in the world to him was of primary importance and Nietzsche resolved it by separating it from theological inquiry with the question, "Under what conditions did man construct value judgments *good* and *evil*"? Nietzsche proposed that "All sciences are now under an obligation to prepare the ground for the future task of the philosopher, which is to solve the problem of value, to determine the true hierarchy of values."

In Trivers' model each individual human is seen as possessing altruistic and cheating tendencies, the expression of which is sensitive to developmental variables that were selected to set the tendencies at a balance appropriate to the local social and ecological environments. Trivers postulated that emotions of friendship and intelligence are prerequisites for the appearance of altruism that transcends the limit of family relationships. The underlying emotional dispositions affecting altruistic behavior have a genetic and thus an instinctive and unconscious component, and display a certain set of universal characteristics:

1. dispositions are sensitive to nuances in behavior; often in such behavior it will pay to cheat and detection of subtle cheating may be difficult;

---

343 Baier, K., *The Moral Point of View,* (Ithaca, N.Y.: Cornell University Press, 1958). Rousseau, J. J., *The Social Contract,* (Chicago: Henry Regnery Co., 1954).

344 Marian Hillar, "Friedrich Nietzsche: Social Origin of Morals, Christian Ethics, and Implications for Atheism in His *The Genealogy of Morals,*" in *Essays in the Philosophy of Humanism,* Vol. 16 (1) Spring-Summer 2008. American Humanist Association, Washington, DC, pp. 59-84.

2. friendship and emotions of liking and disliking will be selected towards those who themselves are altruistic. Moreover, friendship and intelligence are prerequisites for the appearance of such altruism that transcends the limits of family relationship;

3. once emotional dispositions for altruistic behavior have developed the altruist is in a vulnerable position because cheaters will be selected to take advantage of the altruist's emotions. Such a situation produces a selection pressure for the development of a protective mechanism in the form of "indignation" and "moralistic aggression." These dispositions were selected in order to

    a. counteract the altruistic tendencies in the absence of reciprocity to continuing the altruistic acts;

    b. educate the unreciprocating individual by frightening him with immediate or future harm of not receiving moral aid;

    c. and, in extreme cases perhaps, select against the unreciprocating individual by injuring, killing or exiling him.

    Thus much of human aggression has moral overtones motivated by injustice, unfairness and lack of reciprocity.

4. dispositional emotions of gratitude, sympathy, and cost/benefit evaluations:

    Emotion of gratitude has been selected to regulate human response to altruistic acts and is sensitive to the cost/benefit evaluation of such acts.
    Emotion of sympathy has been selected to motivate altruistic behavior as a function of the plight of the recipient of such behavior and increases with the increase of the potential of the benefit even to strangers or disliked individuals.

5. guilt and reparative altruism: Catching a cheater and making him pay dearly will produce a selection for a reparative gesture. This creates an emotion of guilt which is selected to

motivate the cheater to compensate for his misdeed and to behave reciprocally in the future and in this way to prevent the rupture of the reciprocal relationship.

6. mimicking the behavior: Once the emotions favoring altruistic or cooperative behavior develop, they select behavior for mimicking these traits in order to influence the behavior of others to one's own advantage.

7. detection of subtle cheaters: trustworthiness, trust, and suspicion. These dispositions are selected for in order to detect and discriminate against subtle cheaters. In classical philosophical and sociological considerations this issue was presented in terms of a problem how to define altruism, whether in terms of motives – a "real altruism" or "calculated altruism" or in terms of behavior, regardless of the motivation.

8. setting up altruistic relationships: natural selection will favor for establishing reciprocal relationships.

9. multiparty interactions: selection will favor more complex interactions than two-party interactions. This involves:

   a. learning from others indirectly by observation and language;
   b. helping to deal with cheaters;
   c. generalizing altruism;
   d. developing rules of exchange – language facilities formulating and codifying multiparty interactions. Anthropology and cultural history provide abundant evidence for these interactions.

10. developmental plasticity: Human evolution set up a selection pressure for psychological and cognitive powers which contributed to an increase in human brain size during the Pleistocene period (from 2.5 million to 12,000 years ago).

Trivers' model of reciprocal altruism constitutes a biological foundation for the naturalistic social theory. Already Nietzsche had an inkling of it when he attempted to describe the origin of "guilt" or "bad conscience" in the human psyche of emotions and the evolution of punishment and its purpose as an expression of moral rule. Nietzsche explains that the feeling of guilt is a product of the oldest relationship between humans, that of "buyer and seller, creditor and debtor." With this origin is linked the concept of punishment as compensation for the contractual relation between debtor and creditor. Damage produced by not keeping a contract results in rage and for every damage some equivalent for compensation may be found, even in inflicting pain. In older civilizations drastic pledges were made by the debtor in order to guarantee fulfillment of the promise. These compensations were in the form of inflicting bodily harm through which the creditor, in place of material compensation such as land or money, was receiving pleasure. Later this punitive authority was passed on to the legal authority and the creditor then enjoyed seeing the debtor despised and mistreated. Thus through such a process of contracts and legal obligations these moral concepts were developed: guilt, conscience, duty.[345]

Axelrod and Hamilton[346] inspired by the Trivers studies developed computer simulations of his model and created game programs such as Prisoner's Dilemma in which two players have the option to cooperate. It was found that such computer game models evolve and can be maintained between two people if they follow the rule of reciprocity and learning in subsequent encounters. Prisoner's Dilemma games increased in complexity in further studies by allowing a gradation of responses mimicking more closely the complexity that evolved in the behavior of species like ourselves and our close relatives.[347] Also, the studies of reciprocal altruism were extended to many animal species.[348]

Reputation and Reciprocal Altruism Model

But these new models could not explain how large cooperative groups could evolve. In such groups the possibility of re-encountering a person who is helping or who has been helped is quite small. Also one has to consider the situation when some people are cheating and

---

345   Friedrich Nietzsche, *The Birth of Tragedy and The Genealogy of Morals*, translated by Francis Golfing, (New York: Anchor Books, 1956).

346   Axelrod R., Hamilton W. "The Evolution of Co-operation," in *Science*, Vol. 211, pp. 1390-1396, 1981.

347   Nowak M., Sigmund K., "The Dynamics of Indirect Reciprocity by Image Scoring," in *Nature*, Vol. 393, pp. 573-577, 1998. Nowak M, Sigmund K., "The Dynamics of Indirect Reciprocity," in *J. Theor. Biol.*, 194, 561-574, 1998.

348   Connor R, Heithaus M, Barre, L. "Superalliance of Bottlenose Dolphins," in *Nature*, 397, pp. 571-572, 1999. Godin J., Davis S., "Who Dares, Benefits: Predator Approach Behavior in Guppy (*Poecilia reticulata*) Deters Predator Pursuit," in *Proc. Roy. Soc. Lond. B.* 209: pp. 193- 200, 1995.

become freeloaders, others may follow the cheaters and the stability of the group could be jeopardized.

To overcome these problems Martin Nowak and Karl Sigmund[349] developed a mathematical model in which people decide what to do based not only on whether others have helped them but also whether others have helped others. Thus a person with a reputation of a helper can get help even from someone who has not benefited directly from such a person in the past. Such a model was confirmed by Robert Boyd and Peter J. Richerson in 2004 who showed that those who did not help or had a reputation of being freeloaders were shunned.[350]

Punishment and Reciprocal Altruism Model

The reputation model for reciprocal altruism still could not explain fully the cooperative nature of human interactions. Ernst Fehr and others observed in their labor market studies that people tend to be more cooperative than the economic theory would predict. Fairly paid employees worked harder than predicted solely from their self-interest. To explain such behavior he suggested, by using game-playing experiments, that punishment was a factor in cooperative behavior. In a game model, participants could decide whether to keep money they were given or to contribute some or all of it to a group project and, at the same time they had the option to punish non-contributing participants. In this game participants were chose to punish the non-contributors and the majority of those who punished were those whose contributions were above-average. In a situation when punishment was not an option, average contributions dropped. Also, it was demonstrated that a mere threat of punishment was enough to prevent cheating.[351] It is thought that altruistic learning may be instinctive because, in small groups of evolving humans, reputation always counted. Moreover,

349 *Selecta Mathematica*: Volume 1 (German and English Edition) by Karl Menger, Bert Schweizer, Abe Sklar, and Karl Sigmund, eds. (Berlin: Springer, 2002). *Selecta Mathematica*: Volume 2 (German and English Edition) by Karl Menger, Bert Schweizer, Abe Sklar, and Karl Sigmund, eds. (Berlin: Springer, 2003).

350 Robert Boyd and Peter J. Richerson, *The Origin and Evolution* (New York: Oxford University Press, 2005). Peter J. Richerson and Robert Boyd, *Not by Genes Alone: How Culture Transformed Human Evolution* (Chicago: University of Chicago Press, 2006). Robert Boyd, *How Humans Evolved* (New York: W.W. Norton & Co., 2009).

351 Herbert Gintis, Samuel Bowles, Robert T. Boyd, and Ernst Fehr, eds., *Economic Life. Economic Learning and Social Evolution* (Cambridge, MA: MIT Press, 2006). by Joseph Henrich, Robert Boyd, Samuel Bowles, and Colin Camerer, eds., *Foundations of Human Sociality: Economic Experiments and Ethnographic Evidence from Fifteen Small-Scale Societies* (New York: Oxford University Press, 2004). W. Glimcher, Colin Camerer, Russell Alan Poldrack, and Ernst Fehr, *Neuroeconomics: Decision Making and the Brain* (New York: Academic Press, 2008).

punishment had less importance since in human encounters rewards work better than punishment.[352]

Group Selection Model

The other model was developed on the premise that competition among groups can foster co-operation within them. Natural forces may work in different directions, e.g., natural selection may make individuals less cooperative, but competition between groups may push them to cooperate within the group enhancing thus the survivability of the group. This was observed by Darwin and is still observed in modern warring groups and in military history. Archaeological studies, on evidence about 50,000 years ago, and historical reports demonstrated that death from warfare averaged about 14 %, significantly higher than in 20th century Europe with two world wars.[353] This result was confirmed by using game theory simulation. Thus it seems that co-operation between groups increased significantly with time in human evolution.

Co-operation among Viruses and Microbes

It is interesting that co-operation was also observed among such low level organisms as bacteriophages, viruses that live in bacterial cells. Two researchers Joel Sachs and James Bull[354] injected into a bacterial strain two different types of viruses at the same time. After many generations, the two viruses packaged their genomes within a single coating protein thus ensuring the transmission of both of their genomes to the next bacterial host. Other researchers expanded such studies on co-operation between bacterial strains showing that, when they sense the accumulation of other bacteria nearby, so-called *quorum sensing*, they increase secretion of certain biochemicals which are of benefit to all bacteria present.[355] The best known among social microbes is the slime mold *Dictyostelium.* It was shown that these single-cell amoeba organisms often merge to form stalks with fruiting bodies on top, thus allowing some cells to produce spores which may

---

352 Hisashi Ohtsuki, Yoh Iwasa, Martin Nowak, "Indirect Reciprocity Provides only a Narrow Margin of Efficiency for Costly Punishment," in *Nature*, Vol. 457, No. 7225, pp. 79-82.

353 Samuel Bowles, "Did Warfare Among Ancestral Hunter-Gatherers Affect the Evolution of Human Social Behaviors?," in *Science*, 5 June 2009, Vol. 324, no. 5932, pp. 1293-1298.

354 Joel Sachs and James Bull, *Proc. Natl. Acad. Sci.*, 102, 390, 2005.

355 Stuart A. West, Andy Gardner, "Altruism, Spite and Greenbeards," in *Science*, 12 March 2010, Vol. 327, no. 5971, pp. 1341-1344.

disperse to more food-rich places. But among these amoeba cells are also cheaters, cells that mutated, and which infiltrate the fruiting body, thus avoiding becoming the nonreproductive stalk. A large number of genes were discovered that confer the ability to cheat. At the same time studies showed that amoebas can keep cheating in check because mutations that make cheating possible prevent cheaters from getting into the aggregation at all. One of the genes, called the green-beard gene, enables an amoeba to recognize others with the same gene and help perpetuate copies of the gene in others regardless of relatedness.[356]

The existence of such type of genes for co-operation was postulated a long time ago by Hamilton. Many other organisms from termites to meerkats provide examples of co-operation. "The origin of sociality is unlikely to be encompassed by a single explanation. Sociality like multicellularity, has happened numerous times, in diverse taxa, and reached many different levels of integration."[357]

Acknowledgement

Author wishes to express his thanks to Mrs. Claire Stelter for reading the manuscript and he comments.

356   Anupama Khare, Lorenzo A. Santorelli, Joan E. Strassmann, David C. Queller, Adam Kuspa, Gad Shaulsky, "Cheater-Resistance is not Futile," in *Nature 461*, 980-982 (30 September 2009).   Asher Mullard, "Cheating Bacteria Could Treat Infections," *Nature News* (21 January 2009). David C. Queller, "Behavioral Ecology: The Social Side of Wild Yeast," in *Nature* 456, 589-590 (3 December 2008). Lorenzo A. Santorelli, Christopher R. L. Thompson, Elizabeth Villegas, Jessica Svetz, Christopher Dinh, Anup Parikh, Richard Sucgang, Adam Kuspa, Joan E. Strassmann, David C. Queller, et al., "Facultative Cheater Mutants Reveal the Genetic Complexity of Co-operation in Social Amoebae," in *Nature*, 451, 1107-1110 (13 February 2008).
357   Quoted by Elizabeth Pennisi, "On the Origin of Co-operation," in *Science*, 4 September 2009, Vol. 325, pp. 1196-1199.

MODERN PHILOSOPHY AND MODERN SCIENCE. Modern Science provides a biological basis for human behavior and validates philosophical speculation.[358]

Since time immemorial humans were preoccupied with their own behavior and attitudes versus other humans, the rest of the animate world, and the surrounding environment. This is attested by the oldest written documents from the Mesopotamian, Mediterranean, and Far Eastern regions of the World.[359]

In every culture we find the expression "Golden Rule" as the universal principle guiding human behavior. This rule is expressed in religious injunctions as well as in philosophical analyses wherever such attempts were made as is attested again by the history of philosophy.

On the other hand, naturalistic investigation which is today classified as science also attempted to give more critical and natural explanations. These attempts were most often combined with philosophical speculation because of a lack of proper investigative tools to attack the issue from a strictly naturalistic perspective of the human psyche. We observe a continuous thread of attempts starting with ancient pre-Socratics through Aristotle, the Stoics, other ancient philosophers, Michael Servetus, René Descartes, and Friedrich Nietzsche, to mention a few. The serious foundations for modern studies were laid down by Charles Darwin who attempted to gave a biological foundation to philosophical speculation. Serious foundations for modern psychology were produced by William James (1843-1920) and Sigmund Freud (1856-1939). We had to wait, however, till the second half of the twentieth century to see the explosion of studies

---

358 Published in Houston Freethought Alliance Newsletter, Issue 99, January 2008, pp. 5-6.
359 Joseph Campbell, *The Masks of God: Occidental Mythology*, (Penguin Books: Harmondsworth, U.K.; New York, USA, 1976. Joseph Campbell, *The Masks of God: Oriental Mythology*, (Penguin Books: Harmondsworth, U.K.; New York, USA, 1986). W.Y. Evans-Wentz, compiler and editor, *The Tibetan Book of the Dead*, (Oxford University Press: Oxford, UK, 1960). *The Texts of Taoism*, translated by James Legge, Part I, II, (Dover Publications, Inc. : New York, first published, 1962). James B. Pritchard, ed., *The Ancient Near East. Anthology of Texts and Pictures*, Vol. 1, 2, (Princeton University Press: Princeton, 1973). *Hindu Myths. A Sourcebook Translated from the Sanskrit.* With introduction by Wendy Doniger O'Flaherty, (Harmondsworth, UK: Penguin Books, 1975*). The Rig Veda*, translated and annotated by Wendy Doniger O'Flaherty, (Harmondsworth, UK: Penguin Books, 1984). *The Upanishads*, translated by F. Max Müller, Part 1, 2, (Dover Publications: New York, first published 1962). Sarvepalli Radhakrishnan, *Indian Philosophy*, Vol. 1, 2 (first publication, George Allen and Unwin Ltd., 1931). James P. Allen, translator and introduction, *The Ancient Egyptian Pyramid Texts*, (Society of Biblical Literature: Atlanta, GA, 2005). Wing-Tsit Chan, translated and compiled, *Source Book in Chinese Philosophy*, (Princeton University Press: Princeton, 1963).

related to our behavior (morals) from various fields of investigations: experimental psychology, developmental psychology, evolutionary psychology, anthropology, ethology, neurobiology, neurology. Most of such modern studies were recently summarized by Marc D. Hauser in his epoch-making book, *Moral Minds. How Nature Designed Our Universal Sense of Right and Wrong*.[360]

Following Darwin, primatologists like Frans de Waal and other biologists[361] have long argued that the roots of human morality are manifest in social animals like apes and monkeys. They express feelings of empathy and expectations of reciprocity which are essential behaviors for mammalian group life and constitute a counterpart to human morality. Marc D. Hauser summarizing all studies done with animals and in modern psychology and anthropology proposes that people are born with a moral grammar wired into their neural circuits by evolution. He claims that this grammar generates instant moral judgments which are instantaneously inaccessible to the conscious mind. Hauser presents his argument as a hypothesis to be proved, but it is based on solid experimental ground, including work with primates, and in empirical results derived from studies performed by moral philosophers. Hauser argues that moral grammar operates in the same way as the universal grammar proposed by linguist Noam Chomsky for developing language faculty. This universal grammar is a system of rules for generating syntax and vocabulary but does not specify any particular language. That is supplied by the culture in which a child grows up. By analogy, moral grammar, too, is a system composed of neural circuits which generate moral behavior and not a list of specific rules. Basic rules are the same in every society, but it allows for cultural variations, since cultures can put different emphases on its elements.

This proposal has strong and far-reaching implications. It means that parents and teachers do not really teach children the rules of correct behavior rather, they instill the cultural biases and modifications. Also, it demonstrates in a tangible way that religions are not the source of moral codes. On the contrary, moral grammar which operates

---

360 Marc D. Hauser, *Moral Minds. How Nature Designed Our Universal Sense of Right and Wrong*, (New York: HarperCollins Publishers, 2006).

361 Frans de Waal, *Our Inner Ape*, (New York: Riverhead Books, 2005). Francis de Waal, *Primates and Philosophers. How Morality Evolved*, (Princeton and Oxford: Princeton University Press, 2006). Robert Wright, *The Moral Animal. Evolutionary Psychology of Everyday Life*, (New York: Vintage Books, 1995). Robert Trivers, *Natural Selection and Social Theory. Selected papers of Robert Trivers*, (Oxford: Oxford University Press, 2002).

subconsciously is immune to religious doctrines. At best, religions enforce instinctive behavior and most often indoctrinate people with cultural biases.

Moral grammar is a product of the evolutionary process because restraints on behavior are necessary for social living and have been favored by natural selection for survival. Friedrich Nietzsche was among those philosophers who argued for societal origin of rules of behavior which developed as cultures evolved.[362]

Hauser developed his ideas through work with vervet monkeys in Kenya and with birds.[363] Later on, when psychologists developed techniques to study the thinking of human babies, he found that many such studies could be repeated with animals thus setting the cognitive abilities of human babies in an evolutionary framework. His proposal of a moral grammar derived from collaboration with Noam Chomsky who argued that the faculty of language had developed as an adaptation of some neural system in animals. By analogy with language, Hauser thought that moral behavior is also acquired through development of neural circuits which constitute an innate set of rules. Moral grammar, now universal among people, is thought to have evolved to its present shape during the hunter- gatherer stage of our past, some 50,000 years ago through the mechanism of group selection as was suggested already by Nietzsche in a cultural context.

The question arises now, what validity does moral philosophical speculation have in view of scientific theories and the evidence behind them, such as the one postulated by Hauser?[364] The answer which is suggested by Hauser was presented in the form of three models for human behavior incorporating three major themes of philosophical speculation.

The first model, the so-called Humean Model, is based on the entire line of philosophical speculation going back in antiquity to the Stoics, and in modern times has been best expressed by David Hume.

---

362   Friedrich Nietzsche, *The Birth of Tragedy and The Genealogy of Morals*, translated by Francis Golfing, (New York: Anchor Books, 1990).

363   Marc D. Hauser, *The Evolution of Communication*, (Cambridge, MA: The MIT Press, 1997). Marc D. Hauser and Marc Konishi, eds., *The Design of Animal Communication*, (Cambridge, MA: The MIT Press, 2003).

364   Richard Joyce, *The Evolution of Morality*, (Cambridge, MA : The MIT Press, 2006).

Hume assumed that "perceptions" produce feelings and emotional reactions from which follows judgment.

The second model, labeled the Kantian Model, emerges from Kant's moral philosophy misunderstood or interpreted only from one perspective, that of his "categorical imperative." Hauser, who noticed this misconception, introduced a double path in the model. Kant accepted the existence of something he called "good will." It has thus a quality of an instinct. We proceed to evaluate events, actions, etc, either on some principles which he classified as 1. heteronomous (empirical e.g., from principle of happiness, the so-called *moral sense*,[365] inclinations, etc, or rational e.g., from the concept of perfection, transcendental or theological) because they derive from the outside of the individual; 2. an autonomous or categorical imperative which is an autonomous moral law, a law for the will of every rational being. He expressed it as a formula or maxim by which we can judge. It has to be universal to be classified as the moral imperative.

Here seems to lie the crux of the misunderstanding of Kant by philosophers and scientists as well. For before the twentieth century it was generally accepted by philosophers and especially by theologians that the so-called moral behavior, i.e. morality (and I want to emphasize moral behavior not in the sense of an acceptable one, but in the sense of one's interaction with others), was considered a unique characteristic of the human species solely depending on our reflective or rational faculty. There was no room here for instinctive behavior among humans or instinctive judgment. Thus animals could not have "morality" or we could not talk about their "moral behavior;" and vice versa, humans could not have an "instinctive moral behavior." The behavior of animals was classified as "instinctive" thus devoid of any moral value. Kant, in his genius, was able to differentiate between the two, and hence he spoke about the categorical imperative as applying to moral behavior in the "strict sense."

Kant did not go, and in his time it would be very difficult to do so, into the biological foundations of human behavior. It was, anyway, an ideal situation if all humans behaved all the time in a rational, reflective way. He knew that humans do not behave all the time in this way

---

365   In modern terminology it is the *moral faculty* or *moral grammar*.

and do not always use reason for judgment. Thus these heteronomous principles were valid in practice (and still are).

The third model, the Rawlsian Model, is based on the theory of John Rawls who after Stoics postulated an instinctive "moral faculty" which allows us to differentiate moral actions and situations from those which have no moral value, and to differentiate actions which are allowed, permissible, or forbidden.[366] So in this last model we have perception first, then automatically (unconsciously) we judge them, and only then do we develop emotions and feelings about them. Of course in the later stage comes also conscious reflection and reasoning which is then the basis for developing cultural rules, laws, etc. The last model is more realistic and accommodates all previous models as approximations and, at the same time, as is confirmed by evidence from scientific studies in many disciplines, provides an evolutionary basis for human behavior. Still, Kant's model seems to be the most complete though its biological basis could not be developed in the time of Kant. In the following articles we will attempt to present various solutions to the problem of our behavior given by various thinkers in various cultures.

---

366   John Rawls, *A Theory of Justice*, (Cambridge, MA: Harvard University Press, 1990).

MORALITY IS A PRINCIPLE OF NATURE DISCOVERED BY PHILOSOPHY AND EVOLUTIONARY SCIENCES[367]

Marian Hillar

Center for Philosophy, Socinian and Religious Studies

Texas Southern University, Houston, Texas 77004

Abstract

This work concerns metaethics and its goal is to present a short summary 1. How philosophers attempted to justify our moral behavior by postulating the existence of a "natural moral law", and 2. how the achievements of modern psychology, ethology, and evolutionary sciences led to the confirmation of its existence and elucidation of its origin. Author offers a new interpretation of the natural moral law as an unwritten principle which regulates behavior of the entire living world. Our morality, i.e. cooperative behavior in social systems, is a result of biological evolutionary process, and is expressed in the entire living world at the subconscious level in the process of cooperation. When the evolution reached the rational level, it is also expressed in the conscious intellectual constructs.

Introduction

Philosophers when answering the question, How to live our lives and how to treat each other, developed several theories such as hedonism, psychological egoism and altruism, ethical egoism, consequentialism and utilitarianism, deontological theory (Kant's well-being theory), virtue ethical theory, contractarianism and social contract theory, *prima facie* duties theory, natural law theory.[368] The natural law theory seems to be the most fundamental going to the roots conditioning human behavior and all other philosophical speculations. The idea of

---

367   Chapter in *Dialog Filozoficzny o Człowieku*, eds. Paulina Szymczyk, Ewelina Chodźko, Wydawnictwo Naukowe TYGIEL, Lublin 2021, pp. 137 – 159. English version in Journal of Arts, Humanities and Social Sciences, January 15, 2024, Vol. II, issue I, 2024, pp. 42-53.

368   Russ Shafer Landau, *The Fundamentals of Ethics*, (New York, Oxford: Oxford University Press, 2010). Henry Sidgwick, *The Methods of Ethics* (London: Macmillan and Co., 1901; first edition 1877).

a natural law in morality governing our behavior has a long history and was interpreted or understood in a variety of ways. Though it has limited value for formulation of detailed practical maxims to conduct human behavior, nevertheless it is still used by contemporary religious leaders to argue in defense of their particular moral assumptions based on their theological worldview. It has, however, a great historical value for the evaluation of validity of secular philosophical intuition. For modern science, starting with Darwin and his insight into evolution of man, reached the level of sophistication and precision where is able to explain the naturalistic basis for the intuition of philosophers.

This idea of a natural law governing the world can be traced all the way back to the fifth century B.C.E. when the social and political changes on the one hand and ideas about the external world developed by the Presocratic philosophers-scientists led to the rise of intellectual ferment, the age of the ancient Enlightenment.[369] The primary role in this movement was played by the so-called Sophists, professional teachers. They changed the previous focus of interest from the physical reality to the human affairs.[370]

---

369   Jürgen Habermas, contemporary German philosopher calls this age an Axial Age.
370   The words Sophist (*sophistes*) derives from the Greek *sophos* (skilled, wise, clever, learned, subtle, ingenious), *sophia* (skill, cleverness, wisdom, learning), *sophizomai* (practice an art, play tricks, devise skillfully, speculate). The term was widely used in the ancient Greece and designated a poet, as a teacher of men, a knowledgeable and prudent man, a person with a specific skill, expert or adept. In the fifth century this term acquired a specific meaning designating a class of Sophists i.e. of professional teachers, educators, scholars who gave lessons in grammar, rhetoric, politics, mathematics, for money. They taught in small seminars or circles, in public gatherings or private homes. This term became an abusive term in the hands of the satirical writer, Aristophanes, who slandered them and criticized as deceivers. For him Sophists represented an age of decline and breakdown of morals. Athenians were ambivalent about Sophists for they claimed to teach *aretē* (virtue) and how to become a good citizen (Plato, *Protagoras* 319a). Athenians in their democratic outlook did not consider that a special training was necessary for this in contrast to learning specific practical skills (technē). Their opinion was shared by Plato who named them "worthless fellows" primarily for their atheism or agnosticism. In the next century Aeschinus referred to Socrates as "Socrates the sophist" and later Lucian of Samosata (125-180 The Sophists recognized the existence of the "unwritten and necessary natural law,"[371] though considered as originating from gods. And as long as religion was the major factor guiding people god was the author of those standards and it seems that such were the opinions of ancient writers such as Hesiod and Heraclitus.[372] It designated an eternal moral principle universally valid and overruling the positive laws of men. Plato (427-347 B.C.E.) rejects the idea that morals and moral law are changing.[373] He refers us to the unchanging reality, the reality of the Forms (*eidos*) which is accessible only to reason and of which human societies are largely ignorant. Thus, the human behavior in societies is not only subject to the rules established by men in societies, but also to the universal law which is unwritten and to which even gods are subject.[374] Thus it seems that Plato laid the foundation for this original concept of the unchanging natural moral law as part of our natural world. Next who dwelled on the topic of the natural law was Aristotle (384-322 B.C.E.) who distinguished in his *Nicomachean Ethics* between conventional or legal justice, and C.E.) referred to Christ "that crucified sophist" (*Peregrinus* 13). W. K. C. Guthrie, *The Sophists*, Cambridge UK: Cambridge University Press, 1971, reprint 1987), pp. 35-54. The texts of preserved fragments of the Sophists' writings are available in a bilingual collection: *Sofisti. Testimonianze e frammenti. Testo greco a fronte*. A cura di Mario Untersteiner con la collaborazione di Antonio Battegazzore. Introduzione di Giovanni Reale, indici di Vincenzo Cicero, (Milano: Bompiani, 2009). For example Antiphon in Jan Legowicz, *Filozofia Starożytna Grecji i Rzymu*, Warszawa: Państwowe Wydawnictwo Naukowe, 1968), p. 123-124.

The Sophists recognized the existence of the "unwritten and necessary natural law,"[371] though considered as originating from gods. And as long as religion was the major factor guiding people god was the author of those standards and it seems that such were the opinions of ancient writers such as Hesiod and Heraclitus.[372] It designated an eternal moral principle universally valid and overruling the positive laws of men.

Plato (427-347 B.C.E.) rejects the idea that morals and moral law are changing.[373] He refers us to the unchanging reality, the reality of the Forms (*eidos*) which is accessible only to reason and of which human societies are largely ignorant. Thus, the human behavior in societies is not only subject to the rules established by men in societies, but also to the universal law which is unwritten and to which even gods are subject.[374] Thus it seems that Plato laid the foundation for this original concept of the unchanging natural moral law as part of our natural world.

Next who dwelled on the topic of the natural law was Aristotle (384-322 B.C.E.) who distinguished in his *Nicomachean Ethics* between conventional or legal justice, and natural justice. However, both are not unchangeable.[375] Aristotle could arrive at such a conclusion since he viewed nature from the biological perspective observing biological phenomena.

If it so, the question now arises what is human nature, what is human characteristic or human function and this principle that makes us humans? After a lengthy discussion and comparison with other forms of life Aristotle states that:

---

371 For example Antiphon in Jan Legowicz, *Filozofia Starożytna Grecji i Rzymu*, Warszawa: Państwowe Wydawnictwo Naukowe, 1968), p. 123-124.
372 Heraclitus, *The Cosmic Fragments*. Edited with an introduction and commentary by G. S. Kirk (Cambridge: Cambridge University Press, 1954). fr. 114. Hesiod, *The Homeric Hymns and Homerica*, with an English translation and by Hugh G. Evelyn-White (Cambridge, MA: Harvard University Press, 1982), pp. 276-284.
373 Plato, *The Republic, Parmenides*, in *The Republic and Other Works*, translated by B. Jowett, (New York: Anchor Book, 1973).
374 Famous dialogue from *Euthyphro* : "Euthyphro – Yes, I should say that what all the gods love is pious and holy, and the opposite which they all hate, impious. Socrates – Ought we to inquire into the truth of this, Euthyphro, or simply to accept the mere statement on our own authority and that of others? Euthyphro - We should inquire; and I believe that the statement will stand the test of inquiry. Socrates – That, my good friend, we shall know better in a little while. The point which I should first wish to understand is whether the pious or holy is beloved by the gods because it is holy, or holy because it is beloved by the gods." Plato, *Euthyphro* in *The Republic and Other Works, op. cit.,* p. 435.
375 Aristotle, *Nicomachean Ethics*, translated, with introduction and notes by Martin Ostwald, (New York, London: Macmillan Publishing Company, 1962), Bk V. 7.

The proper function of man, then, consists in an activity of the soul (*psuchē*) in conformity with a rational principle or, at least, not without it. In speaking of a proper function of a given individual we mean that it is the same in kind as the function of an individual who sets high standards for himself... the good of man is an activity of the soul in conformity with excellence or virtue, and if there are several virtues, in conformity with the best and most complete.[376]

Aristotle, however, understood the "souls" as a biological phenomenon, function of the body.[377]

The Stoic Philosophy

By stating that reason and rationality is the distinctive human characteristic, Aristotle set the foundations for formulations of the natural law as governing the world and humans which was postulated by the Greek Stoics and explicitly formulated by Cicero. The Stoic philosophy was the most important and influential development in Hellenistic philosophy and it affected Christian writers and their

---

376   Aristotle, *Nicomachean Ethics, op. cit.,* Bk I.7.

377   It is difficult to evaluate the Aristotle's view on the soul from the point of view of modern biology and psychology. Aristotle was not able to explain biological processes and function of the living organisms in modern biological concepts and terms. He tried, however, to do this using available to him analytical approaches. He used his own concepts of nature which were modified Platonic ideas, his own theory of matter and forms. He differentiated three elements in the substance, matter, form, and combination of both, and attempted to show that the soul (or *psyche* in his terminology) is the first actualization of the body which is organized by nature. Form or essence is the element that organizes. It cannot be matter since the soul is the element due to which living organisms are alive and matter is only the potential element. Thus, the soul in every living being is an agent that performs a variety of operations. It is not a substance separate from the body, with which it is connected. So, the nutritive soul in all kinds of living organisms such as plants and animals, must be able to perform nutritive and reproductive functions. All animals have additional sensory perception, at least sense of touch and are able to experience pleasure and pain. These functions are performed by sensory soul. Still other animals have more subtle variety of senses such as vision, hearing, taste, and more complicated perceptions such as memory, imagination, and self-movement. In the Book III Aristotle considers the questions concerning mind which, according to him, belongs only to the human soul. Aristotle argues that thinking is different from both the sensory perception and imagination. He claims that senses cannot deceive, and imagination is an agency that is able to bring back things that were perceived anteriorly while thinking may sometimes be erroneous. Since the mind is able to think whenever it desires, one has to differentiate it into two capabilities: one passive which contains all ideas that belong to mind and can be considered, whereas the second one brings them to action, i.e. the mind is actually thinking about them. In this way Aristotle differentiated possible intellect that is a collection of concepts and universal ideas, and the agent-intellect (proper mind) that is able to recall those ideas and form thoughts. But since Aristotle was not able to find any corresponding organ (Aristotle missed to recognize the function of the brain and of the central nervous system) he thought that it was nonmaterial and able to survive outside the body, thus immortal. He did not consider here the souls of the individual human, but most likely a cosmic power, which he considered as the first mover that was represented by the cosmic mind postulated by Anaxagoras and commonly accepted in his time. Alexander of Aphrodisias, ancient commentator of Aristotle, postulated that human mind that is not yet fully developed is "*nous hylikos,*" inseparable from the body and mortal. The active mind, "*nous poietikos*" through action of which human mind is actualized he identified with god. Chishol H., ed. *Alexander of Aphrodisias*, Encyclopedia Britannica, 11th ed., Cambridge University Press, 1911, p. 566. Aristotle, Περὶ Ψυχῆς *(Peri Psuchēs) Traite, de l'ame*, traduit et annote, par G. Rodier, Ernest Leroux, Éditeur, Paris 1900. Hillar M., The Problem of the Soul in Aristotle's "*De anima*", in *Contributors to the Philosophy of Humanism*, Humanists of Houston, Houston, 1994, pp. 51-82.

moral thinking, and many philosophers. It was revived in the deism and naturalism of the Enlightenment and continues to affect modern thinking as well. It was founded by Zeno of Citium (333-262 B.C.E.) and developed by his successors Cleanthes (303-233 B.C.E.) and Chrysippus (b. ca 280 -d. ca 208/4 B.C.E.).[378]

Like Aristotle, Stoics assumed a reality composed of two fundamental principles: matter and form. Matter constituted a passive, indeterminate principle (το πάσχον εἶναι τὴν ἄποιον οὐσίαν) and form was the governing, active principle (τὸ ποιοὖν λόγον τὸν θεόν) constituting the nature of beings.[379] This form is an active principle that enlivens and vitalizes creatures. Following Heraclitus, the Stoics assumed that it is one and the same principle, *logos*, that governs the thought and structure of the world which was considered ideal because of its orderliness.[380] The Stoic philosophers (Zeno and Cleanthes) initially identified this all-pervasive *logos* with cosmic fire (πῦρ τεχνικόν = artistic, creative fire),[381] but, influenced by contemporary physiology and Diogenes of Apollonia, they came to view it as the creature's breath, that is, *pneuma*, a weightless permeation which was a compound of cosmic fire and air.[382] By analogy with the living creature, the rational principle of the whole world was also identified with *pneuma* as an activating and vivifying principle.

This rational principle and order in nature was described under various names, Logos, Pneuma (πνεὖμα = breath, spirit), Fate, God, Providence, and because of it the world was considered to be fully deterministic. This creative reason, the cosmic rational principle, was anticipated by Plato's either as "soul of the world" or "divine Craftsman."[383]

All these terms – Soul of the world, Mind of the world, Nature, Providence, Craftsman, Logos, God – all refer to one and the same

---

378 *Stoicorum Veterum Fragmenta* collegit Ioannes Ab Arnim, (Stutgardiae: in Aedibus B.G. Teubneri, MCMLXIV), Vol. 1-4, (abbreviated as SVF). Italian edition with translation of the *Fragmenta: Gli Stoici. Opere e Testimonianze* a cura di Margherita Isnardi Parente, Vol. 1-2. (Milano: TEA, 1994). A. A. Long, *Hellenistic Philosophy. Stoics, Epicureans, Sceptics* (Berkeley: University of California Press, 1986), second edition.

379 *SVF* II.300.

380 Cicero, *De natura deorum, op. cit.,* II. 16-39.

381 *SVF* I.120.

382 *SVF* III.300. But in modern religious theistic terminology, spirit. In naturalistic interpretation this *pneuma* is oxygen necessary to maintain life.

383 *SVF* II, 913. Marcus Aurelius wrote: "One god, one substance, one law, common/or universal logos and one truth." Marcus Aurelius, *Meditations,* translated with an introduction by Maxwell Staniforth (Harmondsworth: Penguin Books, 1964). VII, 9.

thing, an artistic and creative fire, fiery and intelligent breath (πνεῦμα νοερόν καὶ πυρῶθδες, πῦρ δυνάμεως, πῦρ τεχνικόν).[384] Inasmuch as it is the principle controlling the universe, it is called the *logos*.[385] And inasmuch as it is the germ from which all other things develop, and their specific types are defined, it is called the *seminal logos* (*logos spermatikos*). Nature taken as a whole, as the governing principle of all things, is equivalent to the *logos*, but as for particular living things, only some possess reason as a natural faculty. This *logos* governing the world is, at the same time, a force, the natural law from which nothing can escape and which leads the entire world to a common end.

Stoics were the first philosophers who maintained systematically that all things are necessarily interrelated "from everything that happens something else follows depending on it by necessity."[386] Chance was for them simply a name for undiscovered causes.[387] Since things in the world are related in one way or the other (mutual relationship and interaction in the world Stoics called "sympathy") Stoics postulated that they are related by relative disposition, that is, they depended upon something else, e.g., being a father entails a relationship with his child or children, etc.[388] This idea may partially correspond to modern concepts of mutual interdependence in ecological terms. But it had much deeper significance for the Stoics since it also included a moral and psychological sense of relating to one's self, society, and the world. To be a happy and good man meant for the Stoics to be related to the universe, "to feel at home in the universe," and to other human beings in a manner according to reason. Marcus Aurelius wrote: "Neither can I be angry with my brother or fall foul of him; for he and I were born to work together...,"[389] and, "The chief good of a rational being is fellowship with his neighbors – for it has been made clear long ago that fellowship is the purpose behind our creation."[390] We find this Stoic principle repeated almost verbatim by Jürgen Habermas as the only justification for the morality and ethics. He develops it into his "moral principle of universalizability" when an individual is integrated into a social order and where his moral obligation comes from the process of

384 *SVF* I.120, 158, 176; II. 1009, 1132; III.323.
385 *SVF* III. 323.
386 *SVF* II. 945.
387 *SVF* II. 67.
388 *SVF* II. 402-404.
389 Marcus Aurelius, *Meditations op. cit.,* II.1.
390 Marcus Aurelius, *op. cit.,* V.16.

socialization. Before Habermas Immanuel Kant developed the same principle into his logical maxim of "categorical imperative."[391]

Concerning human nature, Stoics gave the traditional answer, that it is the Mind that distinguished humans from other things. The concept was borrowed from Diogenes the Cynic (b. ca 412 B.C.E.). This rationality was understood as the practical wisdom of living in accordance with Nature. Individual human beings share this rational principle with Nature; thus, it is a part of the world. They are endowed in varying degrees with "seed powers" (or *spermatikoi logoi*) which were part of the principle or *logos* of Nature. Cosmic events and human actions are both consequences of one thing, the *logos*. Modern psychology, physiology, neurology and psychiatry provide evidence that there are no reasons to deny that mental processes are purely physical processes in the central nervous system.[392] This Stoic concept of rationality acquired a new meaning in Habermas's interpretation as the communicative action in a social context representing a point of convergence for various cultures and societies. This convergence is based on the role played by universal concepts found in every community such as truth, rationality, justification, and consensus. They form a "grammar" for the discourse by analogy to the Chomsky's universal language grammar.[393]

Stoic theory thus has anticipated modern concepts since mind and matter are two constituents or attributes of one thing, the body. A man is a unified substance, but what he consists of is not uniform.

This governing principle, *logos,* is the seat of consciousness and to it belong all the functions which we would associate with the brain. One function is called "impulse," (ὁρμή) a movement of thought towards or away from something"[394] which is initiated by an impression. Impression and impulse provide the causal explanations of goal-oriented animal movements. Creatures are genetically determined to show aversion

---

391   Jürgen Habermas, *Moral Consciousness and Communicative Action,* translated by Christian Lenhardt and Shierry Weber Nicholsen, (Cambridge, Mass: The MIT Press, 1990). Immanuel Kant *Foundations of the Metaphysics of Morals* and *What is Enlightenment?* Translated with an introduction by Lewis White Beck (New York: Macmillan Publishing Company, twenty- first printing 1988).
392   Edward O. Wilson, *Consilience. The Unity of Knowledge* (New York: Alfred A Knopf, 1998). Marc D. Hauser, *Moral Minds. How Nature Designed Our Universal Sense of Right and Wrong,* (New York: HarperCollins Publishers, 2006).
393   Jürgen Habermas, *Between facts and Norms,* translated by William Rehg, (Cambridge, MA: Polity Press, 1998), p. 311.
394   *SVF,* III. 377.

and preference and they are well disposed towards themselves. The technical term describing this relationship to the environment is *oikeiōsis (οἰκείωσις)*, a self-awareness. The behavior depends on animal or human recognition of the object as belonging to itself by its faculty of "assent."[395] But we are not impelled or repelled by things which we fail to recognize as a source of advantage or harm.[396] This faculty impels us to select things necessary for self-preservation and not necessarily by reason. An infant is "not yet rational" and it takes about 7 years to develop the *logos*.[397] Automatic impulse thus governs the behavior of humans in the earliest years, the first thought is self-preservation. Gradually, as the child develops, its governing principle is modified by accretion of the *logos*, then "reason [becomes] supreme as the craftsman of impulse."[398] Reason, however, does not destroy the earlier impulses but they are taken over by reason.

Thus, human nature develops from something which is non-rational to a structure governed by reason.[399] Now new objects of desire develop, and virtue becomes a human characteristic.[400]

Attainment of rationality alters the whole structure of a man's governing principle. Human behavior is a mode of rational conduct which is the use of faculties for the purpose designed by universal natural law.[401] Even the actions which we usually describe as an irrational impulse are in fact governed by the rational principle in the sense that they produce a judgment (intellectual assent) that moves to action, the movement of the soul. So the distinction is between the right reason (*eulogos*) and wrong reason (*alogos*).[402] Therefore, everything that we do is rational in a sense, but the sage or the good man is the criterion, because he alone has the right reason[403] in a consistent way.[404] We fluctuate between right and wrong reason and we make moral progress

---

395 *SVF,* II. 171.
396 *SVF,* II. 979, 991.
397 Aëtius, IV. 11.4 in *Dox. graeci. op. cit.*; Séneque *Lettres à Lucillius* Texte établi par François Préchac et traduit par Henri Noblot (Paris: Société d'Édition "Les Belles Lettres," 1964),. Tome I-VII. T. V. *Ep.* 124.9.
398 D.L. VII. 86.
399 Cicero, *De natura deorum,* II, 29; Sénèque, *Lettres à Lucillius, op. cit.,* T. V. *Ep.* 121, 10.
400 Cicero, *Du bien suprême et des maux les plus graves (De Finibus)* traduction nouvelle avec notice et notes par Charles Appuhn (Paris: Librairie Garnier Frères, 1938). III, 20.
401 *SVF ,*II. 899; III. 5, 175, 438, 466, 488.
402 *SVF ,*I. 203; III. 468.
403 *SVF,* III, 175, 570-571.
404 *SVF,* III. 459.

not by extirpating the desires and emotions but by making them increasingly consistent with the right reason.[405],[406]

Cicero and His Formulation of the Natural Law

Thus, in the Stoic philosophy humans have a natural capacity to act in accordance with the natural law or "right reason" through the impulse to virtue. And we find this understanding of the natural law formulated by Cicero[407] in his *Republic*:

> True law is right reason in agreement with nature; it is of universal application, unchanging and everlasting; it summons to duty by its commands, and averts from wrongdoing by its prohibitions... We cannot be freed from its obligations by senate or people, and we need not look outside ourselves for an expounder or interpreter of it. And there will not be different laws at Rome and at Athens, or different laws now and in the future, but one eternal and unchangeable law will be valid for all nations and all times, and there will be one master and ruler, that is God, over us all, for he is the author of this law, its promulgator, and its enforcing judge. Whoever is disobedient is fleeing from himself and denying his human nature, and by reason of this very fact he will suffer the worst penalties, even if he escapes what is commonly considered punishment...[408]

Cicero in the *Laws* explains why this natural law is called law by differentiating understanding of it by the "populace" and by the "learned men.[409]

It is clear that Cicero defines natural law as "law" by analogy to the human positive law. And such is its popular understanding. However,

---

405 *SVF* III. 278.
406 *SVF* II.979.
407 Marcus Tullius Cicero (106 B.C.E.-46 B.C.E.) was a Roman politician, lawyer, philosopher, and linguist, one of the greatest minds of the ancient Rome. Cicero introduced to the Romans knowledge of the Greek schools of philosophy and created Latin philosophical language. His voluminous writings were influential in the subsequent centuries for developing political and legal thought, and especially Christian ethical thought. His philosophy, Stoic in its outlook, is humanist and still serves as a starting point for modern religious and secular elaborations. Among the most cited works of Cicero one must list *On the Nature of the Gods (De natura deorum)*, *On the Chief Good and Evil (De finibus bonorum et malorum)*, *On Fate (De fato)*, *On Laws (De legibus)*, and *On Duties (De officiis)*.
408 Cicero, *The Republic*, in *De re publica. De legibus*, with an English translation by Clinton Walker Keyes, (Cambridge, MA; London: Harvard University Press, William Heinemann, Ltd, 1988). Bk III. XXII.
409 The Greek term for law is νόμος which Cicero derives from νέμω to distribute, to grant, and the Latin term lex Cicero drives from lego, to choose. Quote from *The laws*, in *De re publica. De legibus, op. cit.*, Bk I.VI.18-19.

in reality it is natural force, mind and reason inherent in human nature regardless of the underlying and accepted metaphysics, recognized by "the most learned men" which directs our behavior on an individual and social level. It is natural because it is proper for human nature: "that animal which we call man, endowed with foresight and quick intelligence, complex, keen, possessing memory, full of reason and prudence, has been given a certain distinguished status by the supreme God who created him; for he is the only one among so many different kinds and varieties of living beings who has a share in reason and thought, while all the rest are deprived of it." And further: "But those who have reason in common must also have right reason in common. And since right reason is law, we must believe that men have Law also in common with gods. Further, those who share Law must also share Justice."[410]

Natural Development of Human Rationality

Thus, in the Stoic view the natural law is the function of our human reason which, however, can be corrupted, and which functions for an individual and for the society. Moreover, Nature works by allowing a stepwise development of rationality, as the development of an individual proceeds, and with it the moral awareness through the mechanism of an "impulse" (*hormē*).[411,412]

Thus, the pattern of human behavior changes from a purely animal-like instinctive pattern to a fully rational one and involves, according to Cicero, five stages. They represent the development of human nature, but only a few people will reach the highest Stages, because the process is not independent of a man's own effort. The "function" or goal of man in this process is attainment of perfection of his nature. The term used by Cicero is *officium* (corresponding to the English office, duty or task, as the office of an official charged with certain duties) and the Greek term is *kathēkon*. One could not talk about the "duty" of an animal or of an infant, but rather of their natural function. The term duty becomes appropriate in stages three-through-five in human development as the changes in behavior become now functions of a

---

410 Cicero, *The Laws*, in *op. cit.*, Bk I.VII.22-23.
411 Diogenes Laertius *Lives of Eminent Philosophers* with an English translation by R. D. Hicks. (Cambridge, MA: Harvard University Press, 1995). Vol 1-2. VII. 85-86.
412 Cicero, *De Finibus*, III. 20-21.

rational being. Similar view on the human moral development was formulated by Lawrence Kohlberg and Kazimierz Dabrowski.[413]

Foundation of Kant's Moral Philosophy and its Reinterpretation

Kant's writings on ethics[414] are the most important since antiquity. Kant argues, following the ancient Stoics, that our moral obligations in the final analysis derive from reason by recognition of the natural moral law, and not from either god, or communities, nor from inclinations or desires. Thus, Kant recognizes the instinctive, subconscious origin of our moral behavior and differentiates several levels of motivation and of the operation of the behavioral rules preserving human autonomy and free choice in our moral decisions.

There are many parallels in Kant's thought with the ideas developed by the ancient Stoics. His thought is thus an elaboration on the themes of the ancient philosophers.[415] It is important for our analysis to keep in mind that the philosophical intuitions we find in various schools in the West and in the East can be reevaluated today in a more precise way due to the progress in the natural sciences, and especially from the evolutionary perspective. This does not mean that such perspective was absent in the previous search, especially in the ancient Greek or Indian thought. The naturalistic outlook represented in the ancient schools and philosophical intuitions today is confirmed by studies of our biological nature. Yet we humans are not automata which follow the prescribed pattern of input/output operating in the mechanical, even highly adaptive systems defined by science. With the rise of sentient

---

413 Lawrence Kohlberg (1927-1987) developed a theory, based on the philosophical intuition of Cicero, of the moral development of children through three levels – the pre-conventional, conventional, and post-conventional, each subdivided into two stages: level 1: stage 1 – morality is understood as obedience and punishment and avoidance of harm to others; stage 2 – morality is understood as satisfying one's own interests and letting others do the same; level 2: stage 3 – morality is understood as playing the role of being a good person, i.e., meeting expectations, following the rules, and being concerned for others; stage 4 – morality is understood as doing one's duty, maintaining the social order and the welfare of the society. Level 3: stage 5 – morality is understood as basic rights, values, and legal contracts of a society. Laws and duties are calculated on overall utility (utilitarian morality); stage 6 – morality is understood as an accord with universal, self-chosen principles (e.g., justice, equality and respect for the dignity of all human beings) which confer validity to maxims and actions (Kantian morality). Kazimierz Dabrowski, *Positive Disintegration*, edited, with an introduction, by Jason Aronson, (Boston: Little, Brown and Company, 1964). Kazimierz Dabrowski, *Personality Shaping through Positive Disintegration*, introduction by O. Hobart Mowrer, (London: J. & A. Churchill Ltd., 1967).

414 *Foundations of the Metaphysics of Morals* (1785), *Critique of Practical Reason* (1788), *Metaphysics of Ethics* (1797).

415 The ancient moral philosophy of the Stoics is still valid. It acquired in Kant's elaboration more precise generalization. But this philosophy still inspires more detailed elaborations and application to modern conditions of life, especially by combining the concepts developed by Kant with general outlook of the Stoics. Such an approach reached the level of a new height of logical analysis in the work of Lawrence C. Becker, *A New Stoicism* (Princeton, NJ: Princeton University Press, 1998).

and rational life appeared a new quality in nature, namely, freedom.[416] Still this freedom should be controlled by reason though we are not always motivated by moral law. Modern science provides today insight into the mechanisms operating in human behavior at several levels.

Kant begins his treatise, *Foundations of the Metaphysics of Morals* (1785),[417] with the classification of our rational knowledge. Kant specified the task of a moral philosopher as clarifying the "principle of morality" on which the rational agent can act insofar as his action is morally good; to justify this principle, that is, to show that this principle is actually binding upon an imperfect agent such as a human being; to apply this principle to build an exposition of human obligations, i.e., duties. In this first work out of the three treatises devoted to moral philosophy[418] Kant dealt with the first task of the moral philosopher. He was not interested in constructing an ethical doctrine or writing a casuistry of morals, but searched for an axiom or principle which might be used for building a general theory of laws of freedom (in contrast to the laws of nature, concerned with physical nature), the science of which he called ethics or theory of morals. In the *Metaphysics of Morals* (1797) Kant defined more precisely what ethics is, namely, as the science of how one is under obligation without regard for any possible external lawgiving, that is, as doctrine of virtue.[419] Just as natural philosophy (physics) has its empirical part so does moral philosophy because it has to determine the human will as it is affected by nature. Kant calls this anthropology.

Thus, the laws of moral philosophy are those according to which everything should happen, allowing for conditions under which what should happen often does not. Though the title contains the word metaphysics it is not about the understanding of ultimate reality, or the metaphysics of nature, but a rigorous search for an establishment of the supreme principle of a possible pure will which cannot be derived from observations of actual behavior of men but can be established by

---

416   Daniel C. Bennett, *Freedom Evolves*, (New York: Viking, 2003).

417   Immanuel Kant, *Foundations of the Metaphysics of Morals and What is Enlightenment?* Translated, with Introduction, by Lewis White Beck. (New York: London: Macmillan Publishing Company, Collier Macmillan Publishers, 1988). Onora O'Neill, "Kantian Ethics." In *A Companion to Ethics*. Peter Singer, ed. (Oxford: Blackwell Publishers, 1997), pp. 175-185

418   Those three treatises are: the *Foundations of the Metaphysics of Morals* (1785), *Critique of Practical Reason* (1788), and *Metaphysics of Morals* (1797).

419   Kant, *Metaphysics of Morals*, introduction, translation, and notes by Mary Gregor, (Cambridge; Cambridge University Press, 1991), XVII, 410.

reason. For Kant defines metaphysics as "a system of *a priori* knowledge from concepts alone ... a practical philosophy, which has not nature but freedom of choice for its object" and as such it requires metaphysics of morals which "every man also has it within himself, tough as a rule only in an obscure way."[420]

Kant starts his considerations with an analysis of the conditions for attaining happiness – namely, of being worthy to be happy i.e., of having a good will that is striving for moral perfection. Our moral obligation in the Greek and Judaic traditions is to achieve this "purity of heart" or "kingdom of god," which means good will. "Nothing in the world – indeed nothing even beyond the world – can possibly be conceived which could be called good without qualification except a good will."[421] This is a spontaneous feeling of respect for moral law and an innate sense of "ought." This postulate is an empirical one derived from the observation of universal human nature. Kant next analyzes in quite a manner of evolutionary approach that nature for achieving its end – preservation of life and its welfare – would select instinct rather than reason:

> For all the actions which the creature has to perform with this intention, and the entire rule of conduct, would be dictated much more exactly by instinct, and that the end would be far more certainly attained by instinct than it ever could be by reason. And if, ... reason should have been granted to the favored creature, it would have served only to let it contemplate the happy constitution of its nature, to admire it, to rejoice in it, and to be grateful for it to its beneficent cause. But reason would not have been given in order that the being should subject its faculty of desire to that weak and delusive guidance and to meddle with the purpose of nature. In a word, nature would have taken care that reason did not break forth into practical use nor have the presumption, with its weak insights, to think out for itself the plan of happiness and the means of attaining it. Nature would have taken over not only the choice of ends but also that of the means, and with wise foresight she would have entrusted both to instinct

---

420 *Ibidem*, II, 216.
421 Kant, *Foundations, op. cit.,* p. 9.

alone… Reason is not, however, competent to guide the will safely with regard to its object and the satisfaction of all our needs … and to this end an innate instinct would have led with far more certainty. But reason is given to us as a practical faculty, i.e., one which is meant to have an influence on the will. As nature has elsewhere distributed capacities suitable to the functions they are to perform, reason's proper function must be to produce a will good in itself and not one good merely as a means, for to the former reason is absolutely essential.[422]

Thus, the function of reason is the establishment of this "good will." Good will is good because of its willingness, that is, it is good in itself without regard to anything else. It is not the sole and complete good but it is the highest good and the condition for of all others. "It dwells already in the natural sound understanding and does not need so much to be taught as only to be brought to light. In the estimation of the total worth of our actions it always takes first place and is the condition of everything else."[423] As an example of such situation Kant gives us an interpretation of the scriptural passages that command us to love neighbors and enemies. It is not done from inclination but from duty, which resides in the will not in feelings or propensities, but in principles of action.

In saying this Kant describes nothing other than common moral consciousness and derives the principle for moral action. Charles Darwin observed that in the time of Kant the origin of this moral consciousness was questioned and Kant himself asked about it.

Darwin was among the first who gave a naturalistic explanation for its origin. He stated in his *The Descent of Man* (1871):[424]

I fully subscribe to the judgment of those writers who maintain that of all the differences between man and the lower animals, the moral sense or conscience is by far the most important. This sense as Mackintosh[425] remarks, 'has

---

422 Kant, *ibid.* p. 11-12.
423 Kant, *ibid.* p. 15.
424 Charles Darwin, *The Descent of Man*, in *The Origin of Species and The Descent of Man*, (New York: The Modern Library, no date). Chapter 4, pp. 471-472.
425 Mackintosh, *Dissertation on Ethical Philosophy*, 1837, p. 231.

a rightful supremacy over every other principle of human action;' it is summed up in that short but imperious word *ought*, leading him without a moment's of hesitation to risk his life for that of a fellow- creature; or after due deliberation, impelled simply by the deep feeling of right or duty, to sacrifice it in some great cause. Immanuel Kant exclaims, 'Duty! Wondrous thought, that workest neither by fond insinuation, flattery, nor by any threat, but merely by holding up thy naked law in the soul, and so extorting for thyself always reverence, if not always obedience; before whom all appetites are dumb, however secretly they rebel; whence thy original'?[426]

This great question has been discussed by many writers of consummate ability; and my sole excuse for touching on it, is the impossibility of here passing it over; and because, as far as I know, no one has approached it exclusively from the side of natural history. The investigation possesses, also some independent interest, as an attempt to see how far the study of the lower animals throws light on one of the highest physical faculties of man.

The following proposition seems to me in a high degree probable – namely, that any animal whatever, endowed with well-marked social instincts, the parental and filial affection being here included, would inevitably acquire a moral sense or conscience, as soon as its intellectual powers have become as well, or nearly as well developed as in man.

We can now add to Kant's postulate that modern science confirms Kant's intuition and provides a biological, naturalistic, evolutionary explanation for the existence of this moral consciousness.

---

426   Immanuel Kant, *Metaphysics of Ethics*, translated by J .W. Semple, (Edinburgh, 1836), p.136. This quote comes from Kant's work *Critique of Practical Reason* (1788). The full quote is: "Duty! Thou sublime and mighty name that dost embrace nothing charming or insinuating but requirest submission and yet seekest not to move the will by thretening aught that would arouse natural aversion or terror, but only holdest forth a law which of itself finds entrance into the mind and yet gains reluctant reverence (though not always obedience) – a law before which all inclinations are mute even though secretly work against it: what origin is worthy of thee, and where is the root of thy noble descent which proudly rejects all kinship with the inclinations and from which to be descended is the indispensable condition of the only worth which men alone can give themselves?" Immanuel Kant, *Critique of Practical Reason*, edited and translated with notes and introduction by Lewis White Beck, third edition, (New York: Macmillan Publishing Company, 1993), p. 90.

Kant insists that in deciding what we ought to do our variable desires are not important – for an action to be truly moral it has to be done in the belief and because of the belief that it is right, i.e., out of respect for moral law.

It is important to indicate at this point that Kant and all philosophers until the post-Darwinian times considered as truly (strictly) moral the actions produced by conscious rational and reflective analysis. This view arose from Origen's account of the Stoic analysis of the motion of objects and action of animals and humans.[427] Origen reported that the Stoics differentiated human beings from all other natural things by a particular kind of movement (action) unique to them. What distinguished those things from others that are moved from without is that they have a certain kind of cause (*aitía*) of motion in themselves. Things like plants and animals have an internal cause of motion, "nature" (*logos* for Stoics) and "soul" (in Origen's view); inanimate objects must have an external agency to be moved along; they move by thrust of external force. Plants and animals by virtue of having "soul" (and "nature") are capable of self-movement or action. In the case of animals, sensory stimulation is a necessary condition of the impulse to self-movement. Those lacking intelligence move and act according to a prescribed pattern. Human beings do not move or act in a set fashion—because the faculty of reason (*logos*) enables them to judge (*krinō*) their sensory presentations—to reject or accept and to be guided. Origen calls this third kind of movement (action) self-movement of which only rational animals are capable, motion (action) "through themselves."[428] We are deserving of praise when we choose the noble and avoid the base, but when we follow the opposite course, we are blameworthy. Origen reasons: It is neither true nor reasonable to lay the blame on external things and release ourselves from the accusation making ourselves analogous to wood and stones inasmuch as they are drawn along by external things that move them; such is

---

427   Origen (185-ca 254) succeeded Clement of Alexandra in the school of Alexandria. Clement was the patriarch of Alexandria who at first supported Origen but expelled him later for being ordained without the patriarch's permission. Origen then moved to Palestine and died there. He wrote commentaries on all the books of the bible. In a treatise, *First Principles* (*Peri Archon*), he formulated one of the first philosophical expositions of Christian doctrine in which he interpreted scripture allegorically. He was a Neo-Pythagorean and Neo-Platonist, and like Plotinus believed that the soul passes through stages of incarnation before reaching god. For him even demons would be reunited with god. He considered god the First Principle, and Christ, the Logos, as subordinate to him. Origen's view was declared anathema in the sixth century.

428   *Stoicorum Veterum Fragmenta* Collegit Ioannes Ab Arnim (Stutgardiae: In Aedibus B.G. Teubneri, MCMLXIV). Vol 1-4. (abbreviated as SVF). SVF 2.989, 879. Origen, *De principiis*, (*On the First Principles*), translated with introduction and notes by G. W. Butterworth, (Gloucester, Mass.: Peter Smith, 1973). III, 1, 2, 3.

the argument of someone who wants to set up a counterfeit notion of autonomy. For if we should ask him what autonomy is, he would say that it obtains "if there are no external causes, when I intend to do something in particular, that incite to the contrary."[429]

The Stoics believed that human beings are capable of self-movement without actually initiating their own motion. Origen's account of the difference in motion (action) between humans and other animals gave rise to the concept of morality as a behavior conditioned by a rational, reflective act. Origen said: "our nature as human beings furnishes the souls for considering the noble and the base and for judging between them. Even though we have no control over the fact that something external causes in us a presentation of this or that sort—the decision (*krisis*) to use this occurrence in one way or another is the function of nothing other than the reason within us."[430] Origen said: "our nature as human beings furnishes the souls for considering the noble and the base and for judging between them. Even though we have no control over the fact that something external causes in us a presentation of this or that sort—the decision (*krisis*) to use this occurrence in one way or another is the function of nothing other than the reason within us."[431] Many actions, even if they produce good results, that are done in accordance with the law do not belong to the realm of moral actions in this strict sense if they are done with some ulterior motives. Thus truly morally good action will not only be in accord with the law but also because the law is acknowledged as absolutely and universally binding. Kant formulated thus the condition of morality in three propositions: 1. It must be done from duty; 2. Moral value is in the maxim by which action is determined and not in the purpose, thus it depends on the principle of volition; 3. Duty is a necessity of an action from the respect of law i.e., consciousness of the submission of the will to a law. And the subjective principle of volition must be distinguished from the objective principle of volition which would serve all rational being also subjectively if they were governed by reason.

Table 1 summarizes Kant's three levels of human behavior. Only the third level, according to Kant, corresponds to the strictly moral

429   SVF II. 990.
430   SVF II.992.
431   SVF II.992.

behavior in Kant's definition. However, this level is reached only by a few individuals and does not reflect how humans actually behave.

Table 1

LEVELS OF BEHAVIORAL RULES

I.   INSTINCTIVE

e.g. food, procreation, fear of the unknown social life in social animals (governed by genes and epigenetic rules only)

II.   HETERONOMOUS

A. Empirical:
From fear, desire; from the principle of happiness from the concept of moral sense
(based on inclinations; all inclinations summed up in the idea of "happiness")
B. Rational motivated by extrinsic values: From the concept of perfection Ontological or transcendental, theological
(These levels corresponds partially to subconscious proto-moral from innate "moral faculty" or "capacity" postulated by natural sciences)

III.   AUTONOMOUS

Categorical Imperative (Autonomous moral law)
A law for the will of every rational being
It only can have as its subject itself considered giving universal law.

Modern Science Provides a Biological Basis for Human Behavior and Validates Philosophical Speculation

We may now present a brief exposition of how the natural law should be understood so far. The natural law postulate formulates recognition of a general principle operating in nature which is innate in humans and governs their behavior. It has character of the law because it is binding to humans; it is universal, because it is independent of particular positive law and applies to all people. Our human understanding of this natural law is growing with the development of our rationality; thus, it is the law of human nature, the law of reason. Our behavior changes from an animal-like instinctive pattern to a fully rational one through stages: "The first appropriate function of a creature is to maintain itself, in its natural condition. The second, that it should seize hold of the things which accord with Nature and banish those which are the opposite." Thus, we can differentiate in the natural law two types of principles, one instinctive, automatic which directs our behavior unconsciously, and the second one, reflective, rational at which we arrive after some rational analysis. For as soon as man acquires the capacity for understanding or rational concepts, he draws rational conclusions that the highest human good is that which is worthy of praise and desirable for its own sake.[432]

These principles are classified as a law from popular understanding of a governing principle by analogy to a written law, that is human positive law which "in written form decrees whatever is it wishes, either by command or prohibition." But in reality "law is intelligence, whose natural function it is to command right conduct and forbid wrongdoing... it is the mind and reason of the intelligent man, the standard by which justice and injustice are measured."

Christian religious thinkers adopted the Ciceronian formulation of the natural law for Thomas Aquinas stated that reason is the rule and measure of human action: "The good of the human being is being in accordance with reason, and human evil is being outside the order of reasonableness... So human virtue, which makes good both the human person and his works, is in accordance with human nature just in so far as it is in accordance with reason; and vice is contrary to human nature

---

432   Cicero's view on human behavior coincides with that of Immanuel Kant who postulated categorical imperative as the maxim for human conduct. This maxim represents the highest level of understanding of morality and therefore he also postulated hypothetical imperative in which human behavior may be governed by other motifs. Immanuel Kant, *Foundations of the Metaphysics of Morals and What is Enlightenment?* Translated, with an Introduction by Lewis White Beck, (New York, London: Macmillan Publishing Company, Collier Macmillan Publishers, 1988). Marian Hillar, "Is a Universal ethics Possible? A Humanist Proposition." In *The Philosophy of Humanism and the Issues of Today.* American Humanist Association, Houston, 1995, pp. 127-148. In the final analysis reason is the basis for morality and philosophy produced very good intuitive theory how it works. Derek Parfit, *Reason and Persons*, (Oxford: Clarendon Press, 1987). Jürgen Habermas, "A Conversation about God and the World," in *Time of Transitions*, edited and translated by Ciaran Cronin and Max Pensky, (Cambridge, UK: Polity Press, 2006), pp. 149-170. Modern science now grounds this philosophical intuition in evolutionary biological processes providing solid empirical foundations.

just in so far as it is contrary to the order of reasonableness."[433] They linked it, however, to their religious speculations.

Since time immemorial humans were preoccupied with their own behavior and attitudes versus other humans, the rest of the animate world, and the surrounding environment. This is attested by the oldest written documents from the Mesopotamian, Mediterranean, and Far Eastern regions of the World.[434] In every culture we find the formulation known as the "Golden Rule" as the universal principle guiding human behavior. This rule is expressed in religious injunctions as well as in philosophical analyses wherever such attempts were made as is attested again by the history of philosophy.

On the other hand, naturalistic investigation which is today classified as science also attempted to give more critical and natural explanations. These attempts were most often combined with philosophical speculation because of a lack of proper investigative tools to attack the issue from a strictly naturalistic perspective of the human psyche. As it was previously indicated, the serious foundations for modern studies were laid down by Charles Darwin who initiated investigations on the biological foundations to philosophical speculations.[435]

Serious foundations for modern psychology were produced by William James (1843-1920) and Sigmund Freud (1856-1939). We had to wait, however, till the second half of the twentieth century to see the explosion of studies related to our behavior (morals) from various fields of investigations: experimental psychology, developmental psychology, evolutionary psychology, anthropology, ethology, neurobiology,

433   Summa Theologiae, op. cit., 1a 2ae, 71, a.2c.
434   Joseph Campbell, The Masks of God: Occidental Mythology, (Penguin Books: Harmondsworth, U.K.; New York, USA, 1976. Joseph Campbell, The Masks of God: Oriental Mythology, (Penguin Books: Harmondsworth, U.K.; New York, USA, 1986). W.Y. Evans-Wentz, compiler and editor, The Tibetan Book of the Dead, (Oxford University Press: Oxford, UK, 1960). The Texts of Taoism, translated by Jmaes Legge, Part I, II, (Dover Publications, Inc. : New York, first published, 1962). James B. Pritchard, ed., The Ancient Near East. Anthology of Texts and Pictures, Vol. 1, 2, (Princeton University Press: Princeton, 1973). Hindu Myths. A Sourcebook Trasnalted from the Sanskrit. With introduction by Wendy Doniger O'Flaherty, (Harmondsworth, UK: Penquin Books, 1975). The Rig Veda translated and annotated by Wendy Doniger O'Flaherty, (Harmondsworth, UK: Penquin Books, 1984). The Upanishads, translated by F. Max Müller, Part 1, 2, (Dover Publications: New York, first published 1962). Sarvepalli Radhakrishnan, Indian Philosophy, Vol. 1, 2 (first publication, George Allen and Unwin Ltd, 1931). James P. Allen, translator and introduction, The Ancient Egyptian Pyramid Texts, (Society of Biblical Literature: Atlanta, GA, 2005). Wing-Tsit Chan, translated and compiled, Ssource Book in Chinese Philosophy, (Princeton University Press: Princeton, 1963).
435   Charles Darwin, The Descent of Man (1871), p. 471-472. In The Origin of Species and The Descent of Man, (New York: The Modern Library no date).

neurology. Most of such modern studies were recently summarized by Marc D. Hauser in his book, *Moral Minds. How Nature Designed Our Universal Sense of Right and Wrong.*[436]

Table 2 lists sciences that provide evidence for the biological basis of our moral behavior. Following Darwin, primatologists and other biologists[437] have long argued that the roots of human morality are manifest in social animals like apes and monkeys. They express feelings of empathy and expectations of reciprocity which are essential behaviors for mammalian group life and constitute a counterpart to human morality. Marc D. Hauser summarizing all studies done with animals and in modern psychology and anthropology proposes that people are born with a moral grammar wired into their neural circuits by evolution. He claims that this grammar generates instant moral judgments which are instantaneously inaccessible to the conscious mind. Hauser presents his argument as a hypothesis to be proved, but it is based on solid experimental ground, including work with primates, and in empirical results derived from studies performed by moral philosophers. Hauser argues that moral grammar operates in the same way as the universal grammar proposed by linguist Noam Chomsky for developing language faculty. This universal grammar is a system of rules for generating syntax and vocabulary but does not specify any particular language. That is supplied by the culture in which a child grows up. By analogy, moral grammar, too, is a system composed of neural circuits which generate moral behavior and not a list of specific rules. Basic rules are the same in every society, but it allows for cultural variations, since cultures can put different emphases on its elements. Table 3 presents comparisons observed between our moral behavior and behavior of higher animals.

---

436 Marc D. Hauser, *Moral Minds. How Nature Designed Our Universal Sense of Right and Wrong*, (New York: HarperCollins Publishers, 2006).

437 Frans de Waal, *Our Inner Ape*, (New York: Riverhead Books, 2005). Frans de Waal, *Primates and Philosophers. How Morality Evolved*, (Princeton and Oxford: Princeton University Press, 2006). Robert Wright, *The Moral Animal. Evolutionary Psychology of Everyday Life*, (New York: Vintage Books, 1995). Robert Trivers, *Natural Selection and Social Theory. Selected papers of Robert Trivers*, (Oxford: Oxford University Press, 2002).

Table 2

NATURAL SCIENCES PROVIDE EVIDENCE FOR THE EXISTENCE OF THE SO-CALLED *MORAL FACULTY* (CAPACITY) IN THE HUMAN PSYCHE

1. Thought experiments and computer games;

2. Developmental psychology – studies of infants and young children; Stages in psychological development; Studies of identical monozygotic twins; (Lawrence Kohlberg, Kazimierz Dąbrowski)

3. Experimental psychology;

4. Anthropology;

5. Ethology (Studies on chimpanzees and bonobos)

6. Evolutionary psychology: Hamilton's Kin Selection

   Triver's Reciprocal Altruism

   Group Selection

   Cooperation in the microbial world

7. Evolutionary process is based on

   a. inherited changes (mutations);

   b. natural selection;

   c. cooperation

8. Universality of the Golden Rule

Table 3

THREE LEVELS OF MORALITY COMPARED FROM ANIMAL STUDIES

Level	Description	Human and Apes Compared
1. Moral sentiments (Kant's instinctive behavior)	Human psychology provides "building blocks" of morality, such as the capacity for empathy, a tendency for reciprocity, a sense of fairness, and the ability to harmonize relationships.	In these areas, there exist evident parallels with other primates.
2. Social pressure (Kant's heteronomous behavior)	Insisting that everyone behaves in a way that favors a cooperative group life behavior. The tools to this end are reward punishment, and reputation building.	Community concern and prescriptive social rules do exist in other primates, but social pressure is less systematic and less concerned with the goals of society as a whole.
3. Judgment and reasoning (Kant's autonomous behavior)	Internalization of others' needs and goals to the degree that these needs and goals figure in our judgment of behavior, including others' behavior that does not directly touch us. Moral judgment is self-reflective (i.e., governs our own behavior as well) and often logically reasoned.	Others' needs and goals may be internalized to some degree, but this is where the similarities end. Humans are the only species to worry about why we think what we think (?).

Frans de Waal, *Primates and Philosophers* (Princeton and Oxford: Princeton University Press, 2006), p.168

This proposal has strong and far-reaching implications. It means that parents and teachers do not really teach children the rules of correct behavior rather, they instill the cultural biases and modifications. Also, it demonstrates in a tangible way that religions are not the source of moral codes. On the contrary, moral grammar which operates subconsciously is immune to religious doctrines. At best, religions enforce instinctive behavior and most often indoctrinate people with cultural biases.

Moral grammar is a product of the evolutionary process because restraints on behavior are necessary for social living and have been favored by natural selection for survival. Friedrich Nietzsche was among those philosophers who argued for societal origin of rules of behavior which developed as cultures evolved.[438]

Hauser developed his ideas through work with vervet monkeys in Kenya and with birds.[439] Later on, when psychologists developed techniques to study the thinking of human babies, he found that many such studies could be repeated with animals thus setting the cognitive abilities of human babies in an evolutionary framework. His proposal of a moral grammar derived from collaboration with Noam Chomsky who argued that the faculty of language had developed as an adaptation of some neural system in animals. By analogy with language, Hauser thought that moral behavior is also acquired through development of neural circuits which constitute an innate set of rules. Moral grammar, now universal among people, is thought to have evolved to its present shape during the hunter-gatherer stage of our past, some 200,000 years ago through the mechanism of group selection as was suggested already by Nietzsche in a cultural context.

The question arises now, what validity does moral philosophical speculation have in view of scientific theories and the evidence behind them, such as the one postulated by Hauser? The answer which is suggested by Hauser was presented in the form of three models for human behavior incorporating three major themes of philosophical speculation.

---

438   Friedrich Nietzsche, The Birth of Tragedy and The Genealogy of Morals, translated by Francis Golfing, (New York: Anchor Books, 1990).

439   Marc D. Hauser, The Evolution of Communication, (Boston: Beacon Press, 1997).

The first model, the so-called Humean Model, is based on the entire line of philosophical speculation going back in antiquity to the Stoics, and in modern times has been best expressed by David Hume. Hume assumed that "perceptions" produce feelings and emotional reactions from which follows judgment.[440]

The second model, labeled the Kantian Model, emerges from Kant's moral philosophy misunderstood or interpreted only from one perspective, that of his "categorical imperative." Hauser, who noticed this misconception, introduced a double path in the model. Kant accepted the existence of something he called "good will." It has thus a quality of an instinct. We proceed to evaluate events, actions, etc, either on some principles which he classified as 1. heteronomous (empirical e.g., from principle of happiness, the so-called *moral sense* (in modern terminology it is the *moral faculty* or *moral grammar*), inclinations, etc, or rational e.g., from the concept of perfection, transcendental or theological) because they derive from the outside of the individual; 2. an autonomous or categorical imperative which is an autonomous moral law, a law for the will of every rational being. He expressed it as a formula or maxim by which we can judge. It has to be universal to be classified as the moral imperative.

But Kant did not go, and in his time, it would be very difficult to do it, into the biological foundations of this mechanism. It was anyway an ideal situation if all humans behaved all the time in such a rational way. He knew that humans do not behave all the time in this way and not always use reason for judgment. Thus, these heteronomous principles were valid in practice (and still are).

The third model, the Rawlsian Model, is based on the theory of John Rawls who postulated an instinctive "moral faculty" which allows us to differentiate moral actions and situations from those which have no moral value and to differentiate actions which are allowed, permissible, or forbidden. So, in this last model we have perception first, then automatically (unconsciously) we judge them and only then we develop emotions and feelings about them. Of course, in the later stage comes also conscious reflection and reasoning which is then the basis

---

440   Author previously discussed Kant's ethics in the context of the possibility of developing a universal moral code: Marian Hillar, "Is a Universal ethics Possible? A Humanist Proposition." In *The Philosophy of Humanism and the Issues of Today.* American Humanist Association, Houston, 1995, pp. 127-148.

for developing cultural rules, laws, etc. The last model is more realistic, and it accommodate all previous models as certain approximations and at the same time is confirmed by evidence from scientific studies in many disciplines and provides evolutionary basis for human behavior. Still Kant's model seems to be the most complete though its biological basis could not be developed in the time of Kant.

Conclusions

The theme of moral behavior was traditionally the subject of inquiry in philosophy and religions. In the ancient world Stoics proposed a natural moral law as a principle that regulates human behavior in society. Immanuel Kant proposed naturalistic theory of human behavior on three levels, instinctive, heteronomous, and autonomous. Kant recognized the existence of subconscious, non-rational principle which he defined as "good will." The function of reason is to expose this principle and bring it to the sphere of consciousness. Then our behavior becomes "moral in the sense that it is directed by reflection" (Origen). Kant posed a question concerning the origin of this subconscious moral sense and Darwin answered Kant's question proposing its evolutionary origin. During the last century natural and evolutionary sciences were successful in explaining the human evolution and particularly in discoveries concerning characteristics of human behavior as a continuation of characteristics of the behavior in animal world and confirmed the suggestions of the Stoics and Kant. Today natural scientists and scholars postulate cooperation, collaboration (moral behavior) as the third element driving and directing the evolutionary process next to mutations and natural selection. It seems that they fully confirm intuitions of philosophers. The thesis about the fundamental status of cooperation in the entire animate world imposes a new reinterpretation of the natural moral law. We must recognize that cooperation is the basic fundamental element of living world and appeared during the process of biological evolution with the development of the neuron. This was laconically asserted by Irene Greaves who stated: "Love is the purpose of evolution."[441]

---

441   Greaves I., *Lovescaping: Building the Humanity of Tomorrow by Practicing Love in Action*, Amazon Publishing, Bellevue, WA 2018.

VI. HUMANIST ETHICS

IS A UNIVERSAL ETHICS POSSIBLE?
A HUMANIST PROPOSITION[442]

Grounds for Morals

Usually, in the philosophical literature ethics is differentiated from morals, being defined as the rational analysis of value-loaded statements and their validity.[1] Morals, on the other hand, are a set of practical statements or opinions about values usually treated in moralistic literature such as sermons and various specific codes of behavior. These normative statements derive from the necessity of coping in human societies with various human interactions. They by necessity cannot be unconditional and are in most cases ambiguous. Moral acts are performed out of a sense of obligation, duty, a moral law. Thus ethics as the theory of morals deals with the justification or grounds of morals and attempts to establish a fundamental principle or principles on which the moral codes could be based.

There were many attempts at finding these grounds of morals, e.g., in the nature of man, in the circumstances of his existence, as given by the transcendental being or as a priori concepts of reason. Most often it is impossible to separate ethics and morality and they are treated together. Though all these grounds may be useful in practice, it seems, however, that if moral action, by definition, is moral in the strictest sense because it is done for its intrinsic value, it should be independent of all motives and conditions. The last position we may call absolutist and it itself can be divided into two trends: rational and transcendental. The rational trend, exemplified by the philosophy of Immanuel Kant (1724-1804), claims only reason as the source of moral statements, whereas the transcendental trend, represented by many religious doctrines, appeals to a supernatural authority in a more or less crypto-legal manner for the set of given moral values and their justification. These two attitudes answer the question of how and on what ground we can know about the content of "ought" statements and whether or not they can be known in any way analogous to knowledge in empirical matters.

---

442   Published in *The Philosophy of Humanism and the Issues of Today,* M. Hillar and F. Prahl, eds., American Humanist Association, Houston, 1995, pp. 127-148.

Grounds for Morals

Empirical   Absolutist
                                    /   \
                            Rational   Transcendental

Empirical and Transcendental grounds lead to conditional moral actions, dependent also on other than strictly rational basis (moral actions in a loose sense). Rational grounds lead to moral actions in a proper, strict sense.

==

The question of the beginning of morality is open but it has to be approached from the evolutionary standpoint of human biological history. It belongs to the realm of historical inquiry to find out when an awareness of the universality of the human condition and moral codes of a universal character emerged for the first time. This awareness is the essence of moral consciousness, and thus decisive to the emergence of humanity as something other than one more zoological species. It is obvious that if the main characteristic of mankind is the possession of reason, then reason as appointed by nature, must be the ruler of our will. But our moral consciousness must have a biological basis in the form of instinctive or intuitive behavior and as such, *mutatis mutandis*, is not significantly different from animal behavior. It is suggested that our moral norms were conceived as an extension of urges which operated universally in nature—namely self-preservation and the preservation of the species. Though we cannot talk about moral behavior of animals in their societies, since moral reflection in a strict sense seems to be specifically human quality. But we can talk about behavior of animals interpreting it in human terms. We find that higher animals have built-in mechanisms which correspond to some moral norms, e.g., the congenital inhibition preventing some animals from killing other members of the same species. Moral customs and human ideas about wrongness or rightness are the codification of the same instincts. As we analyze and discover the laws governing the physical world, so we discover the "laws" governing the social behavior either of animals or of humans. Certainly, in social situations they are not always followed because they reflect a different reality—to be precise moral reality.

They might vary according to the peculiar conditions of the natural life of human tribes, but they derive from a number of fundamental and universal rules, e.g., parents' duties toward children, interdiction of killing useful members of the community. Certain norms operating in primitive societies may be specific for the conditions of human life, e.g., prohibition on incest, that seems to be a universal rule in all human societies, explained as an instrument to preserve the family structure, social roles within the family and the hierarchy of generations.

In human societies, however, these biological mechanisms are less efficient, perhaps due to the development of reflection and hence the possibility of a free choice to follow or not to follow them. The development of humanity, since the moment of appearance of the *nous* (mind), progresses primarily on the second functional level of the human brain. Therefore the biological mechanisms are now compensated through human mind and reason, by development of human culture, including elaborate systems of moral norms, all forms of social organization, scientific knowledge and religions which represented historically in some cultures a unifying intellectual construct.

Epistemological Theories of Moral Judgment

From a certain stage in human evolution, however, moral reflection led to moral awareness which is variously described as a sense of guilt or moral conscience. Moral lore was at this stage in most historically known cultures combined with the mythological interpretation of the world and as the result of this process religion or theistic ideology appeared. During the process the common and non-religious origin of moral foundations was obliterated. People realized that socially inherited moral rules might be verbally challenged and violated in practice by action and decree whereas natural laws cannot be challenged by human will. Thus the question arose as to why this moral prescription should be valid rather than the opposing one? Several answers were given to this question of justification of morals. Materialistic and positivistic philosophies (Hobbes, Spinoza, French naturalists, Hume) converged in the subjectivism that claimed that whatever people say about the moral good and duties is in the realm of personal decision. Nothing is good or evil in itself, such designations are only expressions of our emotional state—our desires or repulsions. The extreme form of this version implies that value judgments and moral norms are exclamatory, expressing emotions and are meaningless because they are neither true nor false. Only logical utterances are meaningful i.e. they can be true or false. Moral and value judgments convey information about the speaker's emotional state. This suggests that people have actually to experience emotions to utter value judgments. The crucial distinction was between the meaningful or empirical statement and the meaningless or moral statement. For example one can design an experiment demonstrating that a stone is heavier than water and thus make a prediction whereas no such operation is possible for the statement "thou shall love your neighbor as yourself." There is an obvious epistemological problem with the value judgment statements. On one hand we may ask why we should accept the rule that verifiability and predictive power are identical with meaningfulness and on the other why should we ban statements that cannot be submitted to the verifiability test? This procedure of defining the conditions of empiricity of statements led to the extraction of rules that operate in science. The rule equating the meaningfulness with verifiability or with predictive power is itself a normative rule and has, arguably, empirico-rational basis. This analysis is valid for phenomena regulated by the laws of nature.

There is however, another set of statements that apply to social situations and they are meaningful in an ordinary sense of the word and its usage. For example when we say "Exploitation is evil" or "Helping one's neighbor in misfortune is our duty" -- these statements describe in a way perfectly understood by all men human relations and human situations. They are not about what is meaningful or meaningless or objective or subjective, yet they may have historically an empirical component—because they evolved from our human experience accumulated throughout history and became certain conventions. This empirical part was unfortunately reflected in mythological ideological traditions.

History indicates that in communities where myth regulated the social order there was no epistemological distinction between the laws in social and natural order—they all were "divine laws" and the punishment inflicted for denying them was the same. But the distinction emerged between various mythological and ideological traditions not only in visualizing the cosmic order and its history, but also in what they forbid or prescribe as obligatory. So the content of moral norms is defined by tradition—e.g., Buddhist or various Christian traditions—itself undergoing historical modifications. Most differences can be settled by adherence to a commonly admitted principle but some can be settled by building consensus through experience just as in empirical matters. In the modern world agreement is shaped in empirical matters by science and its method, but even here it is not suprahistorical (i.e., independent of historical conditioning) either. But informed people have, at least, a common set of criteria in the scientific worldview.

In moral matters the situation is much more complicated than in empirical ones since human beings are affected in their behavior by a variety of psychological and volitive factors. There is therefore much disagreement among people on the content of moral rules and even when accepting them people do not necessarily always follow them.

Another solution for justifying morals which is termed utilitarianism was based on the assertion that there is in fact a good known and defined as such by all people, this good being "happiness" or "pleasure." In accordance with common sense and usage we can by this universal standard assess the wrongness and rightness of human action. Thus all actions which increase happiness are right and the general goal by which we measure all our evaluations is the greatest happiness of the greatest number. The major problem with utilitarianism is that it cannot reduce all the values we cherish to a common scale of the "happiness" or "pleasure" they produce and quantify them to say nothing of the unpredictable consequences our actions may produce. Moreover, what matters is the global amount of pleasure our actions produce. Thus no matter who is producing it, for whom and for what reason, provided the sum is constant. Utilitarian doctrine is based on the assumption that all people seek and desire the same things.

Morality of Intentions in pre- and post-Nicaean Christianity

Other trends in moral thought were based on the intentions of agents as opposed to the effects of their actions. The actions are called good or evil in a derivative sense by reference to good or evil intentions of the authors without regard to the actual effects. This attitude is typical for the various Christian ethics and was summarized by Augustine in saying *Ama et fac quod vis* (Love and do what you wish). This implies that our actions inspired by love are intrinsically good. It remains in line with the message of Jesus and Paul (Mark 12: 29-31; Gal. 5:14): "Love your God ... And love your neighbor as yourself." The term "love" is itself already value-loaded and the injunction raises doubts both in historical and psychological contexts. Love is an emotional experience and cannot be ordered since it does not depend on one's free will. Moreover it is psychologically impossible to love all people and also God, since he remains after all an elusive and abstract idea. Therefore the term "love" has nothing to do with the emotion usually experienced in personal relationships, and it becomes an abstract intellectual notion. No doubt, however, that by upbringing people can be induced to be kind and helpful to each other, or to avoid hatred and envy. But this is irrespective of their religious background. In the final analysis "love" cannot be an actual requirement of morality.[2]

Moreover, the New Testament commandments are not equivalent. They reflect two components of the moral human tradition: one is the theistic mythological value and the other may be treated *mutatis mutandis* as the Christian formulation of the secular empirical anthropic golden rule found in all cultures. The original Messianism (early or pre-Nicaean Christianity) depended heavily on the second component. Thus the pre-Nicaean religion emphasized a code of ethics as its primary element. This code is based on personal decisions which determine the destiny of the individual. To be sure there is here an ultimate theistic motive but right or wrong is decided by action according to or against the independent universal anthropic moral principle. But with time various Christian doctrines were developed from the first component on the relation to the institution of the Church. Morality became a legalistic system based on the acceptance or not of the Church orthodoxy. The doctrine of exclusive truth about unverifiable mythological religious statements led to moral condemnation and persecution of nonbelievers and all who did not accept the party line of the ruling theocrats, both in the Catholic and later Protestant Churches. The myth of original sin led to the pathological distortion of human sexuality and wholesale moral condemnation and oppression of women. Murder of doctrinal or ideological opponents of all sorts became a moral virtue. The theologies of some Protestants and Catholic mystics emphasized the love of God so exclusively that men disappeared as intrinsically valuable creatures. John Calvin (1509-1564), for example, believed that one should limit the amount of sin by all means, including coercion only because sins offend God. In any case, however, according to Christian theologies, our salvation does not depend on our actions. The Christian doctrine of self-perfection works against people who practice charity for the aim of softening human suffering. The ideal of sainthood urges people to practice it in order to merit one's own sainthood. The monastic ideal of a moral life is socially parasitic. The fundamental error, however, as in any theistic system, is that to subordinate relations between people to higher goals—either God's will, satisfaction or "glory," or one's own perfection, is morally risky. It is also very dangerous. In the first case when the concept of divine will consists of the desire for glory and dominion combined with the conception of might and vengeance it leads to development of theocratic totalitarianism as in the rule of the Catholic Church. In the second case it may lead to egocentrism and indifference to others. Both attitudes run against the fundamental anthropic principle of morality.

Kant's Moral Axiom

Kant's work written in 1785, *Foundations of the Metaphysics of Morals*,[3] is one of the most important in the history of ethical philosophy. Kant was not interested in constructing a system or writing a casuistry of morals, but searched for an axiom which might be used for building a general system of laws of freedom (in contrast to the laws of nature, concerned with the nature), the science of which he called ethics or theory of morals. Just as natural philosophy (physics) has its empirical part so does moral philosophy because it has to determine the human will as it is affected by nature. Kant calls this anthropology. Thus the laws of moral philosophy are those according to which everything should happen, allowing for conditions under which what should happen often does not. Though the title contains the word metaphysics it is not about the understanding of ultimate reality, or metaphysics of nature, but a rigorous search for an establishment of the supreme principle of a possible pure will which cannot be derived from observations of actual behavior of men but can be established by reason.

A. Condition of morality

Kant starts his considerations with analysis of the conditions for attaining happiness—namely of being worthy to be happy i.e. of having a good will. Our moral obligation in the Greek and Judaic traditions is to achieve this "purity of heart" or "kingdom of God," which means good will. "Nothing in the world— indeed nothing even beyond the world—can possibly be conceived which could be called good without qualification except a good will." The function of reason is the establishment of this good will. The good will is good because of its willing, that is, it is good in itself without regard to anything else. In saying this Kant describes nothing other than the common moral consciousness and derives the principle for moral action.

He insists that in deciding what we ought to do our variable desires are not important—for an action to be truly moral it has to be done in the belief and because of the belief that it is right, i.e., out of respect for moral law. For the true moral value of our action it is not sufficient that it arise from some good inclination, disposition or temperament even according to duty—it has to arise from the sense of duty, or good will. Whether the action succeeds in its purpose or not, if it is done with a good will it is morally acceptable, the consequences which we consider in passing moral judgment are those intended consequences, implicated in the motive of the action. Many actions, even if they produce good results, that are done in accordance with the law are not moral in this strict sense if they are done with some ulterior motives. Thus truly morally good action will not only be in accord with the law but also because the law is acknowledged as absolutely and universally binding. Kant formulated thus the condition of morality in three propositions: "... the first proposition of morality is that to have moral worth an action must be done from duty. The second proposition is: An action performed from duty does not have its moral worth in the purpose which is to be achieved through it but in the maxim by which it is determined. Its moral value, ... depends on the principle of volition by which the action is done ... The third principle: ... Duty is the necessity of an action executed from the respect for law."

Respect is understood to be the consciousness of the submission of the will to a law. Maxim means the subjective principle of volition whereas the practical law is the objective principle that would serve all rational beings also subjectively if reason had full power over the faculty of desire.

B.   Moral Law or Categorical Imperative

Kant next derives the concept of moral law from consideration of pure reason and will. Everything in nature works according to laws. But only a rational being has the capacity of acting according to the conception of laws, i.e., according to principles. Kant equates this capacity with will. But since reason is required for derivation of actions from laws, will is nothing else but the practical reason that governs human behavior through a conception of law. In human beings, however, reason of itself does not sufficiently determine the will which is also subjugated to subjective conditions which do not always agree with objective ones. But the pure conception of duty and of moral law has the highest influence. Kant emphasizes that moral theory is put together from a mixture of incentives, feelings, inclinations and partially from rational concepts makes the mind vacillate between motives and leads only accidentally to good and often to bad.

The conception of an objective principle to which we refer in governing our actions is a command of reason and the formulation of it is an imperative, an expression containing an "ought." If the action is good as a means to something else, the imperative is hypothetical, thus it is conditional upon circumstances and advisable only. Such a goal cannot be universally held by all men at all times. Further the hypothetical imperatives can be divided into technical (imperative of skill) belonging to art and into pragmatic (imperative of prudence), belonging to welfare of the being.

The moral imperative is unconditional, i.e., it is categorical. It is our moral consciousness that we ought to do our duty regardless of our inclinations and cannot be derived from psychological study. This principle is formulated by pure reason from the concept of "ought." Thus the idea of obligation itself must dictate a criterion for deciding what our obligations are. A moral imperative commands unconditional conformity of our subjective maxim to a law, while the law contains no reference to specific ends on which it depends. The maxim should contain no condition which would prevent it from being itself a law and universally imperative, i.e., valid for all men as rational beings regardless of their specific desires. Thus Kant postulates the principle of universality; the principle of the will that determines its conformity to the law is that one should never act in a way that one could not also will that this maxim should be a universal law. This principle of universality in the imperative form is the categorical imperative:

"Act only according to the maxim by which you can at the same time will that it should become a universal law."

C. The principle of humanity.

Since every rational being exists as an end in himself and not merely as a means to be arbitrarily used by this or that will, a supreme practical principle can be derived that the moral agent should act as if he were a lawgiving member of a realm of ends, i.e., of persons each of whom is an end in himself and an end for all others. Thus Kant formulates the principle of humanity: "Act so that you treat humanity, whether in your own person or in that or another, always as an end and never as a means only."

Moreover, we should act in harmony with the idea of the will of every rational being as making universal laws, therefore should endeavor to further the ends of others: "For the ends of any person, who is an end in himself, must as far as possible also be my end, if that conception for an end in itself is to have its full effect on me." This principle of humanity is the supreme limiting condition on freedom of the action of each man. Thus the principles of universality and of humanity constitute the grounds for all practical judgment.

D. Autonomy of the will, the dignity of man and harmony.

From the moral law Kant derives a conception of the autonomy of the will, the dignity of man and harmony. The will is not only subject to the law but also the lawgiver. The moral law can obligate unconditionally only if it is a law given by man as sovereign in the realm of ends to himself as a subject in this realm. Man thus has a dignity of a lawgiver—the laws he obeys are the laws he gives himself. The being that gives the laws to himself is not merely bound to the law but is freely bound by his own lawgiving activity. This is why Kant calls moral law autonomous (from the Greek word for law *nomos*). The necessity of acting according to that principle is a duty which pertains to each member in the realm of ends (a systematic union of different rational beings through common laws). This duty rests on the relation of rational beings to one another and reason therefore relates every maxim of the will as giving laws to every other will and also to every action toward itself. The imperative form of this principle of autonomy is: "Act by a maxim which involves its own universal validity for every rational being." A being that takes the law from another lawgiver— God, a tyrant, his own cupidity—must be led to obedience by fear or hope. He is not then free but heteronomous. He is not truly moral because all his maxims are hypothetical and he cannot act out of respect for a universal law which takes no account of the contingent and divisive interests of individuals.

The three formulations of the imperative represent three aspects of one moral law that brings the action to intuition as much as possible. The will is unconditionally good which follows this maxim of the moral law. But a rational being cannot expect that every rational being be true to it; so Kant reformulates the law into still another, practical version: "Act according to the maxim of a universally legislative member of an only potential realm of ends." But still it commands categorically and Kant emphasizes that it suffices that the dignity of humanity as rational nature and respect for the idea should serve as the inflexible precept of the will. Moreover, the worthiness of every rational subject to be a legislative member consists in independence of the maxims from such incentives. Hence morality is the relation of actions of possible universal lawgiving by maxims of the will. Action compatible with the authority of the will is permitted. The will whose maxims necessarily are in harmony with the laws of autonomy is an absolutely good will. The dependence of a will not absolutely good on the principle of autonomy is obligation. And the objective necessity of an action from obligation Kant calls duty.

In the concept of duty we usually think of subjection, yet there is dignity in it so far as the person who fulfills his/her duties is a legislator of the law and subject to it for that reason. Also no fear or inclination to the law may give a moral sanction in the strict sense of the word to action. Thus autonomy of the will is the supreme condition of morality: "Never choose except in such a way that the maxims of the choice are comprehended in the same volition as a universal law." If the will seeks the determination of the law outside itself in the property of any of its objects, heteronomy results and becomes the source of the spurious principles of morality based on hypothetical imperatives in the terminology of Kant (see the list below). An example will illustrate this. According to the rule of heteronomy and hypothetical imperative—"I should not lie if I wish to keep my reputation. According to the rule of autonomy and categorical imperative—"I should not lie even though it would not cause me the least injury."

But Kant, being a realistic man, admits that among all spurious principles he would admit as most tolerable the principle derived from the concept of moral sense because it preserves the idea of a will good in itself. He defines this moral sense as "The subjective effect which the law [his moral law of categorical imperative] has upon the will to which reason alone gives objective grounds.

Table 1

Kant's List of Conditional (or Spurious) Principles of Morality from the Principle of Heteronomy

===

Empirical	Rational
a. from principle of happiness physical or moral; the moral feeling.	from principle of perfection
b. as concept of moral sense the moral feeling.	a. ontological concept of perfection as a possible result;
	b. theological concept of independent perfection (the will of God).

===

E.   Possibility of the Categorical Imperative

So far Kant dealt with the question: "What is morality, such that we could say that an action with such and such characteristics would be moral?" Now Kant has to deal with another question: "Can such a question actually take place?" Answers to both questions cannot be given by citing examples, they have to be answered by reason. The key to the answer to the second question lies in the freedom of the will—otherwise morality is impossible, because something else would determine it and the categorical imperative would become hypothetical imperative. Thus freedom cannot be a law of nature, rather an autonomy of the will that is the property of the will to be law to itself. For reason must regard itself as the author of its principles and thus practical reason or the will of a rational being must regard itself free, independent of foreign influences. Kant, following in principle Aristotle's reasoning, explains this freedom through his theory of knowledge that there is something else in man behind the appearance of man, namely the ego or consciousness in itself or the pure activity of reason which is free from causal determination in the world of appearance i.e., things which we perceive. Thus man can be apart from nature and free from its laws, when reason exclusively determines his action, but also is a part of the world of sense under the laws of nature and as such not free. Freedom is expressed by the categorical imperative and the hypothetical imperative expresses inclinations in the world of sense. Kant summarizes this by saying: "As a rational being and thus as belonging to the intelligible world, man cannot think of the causality of his own will except under the idea of freedom, for independence from the determining causes of the world of sense (an independence which reason must always ascribe to itself) is freedom. The concept of autonomy is inseparably connected with the idea of freedom, and with the former there is inseparably bound the universal principle of morality, which ideally is the ground of all actions of rational beings, just as natural law is the ground of all appearances."

Categorical imperatives are possible because the idea of freedom makes man a member of the intelligible world. If one were a member only of this world, all actions would be always in accordance with the autonomy of the will. But since man is at the same time a member of the world of sense, his actions ought to conform to the autonomy

251

of the will as belonging to the intelligible world, which according to reason should dominate the sensuously affected will. Anyone who is accustomed to using his reason is conscious of the good will which constitutes the law for his bad will as a member of the world of sense and acknowledges the authority of this law even while transgressing it. The moral "ought" is one's own volition as a member of the intelligible world. It is conceived as an "ought" only in so far as one regards himself at the same time as a member of the world of sense.

Kant next asserts, however, that philosophy has no knowledge of this supersensible world, it only can indicate its possibility and thus defends foundations of morality.

To summarize briefly Kant's foundations of morals:

Kant believed that ethics not only can but has to be validated without appeal to God's will or God's orders. Otherwise it would not be moral law in the proper sense, that is, ethics would not be autonomous and thus would not be ethics properly so called. He believed that moral law was to be validated not only independently of utility, pleasure, happiness, natural desires, or positive law, but independently of God's will as well. This is a specification of Kant's general concept of moral actions: if we were acting in conformity with moral law not because it is moral law but because God wants us to do so, or because we risk divine retribution in the afterlife, we would not act morally in the strict sense. This principle of autonomy is so conceived that it excludes from moral motivations in the strict sense not only the fear of hell and purgatory, but even the pure readiness to subordinate one's will to God's orders; the motive for doing God's will is not a moral motive. Kant states that only the good will is good in a moral sense of the word, the strict sense. More, he says, there is only one motive which is morally good and this is the will to act according to duty as expressed in a general principle. Thus an act is morally praiseworthy if it is done out of a sense of duty as such, and not, for instance, from mere inclination or compassion. If what is my duty happens to coincide with what I will spontaneously, my act is morally empty (in the strict sense); a duty should be performed merely because it is duty and not for any other reason. Kant also realized that people being what they are may act from various motives. Thus the rational act performed out of a sense of moral duty is the supreme ideal of moral acts.

Kantian morality has a supreme normative principle, the Categorical Imperative, recommending us to act in such a way that we would wish the particular rule governing a given action to become a universal law. This principle has a formal character and it states the condition on which any particular moral rule may claim to be valid.

Kantian ethics enjoins us to treat each person as a goal, never as a means. It is not a monistic system: it has, to be sure, a supreme normative principle, categorical imperative, yet this principle does not contain any supreme material value; it has an admittedly formal character and it merely states the condition on which any particular moral rule claims to be valid.

Monism and Troubles with Ethical Systems

From the above considerations we may conclude that in an actual situation of the human condition any attempt to base morals on only one intrinsic value and to subordinate all others as means must lead to failure. It is tempting to build ethics on a single value whether it is "God's glory," "happiness" or "freedom." It seems that such ethics would eliminate all moral conflicts and ambiguities. However, it is not realistic and practical, since it does not reflect the basic psychological and social facts of human life, therefore it must lead to failure.

The rules of morality must be conditional and unescapably are ambiguous, and in each case of conflict we are led by a vague intuition rather than by a precise reckoning to a decision. In most cases we arrive at the decision almost mechanically, in other cases we are faced with a decision for which we have no precise rules and no reliable knowledge about the possible results of action. Then we are only too happy if someone else, a person or an institution, either makes the decision for us or convinces us that there is an absolute rule to take a decision for us. This makes of us moral automata, but such a behavior constitutes the psychological basis for survival of religious worldviews and religious institutions.

The postulate of ambiguity of morals does not mean that no rules can be safely recognized in absolute form. Some principles are valid unconditionally and some actions are morally wrong in all circumstances. But such principles should be specific and should leave almost no doubt whether the situation described actually occurs. Leszek Kołakowski[2] proposes among such principles e.g., prohibition of torture, including encouraging, condoning or passing it over in silence, prohibition of rape, and condemnation of people abandoning or not assisting others in danger who are helpless and dependent on them.

Other problems arise for various models of ethics. The utilitarian model runs against our ingrained moral intuition and probably against the normal meaning of the adjective "moral." In the case when we claim that only intentions count in morals we encounter another difficulty in that in many instances we can guess people's intentions, though very often we cannot. Moreover, people are not always aware themselves of their own intentions. Ethics, being a practical knowledge, is subject to objection if it does not have a method to test its distinctions. Moreover, its norms are instruments whereby people impose on each other ways of behaving that run against their spontaneous inclinations, thus the more so it must have a method to test them. There is a room here, especially in theistically motivated morality, for self-justification by skillful casuistry. This is a contrivance easy to learn and apply, and Jesuits were famed for its practice.[4] A Christian moralist might say that in God's all seeing eyes no motive or intention can be hidden, but this defers the judgment and leaves a large area of temporal life exempt from moral evaluation.

Similarly the rigorous insistence on good intention or will (either commanded by a Practical Reason or God-given) produces difficulty in assessing the difference between actions which intentionally produce reasonably good results yet were inspired by selfish or suspected motives, on one hand, and actions that are undoubtedly vicious and evil on the other. For example, it is better not to steal because one believes that stealing is intrinsically bad than not steal out of fear. Thus we might make a distinction between a minimum and a maximum requirement for morality and introduce a gradation in its evaluation. This confusion derives from the assessment that moral rules are about subjective attitudes and conduct which may have various degrees of perfection. We acquire them in a variety of ways e.g., children imitate grown-up people not because they apprehend the intrinsic virtues of these rules or we may develop good habits as a result of snobbery, yet subsequently they become our natural way of conduct. Thus it seems that in an ideal situation the moral education process should develop motivations, that is, convictions about what is right or wrong and should not be based on external sanctions legal or divine.

Practice thus indicates that we have to differentiate between what is perfect and what is reasonably good, what is more evil and what is less evil. Moreover, it has to be assured that there are few people who achieve the highest degree of moral excellence. Kołakowski[2] makes a mistake here assuming that, e.g., chastity, or the ideal of poverty practiced by Francis of Assisi, may be considered as such criteria of moral perfection. They are obviously anomalies, and by themselves have nothing to do with moral perfection. But when practiced with moderation they may be elements of character building, and therefore derivative goods. Most people, however, may be decent persons without being perfect. Yet he admits there are minimal rules which may safely be enumerated:

1. that no particular political ideology can ever be deduced from moral principles;

2. that moral rules by definition are universal. Those that we consider valid in private life are also valid in public life, because there is no clear boundary between them. The most modest requirement would be to be aware that when we violate moral norms we do in fact violate them.

3. that no moral precepts follow from historical knowledge or from a philosophical history. It means that if in the past the moral norms were violated though admirable actions were performed this does not invalidate the norms.

Need for Global Ethics

A. Do we need a new ethics ?

The suggestion is frequently voiced that since the moral corpus inherited from the Christian legacy cannot cope with the needs of modern society we now have to elaborate new codes better adapted to contemporary problems. Kołakowski[2] aptly dismisses the idea by presenting convenient examples demonstrating no reason for change—indeed his examples do not validate the need. Indeed moral codes should not conform to actually prevailing customs since ethics has always been about how people ought to behave irrespective of how they behave in fact. Moreover, availability of new techniques does not make, e.g., the problem of war more or less soluble by, e.g., making it easier to justify. He ignores, however, certain new discoveries that explain on a biological basis, independent of human decisions, that what was once assumed to be morally evil, e.g. homosexuality. But he contradicts himself saying that "the body of Christian ethics is not construed in such a way that it can settle all our particular moral conflicts" -- historically it pretended just to do so.

B. Ethical revolution, process of democratization and globalization

There is also another need for a new ethics connected with global processes. Each religion or culture tended to be very certain that it alone had the complete explanation of the ultimate meaning of life, and how to live accordingly. In non-democratic societies it was easy to impose dominion of ideologies through political control of life. But from the XVIIth century a process of democratization of societies was set in motion accompanied by revolutions in understanding the limitedness of all statements about the meaning of things. So now different religions, cultures and ideologies are drawn into dialogue with each other. As the globe becomes more and more a small village there is an additional need for a new unifying tendency toward universally accepted rational premises. A first step in this direction would be the formulation of a universal declaration of global ethics. It seems that declaration of global ethics in every detail is impossible—but what is possible is the consensus on fundamental attitudes toward good and evil in terms of basic and middle principles. This consensus must be arrived at through a dialogue.

Leonard Swidler[5] even proposes a plan of action in drafting this universal declaration of global ethics which would serve as a minimal ethical standard for humankind to live up to much as the United Nations' 1948 Declaration of Human Rights. It would serve as a complementary document. The guidelines for drafting such a Declaration should include:

1. The language should be acceptable to major religious and ethical groups, and therefore it ought to be anthropo-cosmo-centric.

2. The affirmation must be susceptible to being reinterpreted in a larger framework.

3. The declaration should set an inviolable minimum and open-ended maximum.

4. The declaration should be focused first on the self and then expanded to the family, friends, community, nations, world and cosmos.

5. Human beings should be always treated as ends not mere means i.e., as subjects, never as objects.

6. The declaration should be a kind of constitutional set of basic and middle ethical principles from which more detailed applications could be drawn.

7. The starting point and the practical basis for evaluation of moral statement could be the anthropic universal principle known as the Golden Rule.[6] It was popularized in the western world in the Judean culture ("Do to no one what you would not want done to you," Leviticus 19:18; Tobit 4:16) but is found empirically in all cultures and religions of the world: from Zoroastrianism through Confucianism, Buddhism, Judaism, New Testamental Christianity and Islam, to modern religious and secular ethical systems. Its rational basis was discovered by Kant as the universal moral law. Though Kant did not recognize this rule as a universal law in the strict sense, he most certainly would agree on its practical value. The golden rule has advantages over the Kantian imperative: It is accepted in all cultures and religions, is practical and easy to understand. Moreover, it was the underlying fundamental principle for morals in the theistic ideologies before they became corrupted by the secondary doctrines.

Universal Declaration of Global Ethics

The Universal Declaration, though proposed for the first time by a Roman Catholic, was promulgated in the ecumenical spirit to unite religious and non-religious positions, thus it is fundamentally a humanist endeavor. The following text is based on the Declaration published by Swidler.[5]

Preamble

All women and men from various ethical and religious traditions recognize common convictions: support of universal human rights— freedom and equality before the law—a call to work for justice and peace, support of democracy and concern for conservation of the earth.

The conditions of the global order demand that the mankind should look beyond the divisions of particular groups and build a global ethic based on the universally recognized norms and principles. Therefore the Universal Declaration of a Global Ethics is proposed as a document standing in conjunction with the 1948 Declaration of Human Rights of the United nations. This document takes for granted several fundamental presumptions:

1. Every human possesses an inalienable and inviolable dignity.

2. No person or social institution exists beyond the scope of moral order.

3. Humans as beings endowed with reason and conscience should act rationally.

4. Humans are an inextricable part of the universe and as such should act in harmony with nature.

Basic Rule

The basic rational principle of morals is the axiom of moral law formulated in the principles: of universality, of humanity and of the autonomy of the human will.

This principle, as the supreme criterion of moral acts, was recognized, accepted, and empirically formulated in all cultures, religious and secular ethical traditions as a practical precept of the Golden Rule

What you do not wish done to yourself, do not do to others

Basic Principles

1. Every person is free to experience and develop every capacity as long as it does not infringe on the rights of others or does not disrupt the harmony with the rest of the universe.

2. All humans should treat each others as ends, never as means, respecting their intrinsic dignity. This respect should be extended to the community, nation, world and cosmos—to all living creatures and non-living parts of the universe according to their intrinsic values.

3. All humans should be granted a right to hold their own beliefs and strive to achieve explanations for meaningful life. A rational dialogue is the only method of arriving at a consensus whereby people can live together.

Middle Principles

1. Legal Responsibilities

All individuals and communities should be treated equally before the law. They should follow all just laws arrived at through a democratic process and consensus.

2. Responsibilities Concerning Conscience

All individuals and communities should have the right to freedom of thought, inquiry, conscience and a belief. At the same the exercise of these freedoms should respect the rights of others.

3. Responsibilities Concerning Speech and Information

Individuals and communities should be granted the right to free expression and information. At the same time this right should be exercised with a sense of responsibility avoiding distortions, falsifications or manipulations of others.

4. Responsibilities Concerning Participation in the Political Process and Self-Governance

All individuals and communities should have a right to free participation in all aspects of the political process and self-governance. They should at the same time exercise their right responsibly for the benefit of all involved.

5. Responsibilities Concerning the Relations between Women and Men

All humans, women and men, should have equal civil rights and the opportunity to develop fully their talents. Marriage, as an institution, should be a partnership of equal individuals with mutual respect of each other's dignity, equality and freedom.

6. Responsibilities Concerning Property

All individuals and communities should have the right to own property of various kinds. At the same time society should be organized in such a way that the property would be used to benefit not only the owners, but also their fellow humans and the world at large.

7. Responsibilities Concerning Work and Leisure

All individuals and communities should strive to organize society as to provide meaningful work and recreative leisure for authentic human life. At the same time it is the responsibility of the individuals to work appropriately with their obligations and duties.

8. Responsibilities Concerning Children and Education

All individuals and communities have an obligation to strive to provide the most humane care possible, physical, mental and social to children. They should strive to provide education directed to full development of the human person.

9. Responsibilities Concerning Peace

All individuals and communities should respect the need for justice and peace, and should strive to further their growth.

10. Responsibilities Concerning the Preservation of the Environment
All individuals and communities should respect the ecosphere within which they live, preventing its destruction and replacing materials that were used.

Bibliography

1. Andrew G. Oldenquist. *Moral Philosophy. Text and Readings. (Prospect Heights, Illinois:* Waveland Press, Inc., 1978).

2. Leszek Kołakowski, "Ethics," in *Dialogue and Humanism, The Universalist Journal,* Vol. IV, No. 4, 1994, pp. 5-44

3. Immanuel Kant, *Foundations of the Metaphysics of Morals and What is Enlightenment.* Translated, with Introduction, by Lewis White Beck. (New York, London: Macmillan ublishing Company, Collier Macmillan publishers, 1988).

4. Blaise Pascal, *Provinciales, in Oeuvres complètes.* Préface d'Henri Gouhier de L'Institut. Présentation et notes de Louis Lafuma. (Paris: Aux Éditions du Seuil, 1963).

5. Leonard Swidler, "Toward a Universal Declaration of a Global Ethic," in *Dialogue and Humanism, The Universalist Journal,* Vol. IV, No. 4, 1994, pp. 51-64.

6. Marian Hillar. "Justification of Morals in the Philosophy of Thomas Aquinas," in *Ethics and Humanism. Anthology of Essays,* (Houston: Humanists of Houston, 1992).

REINTERPRETATION OF KANT'S UNIVERSAL MORAL PHILOSOPHY. A QUINTESSENTIAL HUMANISTIC DOCTRINE[443]

Kant's Life and Work

Immanuel Kant,[444] is considered the founder of modern philosophy, was born in Königsberg, East Prussia, (which today is Kaliningrad in Russia) on April 22, 1724. He came from a Protestant family of Pietists. Kant attended the University of Königsberg and became an instructor at the university. For fifteen years he lectured and wrote on various topics in metaphysics, logic, natural sciences: physics, astronomy, geology, meteorology.

In 1770 he became a university professor of logic and metaphysics. In 1781 he published his important work, Critique *of Pure Reason,* which was a starting point for a new field of studies and extensive writing. Second edition which contains many revisions was published in 1787. His reaction to critique to his first edition is found in *Prolegomena to Any Future Metaphysics* (1783). Both these works represent his transcendental idealism (also termed "formal" or "critical"). This doctrine maintains that our theoretical knowledge is limited to systematization of spatiotemporal appearance. Subsequently Kant published almost every year a new book: *Idea of a Universal History* (1784), *Foundations of the Metaphysics of Morals* (1785), *Metaphysical Foundations of Natural Science* (1786), *Critique of Practical Reason* (1788), *Critique of the Faculty of Judgment* (1790), *Religion within the Limits of Reason Alone* (1793), *Perpetual Peace* (1795), *Metaphysics of Ethics* (1797), *Anthropology from a Pragmatic Point of View* (1798), *The Conflict of the Faculties* (1798).

Kant differentiated between pure reasons and practical reason. Pure reason or pure theoretical reason does not depend on any

---

443 Published in *Essays in the Philosophy of Humanism,* Vol. 17 (1), 2009, pp. 71-90. An earlier version of it was published in *Essays in the Philosophy of Humanism,* Vol. 8, pp. 63-73, 2000.

444 General description of Kant's philosophy is summarized in Robert Audi, general editor, The Cambridge Dictionary of Philosophy, (Cambridge, UK: Cambridge University Press, 1995), 398-403.

experience thus it can make determination of the realm of nature *a priori*. Pure practical reason (or *Wille* = will) determines the rules for the faculty of desire and will independently of sensibility. It deals with the realm of freedom and of what ought to be. It is opposed to the faculty of cognition and of feeling and it deals with laws which have unconditional character (in one aspect of his theory) and apply to a being with absolute freedom, that is, the faculty to choose (*Willkür*) to will or not to will to act. Thus Kant argued that human freedom does not derive from the empirical knowledge of ourselves as part of the spatiotemporal nature. But Kant also argued that there is this empirical and spatiotemporal realm but it does not exhaust the reality. Its principles Kant terms as "metaphysics of experience" and they do not define the ultimate reality hence the term used for his philosophy – "transcendental idealism."

What he meant by this can be exemplified by his treatment of mathematics. Mathematical principles are transcendental, *a priori*, that is the philosophical argument that these principles apply in experience. The mathematical proof of these principles is not in itself transcendental. In other knowledge we may start with proposition that there is experience and then discover *a priori* principles necessary for that specific knowledge. The metaphysical *a priori* judgments Kant labels as "synthetic." He claimed, we know that the proposition is necessary and objective. And Kant emphasizes that synthetic judgments rely on intuition (*Anschauung*) and this is not part of their definition. Intuition is a technical term for Kant and is defined as a representation that has an immediate relation to its object. Intuitions can be sensible (sensuous) or passive, but can be also "intellectual" and can have a singular or general object.

The other type of propositions Kant labeled as analytic which are defined as the ones whose predicate is "contained in the subject" that is what is contained in the concepts of the subject term and the predicate term. And they are known through concepts alone. Concepts are representations of representations referring to what is common to a set of representations. But we do not have ready definitions for *a priori* or empirical concepts. He seems to rely on an intuitive process connecting subject with the predicate.

In analysis of the outer world Kant came to the conclusion that we do not perceive the objects as "things-in-themselves" (*Dinge an sich*) (*noumena*) apart from our intrinsic cognitive relation to our representations (that is as unknown and beyond our experience or knowable in some non-sensible way). Rather we find in objects through our faculties of representation something that determines how objects must be, at least as objects of experience or *phenomena*. In our faculty of sensibility receiving impressions we find not only contingent contents but also two pure "forms of intuition": space which structures all outer representations, and time, which structures all inner representations. And this explains why synthetic *a priori* propositions of mathematics apply with certainty to all objects of our experience which necessarily conform to our representations. Thus mathematics and metaphysics of our notions of space and time can reveal an evident proposition that there is one infinite space.

Kant's doctrine is not an empirical one, but a metaphysical thesis which enriches empirical explanations with an *a priori* postulate. But this postulate itself is explained as being "constitution of human sensibility."

Sensible representations, impressions, structured by these two forms of space and time have to be grasped in concepts in order to yield knowledge and then intuitions and concepts are combined in judgment. Otherwise "thoughts without content are empty, intuitions without concepts are blind." Any judgment involves a unity of thought comprising all representations that can be judged by us as subject to a unity of thought which is termed by Kant as *apperception*. Kant contrasts it with the mere temporal representations in our mind.

This need for concepts and judgments suggests that our constitution may require not only the intuitive forms, but also conceptual forms i.e., "categories" or "pure concepts of understanding." The evidence for this comes from the transcendental deduction of the categories or the objective validity of the "pure concepts of understanding." They are structures of our sensibility and we cannot imagine anything given to us without them. Nevertheless, Kant admits that the representations once given need not to be combined in terms of such pure concepts. He proposed that a list of putative categories could be produced from a list of necessary forms of the logical table of judgments. This table is a collection of all possible judgment forms organized under four headings: 1. quantity (universal, particular, singular); 2. quality (affirmative, negative, infinite); 3. relation (categorical, hypothetical, disjunctive); 4. modality (problematic, assertoric, apodictic). Kant develops next an intricate network of "metaphysical deductions" of the categories and matching with the form of judgment.

Kant's life was highly organized and regular to the extent that, according to the anecdote, housewives could adjust their clocks by the regular afternoon walk which was his daily routine.

Kant had broad philosophical and scientific interests. He examined Leibnitz, Wolff, Baumgarten, Crusius, Hume, Rousseau; he was keenly interested in the progress of science and studied the works of Newton and Kepler. His personality and intellectual attitude were characterized by Johann Gottfried Herder, his disciple in these words: "He was indifferent to nothing worth knowing. No cabal, no sect, no prejudice, no desire for fame could ever tempt him in the slightest way from broadening and illuminating the truth. He incited and gently forced others to think for themselves; despotism was foreign to his mind. This man, whom I name with the greatest gratitude and respect, was Immanuel Kant."[445] Kant died in Königsberg, February 12, 1804.

Introduction

Kant's writings on ethics (*Foundations of the Metaphysics of Morals* (1785), *Critique of Practical Reason* (1788), *Metaphysics of Ethics* (1797)) are the most important since antiquity. Kant argues, following the ancient Stoics, that our moral obligations in the final analysis derive from reason by recognition of the natural moral law, and not from either god, or communities, nor from inclinations or desires. But being a practical realist, Kant differentiates several levels of motivation and of the operation of the behavioral rules preserving human autonomy and free choice in our moral decisions. Thus his theory, just as its sources (Aristotle's psychology and the Stoic doctrine), is deeply humanistic. He considered himself a philosopher of the Enlightenment and believed that one should submit everything to the test of criticism and that our reason is the source of its own principles.

---

445   Quoted by Lewis White Beck in his translation of Kant's *Critique of Practical Reason*. Immanuel Kant, *Critique of Practical Reason*, edited and translated with notes and introduction by Lewis White Beck, third edition, (New York: Macmillan Publishing Company, 1993), p. xxii.

There are many parallels in Kant's thought with the ideas developed by the ancient Stoics (Zeno of Citium, Cleanthes, Chrysippus, Cicero, and others) and Eastern thought developed in Indian culture and in China. His thought is thus an elaboration on the themes of the ancient philosophers.[446] Previously we have reviewed moral philosophy of the Stoic school in a series of six articles published in the *Houston Freethought Alliance Newsletter* (issues 101-106, 2008).[447] In this paper we shall present the moral philosophy of Kant as a culminating point in an effort of the human mind to grasp the issue of human behavior in society. What is important for this analysis is to keep in mind that the philosophical intuitions we find in various schools in the West and in the East can be reevaluated today in a more precise way due to the progress in the natural sciences, and especially from the evolutionary perspective. This does not mean that such perspective was absent in the previous search, especially in the ancient Greek or Indian thought. The naturalistic outlook represented in the ancient schools and philosophical intuitions today is confirmed by studies of our biological nature. Yet we humans are not automata which follow the prescribed pattern of input/output operating in the mechanical, even highly adaptive systems defined by science. With the rise of sentient and rational life appeared a new quality in nature, namely, freedom.[448] Still this freedom should be controlled by reason though we are not always motivated by moral law. Modern science provides today some insight into the mechanisms operating in human behavior at several levels which we will discuss at another occasion.[449]

---

446   The ancient moral philosophy of the Stoics is till valid. It acquired in Kant's elaboration reviewed moral philosophy of the Stoic school in a series of six articles published in the *Houston Freethought Alliance Newsletter* (issues 101-106, 2008).[447] In this paper we shall present the moral philosophy of Kant as a culminating point in an effort of the human mind to grasp the issue of human behavior in society. What is important for this analysis is to keep in mind that the philosophical intuitions we find in various schools in the West and in the East can be reevaluated today in a more precise way due to the progress in the natural sciences, and especially from the evolutionary perspective. This does not mean that such perspective was absent in the previous search, especially in the ancient Greek or Indian thought. The naturalistic outlook represented in the ancient schools and philosophical intuitions today is confirmed by studies of our biological nature. Yet we humans are not automata which follow the prescribed pattern of input/output operating in the mechanical, even highly adaptive systems defined by science. With the rise of sentient and rational life appeared a new quality in nature, namely, freedom.[448] Still this freedom should be controlled by reason though we are not always motivated by moral law. Modern science provides today some insight into the mechanisms operating in human behavior at several levels which we will discuss at another occasion.[449]

447   Marian Hillar, The Stoic Ethics: Natural Development, Rationality, and Responsibility. In *Houston Freethought Alliance Newsletter*, issues 101-106, 2008.

448   Daniel C. Bennett, *Freedom Evolves*, (New York: Viking, 2003).

449   Some discussion of the issues of modern science and its relation to philosophical intuition we presented previously in Marian Hillar, *Moral Philosophy and Modern Science. Modern Science Provides a Biological Basis for Human Behavior and Validates Philosophical Speculation*, published in Houston Alliance Newsletter, issue 99, January 2008, pp. 5-6, and in a seminar presented to the Ideas Club, Humanists of Houston, March 23, 2008. Houston, *Philosophy and Modern Science*.

We will attempt to present Kant's moral philosophy and emphasize its various aspects which are usually ignored by philosophers.

The Condition of Morality

Kant begins his treatise, *Foundations of the Metaphysics of Morals* (1785),[450] with the classification of our rational knowledge (Table 1). In the Preface to his work Kant specified the task of a moral philosopher as clarifying the "principle of morality" on which the rational agent can act insofar as his action is morally good; to justify this principle, that is, to show that this principle is actually binding upon an imperfect agent such as a human being; to apply this principle to build an exposition of human obligations, i.e., duties. In this first work out of the three treatises devoted to moral philosophy[451] Kant dealt with the first task of the moral philosopher. He was not interested in constructing an ethical doctrine or writing a casuistry of morals, but searched for an axiom or principle which might be used for building a general theory of laws of freedom (in contrast to the laws of nature, concerned with physical nature), the science of which he called ethics or theory of morals. In the *Metaphysics of Morals* (1797) Kant defined more precisely what ethics is, namely, as the science of how one is under obligation without regard for any possible external lawgiving, that is, as doctrine of virtue.[452] Just as natural philosophy (physics) has its empirical part so does moral philosophy because it has to determine the human will as it is affected by nature. Kant calls this anthropology.

Thus the laws of moral philosophy are those according to which everything should happen, allowing for conditions under which what should happen often does not. Though the title contains the word metaphysics it is not about the understanding of ultimate reality, or the metaphysics of nature, but a rigorous search for an establishment of the supreme principle of a possible pure will which cannot be derived from observations of actual behavior of men but can be established by reason. For Kant defines metaphysics as "a system of *a priori* knowledge

---

450 Immanuel Kant, *Foundations of the Metaphysics of Morals and What is Enlightenment?* Translated, with Introduction, by Lewis White Beck. (New York: London: Macmillan Publishing Company, Collier Macmillan Publishers, 1988). Onora O'Neill, "Kantian Ethics." In *A Companion to Ethics.* Peter Singer, ed. (Oxford: Blackwell Publishers, 1997), pp. 175-185.

451 Those three treatises are : the *Foundations of the Metaphysics of Morals* (1785), *Critique of Practical Reason* (1788), and *Metaphysics of Morals* (1797).

452 Kant, *Metaphysics of Morals*, introduction, trnbaslation, and notes by Mary Gregor, (Cambridge; Cambridge University Press, 1991), XVII, 410.

from concepts alone ... a practical philosophy, which has not nature but freedom of choice for its object" and as such it requires metaphysics of morals which "every man also has it within himself, tough as a rule only in an obscure way."[453]

Table 1

CLASSIFICATION OF RATION
KNOWLEDGE

Material / Formal

Material → Logic (no empirical part)

Formal → With definite object

Logic → Deals with laws of nature

With definite object → Deals with laws of freedom

Deals with laws of nature → Physics (theory of nature)

Deals with laws of freedom → Ethics (theory of morals)

Empirical part

Physics (theory of nature) → Deals with laws of nature concerning objects

Ethics (theory of morals) → Deals with laws of morals concerning human
Practical anthropology

"Pure"part
(on *a priori* principles)
Metaphysics

Deals with laws of nature concerning objects → Laws of how everything happes
Methaphicas of Nature

Deals with laws of morals concerning human → Laws of how everything should happen
Metaphysics of Morals
(Theory of Morals)

---

453   Ibidem, II, 216.

Kant starts his considerations with an analysis of the conditions for attaining happiness – namely, of being worthy to be happy i.e., of having a good will that is striving for moral perfection. Our moral obligation in the Greek and Judaic traditions is to achieve this "purity of heart" or "kingdom of god," which means good will. "Nothing in the world – indeed nothing even beyond the world – can possibly be conceived which could be called good without qualification except a good will." This is a spontaneous feeling of respect for moral law and an innate sense of "ought." This postulate is an empirical one derived from the observation of universal human nature. The function of reason is the establishment of this "good will." Good will is good because of its willingness, that is, it is good in itself without regard to anything else. In saying this Kant describes nothing other than common moral consciousness and derives the principle for moral action. Charles Darwin observed that in the time of Kant the origin of this moral consciousness was questioned. Darwin was among the first who gave a naturalistic explanation for its origin. He stated in his *The Descent of Man* (1871)[454]:

I fully subscribe to the judgment of those writers who maintain that of all the differences between man and the lower animals, the moral sense or conscience is by far the most important. This sense as Mackintosh[455] remarks, 'has a rightful supremacy over every other principle of human action;' it is summed up in that short but imperious word *ought*, leading him without a moment's of hesitation to risk his life for that of a fellow-creature; or after due deliberation, impelled simply by the deep feeling of right or duty, to sacrifice it in some great cause. Immanuel Kant exclaims, 'Duty! Wondrous thought, that workest neither by fond insinuation, flattery, nor by any threat, but merely by holding up thy naked law in the soul, and so extorting for thyself always reverence, if not always obedience; before whom all appetites are dumb, however secretly they rebel; whence thy original?'[456]

454 Charles Darwin, *The Descent of Man*, in *The Origin of Species and The Descent of Man*, (New York: The Modern Library, no date). Chapter 4, pp. 471-472.

455 Mackintosh, *Dissertation on Ethical Philosophy*, 1837, p. 231.

456 Immanuel Kant, *Metaphysics of Ethics*, translated by J .W. Semple, (Edinburgh, 1836), p. 136. This quote comes from Kant's work Critique of Practical Reason (1788). The full quote is: "Duty! Thou sublime and mighty name

This great question has been discussed by many writers of consummate ability; and my sole excuse for touching on it, is the impossibility of here passing it over; and because, as far as I know, no one has approached it exclusively from the side of natural history. The investigation possesses, also some independent interest, as an attempt to see how far the study of the lower animals throws light on one of the highest physical faculties of man.

The following proposition seems to me in a high degree probable – namely, that any animal whatever, endowed with well-marked social instincts, the parental and filial affection being here included, would inevitably acquire a moral sense or conscience, as soon as its intellectual powers have become as well, or nearly as well developed as in man.

We can now add to Kant's postulate that, precisely, modern science confirms Kant's intuition and provides a biological, naturalistic, evolutionary explanation for the existence of this moral consciousness.

Kant insists that in deciding what we ought to do our variable desires are not important – for an action to be truly moral it has to be done in the belief and because of the belief that it is right, i.e., out of respect for moral law. For the true moral value of our action it is not sufficient that it arises from some good inclination, disposition or temperament even according to duty – it has to arise from a sense of duty, or good will. Whether the action succeeds in its purpose or not, if it is done with a good will, it is morally acceptable. The consequences which we consider in passing moral judgment are those intended consequences, implicated in the motive of the action.

It is important to indicate at this point that Kant and all philosophers until the post-Darwinian times considered as truly (strictly) moral the actions produced by conscious rational and reflective analysis. This view arose from Origen's account of the Stoic

that dost embrace nothing charming or insinuating but requirest submission and yet seekest not to move the will by threatening aught that would arouse natural aversion or terror, but only holdest forth a law which of itself finds entrance into the mind and yet gains reluctant reverence (though not always obedience) – a law before which all inclinations are mute even though secretly work against it: what origin is worthy of thee, and where is the root of thy noble descent which proudly rejects all kinship with the inclinations and from which to be descended is the indispensable condition of the only worth which men alone can give themselves?" Immanuel Kant, Critique of Practical Reason, edited and translated with notes and introduction by Lewis White Beck, third edition, (New York: Macmillan Publishing Company, 1993), p. 90.

analysis of the motion of objects and action of animals and humans.[457] Origen reported that the Stoics differentiated human beings from all other natural things by a particular kind of movement (action) unique to them. What distinguished those things from others that are moved from without is that they have a certain kind of cause (*aitía*) of motion in themselves. Things like plants and animals have an internal cause of motion, "nature" (*logos* for Stoics) and "soul" (in Origen's view); inanimate objects must have an external agency to be moved along; they move by thrust of external force. Plants and animals by virtue of having "soul" (and "nature") are capable of self-movement or action. In the case of animals, sensory stimulation is a necessary condition of the impulse to self-movement. Those lacking intelligence move and act according to a prescribed pattern. Human beings do not move or act in a set fashion—because the faculty of reason (*logos*) enables them to judge (*krinō*) their sensory presentations—to reject or accept and to be guided. Origen calls this third kind of movement (action) self-movement of which only rational animals are capable, motion (action) "through themselves."[458] We are deserving of praise when we choose the noble and avoid the base, but when we follow the opposite course we are blameworthy. Origen reasons: It is neither true nor reasonable to lay the blame on external things and release ourselves from the accusation making ourselves analogous to wood and stones inasmuch as they are drawn along by external things that move them; such is the argument of someone who wants to set up a counterfeit notion of autonomy. For if we should ask him what autonomy is, he would say that it obtains "if there are no external causes, when I intend to do something in particular, that incite to the contrary."[459]

The Stoics believed that human beings are capable of self-movement without actually initiating their own motion. The beginning of motion of external objects, and self-movement, consists of the response of a sentient creature to those external causes. Moreover, it is clear that the faculty of reason, which informs assent to sensory presentation, makes the self-movement of human beings different in kind from that

---

457 Origen (185-ca 254) succeeded Clement of Alexandra in the school of Alexandria. Clement was the patriarch of Alexandria who at first supported Origen but expelled him later for being ordained without the patriarch's permission. Origen then moved to Palestine and died there. He wrote commentaries on all the books of the bible. In a treatise, *First Principles* (*Peri Archon*), he formulated one of the first philosophical expositions of Christian doctrine in which he interpreted scripture allegorically. He was a Neo-Pythagorean and Neo-Platonist, and like Plotinus believed that the soul passes through stages of incarnation before reaching god. For him even demons would be reunited with god. He considered god the First Principle, and Christ, the Logos, as subordinate to him. Origen's view was declared anathema in the sixth century.

458 *Stoicorum Veterum Fragmenta* Collegit Ioannes Ab Arnim (Stutgardiae: In Aedibus B.G. Teubneri, MCMLXIV). Vol 1-4. (abbreviated as SVF). SVF 2.989, 879. Origen, *De principiis*, (*On the First Principles*), translated with introduction and notes by G. W. Butterworth, (Gloucester, Mass.: Peter Smith, 1973). III, 1, 2, 3.

459 SVF 2,990.

of any other living being. Origen's account of the difference in motion (action) between humans and other animals gave rise to the concept of morality as a behavior conditioned by a rational, reflective act. Origen said: "our nature as human beings furnishes the souls for considering the noble and the base and for judging between them. Even though we have no control over the fact that something external causes in us a presentation of this or that sort— the decision (*krisis*) to use this occurrence in one way or another is the function of nothing other than the reason within us."[460]

Many actions, even if they produce good results, that are done in accordance with the law do not belong to the realm of moral actions in this strict sense if they are done with some ulterior motives. Thus truly morally good action will not only be in accord with the law but also because the law is acknowledged as absolutely and universally binding. Kant formulated thus the condition of morality in three propositions (Table 2) :

1. "... the first proposition of morality is that to have moral worth an action must be done from duty as obedience to the moral law.

2. The second proposition is: An action performed from duty does not have its moral worth in the purpose which is to be achieved through it but in the maxim by which it is determined. Its moral value, ... depends on the principle of volition by which the action is done ...

3. The third principle: ... Duty is the necessity of an action executed from the respect for law." Respect is understood to be the consciousness of the submission of the will to a law. Maxim means the subjective principle of volition whereas practical law is the objective principle that would serve all rational beings also subjectively if reason had full power over the faculty of desire.

Moral Law or Categorical Imperative

Kant next derives the concept of moral law from consideration by pure reason and will. Everything in nature works according to laws.

460 SVF 2.992.

But only a rational being has the capacity of acting according to the conception of laws, i.e., according to principles.

This conception of law derives from the Stoic philosophy as a natural capacity to act in accordance with "right reason" through the impulse to virtue. We find such formulation of the "natural law" in Cicero's *Republic*:

> True law is right reason in agreement with nature; it is of universal application, unchanging and everlasting; it summons to duty by its commands, and averts from wrongdoing by its prohibitions. And it does not lay its commands or prohibitions upon good men in vain, though neither has any effect on the wicked. It is a sin to try to alter this law, nor is it allowable to attempt to repeal any part of it, and it is impossible to abolish it entirely. We cannot be freed from its obligations by senate or people, and we need not look outside ourselves for an expounder or interpreter of it. And there will not be different laws at Rome and at Athens, or different laws now and in the future, but one eternal and unchangeable law will be valid for all nations and all times, and there will be one master an ruler, that is God, over us all, for he is the author of this law, its promulgator, and its enforcing judge. Whoever is disobedient is fleeing from himself and denying his human nature, and by reason of this very fact he will suffer the worst penalties, even if he escapes what is commonly considered punishment...[461]

---

461   Cicero, *The Republic*, in *De re publica. De legibus*, with an English translation by Clinton Walker Keyes, (Cambridge, MA; London: Harvard University Press, William Heinemann, Ltd, 1988). Bk III. XXII.

Table 2
THREE PROPOSITIONS OF MORALITY
(Condition of Morality)

---

1. Done from duty.
2. Moral value is in the maxim by which action is determined and not in the purpose;
    Depends on the principle of volition.
3. Duty is a necessity of an action from the respect of law i.e., consciousness of the submission of the will to a law.

MAXIM:

> Subjective principle of volition.
> Subjective principle of acting, must be
> distinguished from the objective principle, i.e., the practical law.

PRACTICAL LAW:

> Objective principle of volition serving all rational beings also subjectively if they were governed by reason.

We do not need to be alarmed by the use of the term "God" by Cicero. For the Stoics used this term for the totality of what existed – Nature. The concept and existence of God as divinity of nature was important in the Stoic philosophy. But again it is not the detached and transcendental God of the Hebrews, Plato or Aristotle. Chrysippus reasoned that if there is something capable of producing, which human reason is incapable of, it must be better than man, "And what name rather than God would you give to this?"[462]

Cicero in the *Laws* explains why this natural law is called law by differentiating understanding of it by the "populace" and by the "learned men;" and at the same time he explains the etymology of the term "law":

---

462 Chrysippus, in Cicero, *The Nature of the Gods (De natura deorum),*translated by Horace P. McGregor, (Harmondsworth, UK: Penguin Books, 1986), II, 16.

Well then, the most learned men have determined to begin with Law, and it would seem that they are right, if, according to their definition, Law is the highest reason, implanted by Nature, which commands what ought to be done and forbids the opposite. This reason, when firmly fixed and fully developed in the human mind, is Law. And so they believed that Law is intelligence, whose natural function it is to command right conduct and forbid wrongdoing. They think that this quality derived its name in Greek from the idea of granting to every man his own, and in our language I believe it has been named from the idea of choosing. For as they have attributed the idea of fairness to the word law, so we have given it that of selection, though both ideas properly belong to Law. Now, if this is correct as I think it to be in general, then the origin of Justice is to be found in Law, for law is a natural force; it is the mind and reason of the intelligent man, the standard by which Justice and Injustice are measured. But since our whole discussion has to do with the reasoning of the populace, it will sometimes be necessary to speak in the popular manner, and give the name of law to that which in written form decrees whatever it wishes, either by command or prohibition. For such is the crowd's definition of law. But in determining what Justice is, let us begin with that supreme Law which had its origin ages before any written law existed and or any State had been established.[463]

It is clear that Cicero defines natural law as "law" by analogy to the human positive law. And such is its popular understanding. However, in reality it is natural force, mind and reason inherent in human nature regardless of the underlying and accepted metaphysics, recognized by "the most learned men" which directs our behavior on an individual and social level. It is natural because it is proper for human nature: "that animal which we call man, endowed with foresight and quick intelligence, complex, keen, possessing memory, full of reason and prudence, has been given a certain distinguished status by the supreme God who created him; for he is the only one among so many different kinds and varieties of living beings who has a share in reason and

---

463   The Greek term for law is νόμος which Cicero derives from νέμω, to distribute, to grant, and the Latin term lex Cicero drives from lego, to choose. Quote from *The laws*, in *De re publica. De legibus, op. cit.,* Bk I.VI.18-19.

thought, while all the rest are deprived of it." And further: "But those who have reason in common must also have right reason in common. And since right reason is law, we must believe that men have Law also in common with gods. Further, those who share Law must also share Justice."[464]

Kant equates this capacity to act according to the conception of laws with will. But since reason is required for the derivation of actions from laws, will is nothing else but the practical reason that governs human behavior through a conception of law. In human beings, however, reason by itself does not sufficiently determine the will which is also subjugated to subjective conditions which do not always agree with objective ones. But the pure conception of duty and of moral law has the highest influence. Kant emphasizes that moral theory that is put together from a mixture of incentives, feelings, inclinations and partially from rational concepts makes the mind vacillate between motives and leads only accidentally to good and often to bad. The conception of an objective principle to which we refer in governing our actions is a command of reason and the formulation of it is an imperative, an expression containing an "ought" (Table 3).

If the action is good as a means to something else, the imperative is hypothetical, thus it is conditional upon circumstances and advisable only. Such a goal cannot be universally held by all men at all times. Further, the hypothetical imperatives can be divided into technical (imperative of skill), belonging to art and into pragmatic (imperative of prudence), belonging to welfare of the being.

The moral imperative (in the strict sense) is unconditional, i.e., it is categorical. It is our moral consciousness that we ought to do our duty regardless of our inclinations and cannot be derived from psychological study. Now the question arises: How is it possible, i.e., how is the constraint of will possible? This principle is formulated by pure reason from the concept of "ought." Thus the idea of obligation itself must dictate a criterion for deciding what our obligations are. A moral imperative commands unconditional conformity of our subjective maxim to a law, while the law contains no reference to specific ends on which it depends. With this are associated three principles of the will.

---

464   Cicero, *The Laws*, in *op. cit.*, Bk I.VII.22-23.

Three Principles of the Will

1. The principle of universality

The maxim should contain no condition which would prevent it from being itself a law and universally imperative, i.e., valid for all men as rational beings regardless of their specific desires. Thus Kant postulates the principle of universality; the principle of the will that determines its conformity to the law is that one should never act in a way that one could not also will that this maxim should be a universal law. This principle of universality in the imperative form is the categorical imperative: "Act only according to the maxim by which you can at the same time will that it should become a universal law." In terms of the law of nature the same principle is formulated: "Act as though the maxim of your action were by your will to become a universal law of nature."

2. The principle of humanity.

Since every rational being exists as an end unto himself and not merely as a means to be arbitrarily used by this or that will, a supreme practical principle

Table 3

PRINCIPLES OF VOLITION (ACTION) (IMPERATIVES)

A.	HYPOTHETICAL (Conditional)
	Principles of volition
	Rules of skill (as in science) Technical
	Pragmatic (for happiness as an end)
	Counsels of prudence
B.	CATEGORICAL (Unconditional)
	Laws; Commands of morality
	Unconditional
	Objective
	Universally valid
	Binding even against inclinations
	Belonging to free conduct
	Absolutely necessary

can be derived that the moral agent should act as if he were a lawgiving member of a realm of ends, i.e., of persons each of whom is an end unto himself and an end unto all others. Thus Kant formulates the principle of humanity: "Act so that you treat humanity, whether in your own person or in that of another, always as an end and never as a means only." This principle of humanity is the supreme limiting condition on freedom of action for each man.

3. The principle of harmony with universal practical reason.

Moreover, we should act in harmony with the idea of the will of every rational being as making universal laws, and therefore should endeavor to further the ends of others: "For the ends of any person, who is an end unto himself, must as far as possible also be my end, if that conception for an end in itself is to have its full effect on me" and hence the third principle of the will as the supreme condition of its harmony with universal practical reason can be formulated as: the idea of the will of every rational being as making universal law. Thus the principles of universality and of humanity constitute the grounds for all practical judgment.

Autonomy of the will, the dignity of man and harmony

From moral law Kant derives a conception of the autonomy of the will, the dignity of man and harmony. The will is not only subject to the law but also the lawgiver. Moral law can obligate unconditionally only if it is a law given by man as sovereign in the realm of ends unto himself as a subject in this realm. Man thus has the dignity of a lawgiver – the laws he obeys are the laws he gives himself. The being that gives the laws to himself is not merely bound to the law but is freely bound by his own lawgiving activity. This is why Kant calls moral law autonomous (from the Greek words self, *auto,* and law, *nomos*). The necessity of acting according to that principle is a duty which pertains to each member in the realm of ends (a systematic union of different rational beings through common laws in a society). This duty rests on the relation of rational beings to one another, and reason therefore relates every maxim of the will as giving laws to every other will and also to every action toward itself. The imperative form of this principle of autonomy is: "Act by a maxim which involves its own universal validity for every rational being."

A being that takes the law from another lawgiver – god, a tyrant, his own cupidity – must be led to obedience by fear or hope. He is not then free but heteronomous. His actions are not truly moral[465] (in the strict sense) because all his maxims are hypothetical and he cannot act out of respect for a universal law which takes no account of the contingent and divisive interests of individuals.

The three formulations of the imperative (from the principles of universality in two forms, humanity, and harmony) represent three aspects of one moral law that brings the action to intuition as much as possible. These formulations are summarized in Table 4. The will is unconditionally good which follows this maxim of moral law. But a rational being cannot expect that every rational being be true to it; so Kant reformulates the law into still another, practical version: "Act according to the maxim of a universally legislative member of an only potential realm of ends" (where "realm of end" refers to a society as a union of rational beings through the common laws). But it still commands categorically and Kant emphasizes that it suffices that the dignity of humanity as rational nature and respect for the idea should serve as the inflexible precept of the will. Moreover, the worthiness of every rational subject to be a legislative member consists of independence of the maxims from such incentives. Hence morality is the relation of actions of possible universal lawgiving by maxims of the will. Action compatible with the authority of the will is permitted.

The will whose maxims necessarily are in harmony with the laws of autonomy is an absolutely good will. The dependence of a will not absolutely good on the principle of autonomy is obligation. And the objective necessity of an action from obligation Kant calls duty.

In the concept of duty we usually think of subjection, yet there is dignity in it so far as the person who fulfills his/her duties is a legislator of the law and is subject to it for that reason. Also no fear or inclination to the law may give moral sanction in the strict sense of the word to the action. Thus autonomy of the will is the supreme condition of morality: "Never choose except in such a way that the maxims of the choice are comprehended in the same volition as a universal law." If the will seeks the determination of the law outside itself in the property of any of its objects, heteronomy results and becomes the source of

---

465   The term moral here as well as throughout the text does not designate an action morally acceptable or good as the colloquial usage of this term would indicate. It refers to the realm of actions which we designate as morality, i.e., actions affecting interpersonal relations.

spurious principles of morality based on hypothetical imperatives in the terminology of Kant (see the list below in Table 5). An example will illustrate this. According to the rule of heteronomy and hypothetical imperative – "I should not lie if I wish to keep my reputation. According to the rule of autonomy and categorical imperative – "I should not lie even though it would not cause me the least injury."

Table 4
FORMULATIONS
OF THE CATEGORICAL IMPERATIVE

1. From the principle of universality:

    Act only according to the maxim by which you can at the same time will that it should become a universal law

2. From the concept of nature:

    Act as though the maxim for your action were by your will to become a universal law of nature

3. From the principle of humanity (human as a rational being as an end unto himself): Act so that you treat humanity, whether in your own person or in that of another, always as an end and never as a means only

4. From the principle of autonomy of the will:

    Act by a maxim which involves its own universal validity for every rational being.

But Kant, being a realistic man, admits that among all spurious principles he would admit as most tolerable the principle derived from the concept of moral sense because it preserves the idea of a will good in itself. He defines this moral sense as "The subjective effect which the law [his moral law of the categorical imperative] has upon the will to which reason alone gives objective grounds." These are imprecise formulations but Kant probably meant by moral sense the unconscious "feeling" of what is right and wrong. It derives from a verity of inner psychological sources and external influences from others due to our living in a society. Generally moral sense expresses our evaluation of the behavior of others and our expectations of reciprocity which was grasped well by Friedrich Nietzsche.[466] Moral consciousness on the

---

466   Marian Hillar, "Friedrich Nietzsche: Social Origins of Morals. Critique of Christian Ethics, and Implications for Atheism in His *The Genealogy of Morals*." In *Essays in the Philosophy of Humanism*, Vol. 16 (1), Spring-Summer, 2008, pp. 59-84.

other hand is an expression of the natural, evolutionary, and biological "moral faculty" postulated by modern science and which constitutes the intuitive basis for our conscious and reflective moral judgment (strictly moral).

Table 5

Kant's List of Conditional (or Spurious) Principles of Morality from the Principle of Heteronomy

Empirical	Rational
a. from the principle of happiness based on a physical or moral feeling; b. as a concept of moral sense, the moral feeling; (it has no uniform standard, but preserves the idea of the good will in itself).	from the principle of perfection a. an ontological concept of perfection as a possible result; b. a theological concept of independent perfection (the will of god as a determining cause of our will; a desire for glory and dominion, feelings opposed to morality).

Possibility of the Categorical Imperative

So far Kant dealt with the question: "What is morality, such that we could say that an action with such and such characteristics would be moral?" Now Kant has to deal with another question: "Can such an action actually take place?" Answers to both questions cannot be given by citing examples; they have to be answered by reason. The key to the answer to the second question lies in freedom of the will – otherwise morality is impossible, because something else would determine it and the categorical imperative would become a hypothetical imperative. Thus freedom cannot be a law of nature, rather an autonomy of the will that is the property of the will to be law to itself. For reason must regard itself as the author of its principles and thus practical reason or the will of a rational being must regard itself free, and independent of foreign influences. Kant, following in principle Aristotle's reasoning, explains this freedom through his theory of knowledge that there is something else in man behind the appearance of man, namely the ego or consciousness in itself or the pure activity of reason which is free from causal determination in the world of appearance i.e., things which we perceive. Thus man can be apart from physical nature and free from its laws when reason exclusively determines his action, but also is a part of the world of sense under the laws of nature and as such not free. Freedom is expressed by the categorical imperative and the hypothetical imperative expresses inclinations in the world of sense. Kant summarizes this by saying: "As a rational being and thus as belonging to the intelligible world, man cannot think of the causality of his own will except under the idea of freedom, for independence from the determining causes of the world of sense (an independence which reason must always ascribe to itself) is freedom. The concept of autonomy is inseparably connected with the idea of freedom, and with the former there is inseparably bound the universal principle of morality which ideally is the ground for all actions of rational beings, just as natural law is the ground of all appearances."

Accordingly, Kant differentiated three levels of behavioral rules operating in the living world (Table 6): 1. the instinctive rules to which belong human urges satisfying our physiological and biological needs, as well as behavior of lower social animals. They are controlled by genes or epigenetic rules. 2. the heteronomous rules (hypothetical imperative, where the action is a means to something else or the will is subjected to extraneous motivations) which Kant divided into two types. A. One type, empirical, is associated with desires, fear, and other motivations. Here belong also the rules produced by the so-called moral sense which is responsible for subconscious or vaguely perceived, non-reflective actions and reactions. They may operate as well in higher animals. Modern science enlarges this intuition of Kant indicating that there is an subconscious, quasi instinctive component in human behavior which may be controlled genetically and/or a result of habituation.[467] Also behavior of higher animals like apes may be controlled by this unconscious mechanism. It cannot be termed "moral," however, using the Kantian definition of morality (morality in the strict sense). Once these rules are consciously recognized they constitute the basis for moral reflective behavior (morality in the strict sense). Nevertheless higher animals have a certain subconscious recognition of rules of behavior common with humans which we prefer to classify as proto-morality. B. The second type, rational, refers to heteronomous rules

---

[467] This aspect of human behavior was amply discussed and elaborated by the Stoics. In ce of social pressures on a society for the development of moral rules. Friedrich Nietzsche, *The Birth of Tragedy and The Genealogy of Morals*, translated by Francis Golfing, (New York: Anchor Books, 1990).

which are produced by reflection; however, they are motivated by extrinsic values like achieving perfection or theological considerations. 3. the autonomous rules (categorical imperative) which are attained by conscious reflection representing the categorical imperative. These are moral rules in the true strict sense of morality proper only to humans.

Table 6
LEVELS OF BEHAVIORAL RULES

I.   INSTINCTIVE
    e.g. food, procreation, fear of the unknown social life in
      social animals
      (governed by genes and epigenetic rules only)
II. HETERONOMOUS
    A. Empirical:
      1. From fear, desire; from the principle of happiness
      from the concept of moral sense
      (based on inclinations; all inclinations summed up in the
      Idea of "happiness")
      2. Subconscious proto-moral from the moral faculty
    B. Rational motivated by extrinsic values:
      From the concept of perfection
      Ontological or transcendental, theological
III. AUTONOMOUS
    Categorical Imperative (Autonomous moral law)
    A law for the will of every rational being
    It only can have as its subject itself considered
      giving universal law.

This classification of the behavioral levels derives from the Stoic doctrine[468] and corresponds to the stages of moral development of man through which community life and virtue are recognized as pre-eminently "things belonging to man" in their terminology and are related to the autonomous behavioral level (categorical imperative of Kant). In modern times such Stoic view of moral development of man in the Kantian modification was wholly confirmed by modern psychology and philosophy. Lawrence Kohlberg (1927-1987) suggested six stages of moral development of children through three levels – the pre-conventional, conventional, and post-conventional, each subdivided into two stages. The first two levels correspond to the heteronomous behavioral level of Kant. Level 1: stage 1 – morality is understood as obedience and punishment and avoidance of harm to others; stage 2 – morality is understood as satisfying one's own

---

468   SVF 1.197.

interests and letting others do the same; Level 2: stage 3 – morality is understood as playing the role of being a good person, i.e., meeting expectations, following the rules, and being concerned for others; stage 4 – morality is understood as doing one's duty, maintaining the social order and the welfare of the society. In the third level in stage 5 morality is understood as the basic rights, values, and legal contracts of a society. Positive laws and duties are calculated on overall utility (utilitarian morality); in stage 6 morality is understood as an accord with universal, self-chosen principles (e.g., justice, equality and respect for the dignity of all human beings) which confer validity to maxims and actions. This level corresponds completely to the autonomous behavioral level (categorical imperative) in Kant's classification.

This scheme was adopted by Jürgen Habermas (b. 1929), a popular contemporary German philosopher-sociologist, with only a small modification.[469] Habermas develops Kantian ethics into a discourse of social consensus. Since Habermas considers modernity as a process in which subjects liberate themselves from traditional roles and values, and create a new social order through communication and discourse, it follows that they create new "normativity" out of their own discourses. And he understands "normativity" as new meanings and understandings which are shared and rational i.e., based on mutual recognition of validity claims. The issue here is the emergence of secular morality from the Judeo-Christian tradition, namely the question of how to live one's life. Habermas contends that gradually a normative ethics as an exposition of detailed norms based on religious tradition was replaced by competing conceptions of the good and transformed from a set of commands to a system of principles and valid norms which are universal and unconditional. Though they are a legacy of the religious tradition, they function in a new social order. This consideration would refer to the existing morality in practice.

Similarly, one could consider history of the moral theory, and Habermas emphasizes that Kant was the first among moral philosophers who pointed to the modern conception of morality, namely, the "formula of the universal law," maxims which are incorporated into the

---

469 Lawrence Kohlberg, *Essays on Moral Development,* (San Francisco: Harper & Row, 1981, 1984), Vols. 1, 2. Jürgen Habermas, *Moral Consciousness and Communicative Action,* translated by Christian Lenhardt and Shierry Weber Nicholsen, (Cambridge, Mass: The MIT Press, 1990 [1983]).

will: "Act only on that maxim by which you can at the same time will it to be a universal law." In Kant's ethics moral actions are expressions of a free act, and based on establishing the validity of moral norms by each individual. Habermas, as a sociologist, criticizes Kant for this individualistic twist and considers morality a collective process of reaching a consensus: "The emphasis shifts from what each can will without contradiction to be a general law, to what all can will in agreement to be a universal law." But this critique is not justified, he simply overlooked Kant's principle of universality at the same time he contradicts himself by introducing "moral discourse" which is equivalent to the Kant theory of morals and concerns norms which are absolute and are either unconditionally valid or non valid and hold across competing cultural traditions. They are evaluated either as right or wrong, just or unjust, and are deontological, and their validity is unconditional. But the detailed rules of behavior conditioned by social situations Habermas labels as "ethical discourse" and claims that in many situations it is difficult to separate these two discourses. Habermas, nevertheless insists on the priority of moral discourse and moral norms which always trump the ethical values, just confirming Kant's theory of the moral. This is due to the fact that in this discourse values are cut off the justification process; moral norms are not cultural values but they are communicative ideals of universal validity; moral discourse is not rooted in any particular cultural tradition but belongs to the post-conventional level of the understanding of morality.

Categorical imperatives are possible because the idea of freedom makes man a member of the intelligible world. If one were a member only of this intelligible world, all actions would be always in accordance with the autonomy of the will. But since man is at the same time a member of the world of sense, his actions ought to conform to the autonomy of the will as belonging to the intelligible world, which, according to reason, should dominate the sensuously affected will. Anyone who is accustomed to using reason is conscious of the good will which constitutes the law for his bad will as a member of the world of sense and acknowledges the authority of this law even while transgressing it. The moral "ought" is one's own volition as a member of the intelligible world. It is conceived as an "ought" only insofar as one regards himself at the same time as a member of the world of sense.

Kant next asserts, however, that philosophy has no knowledge of this supersensible world; it only can indicate its possibility and thus defends the foundations of morality.

To summarize briefly Kant's foundations of morals:

Kant believed that ethics not only can but has to be validated without appeal to god's will or god's orders. Otherwise it would not be moral law in the proper sense, that is, ethics would not be autonomous and thus would not be ethics properly so called. He believed that moral law was to be validated not only independently of utility, pleasure, happiness, natural desires, or positive law (law created by humans for regulating society), but independently of god's will as well. This is a specification of Kant's general concept of moral actions: if we were acting in conformity with moral law not because it is moral law but because god wants us to do so, or because we risk divine retribution in the afterlife, we would not act morally in the strict sense. This principle of autonomy is so conceived that it excludes from moral motivations in the strict sense not only the fear of hell and purgatory, but even the pure readiness to subordinate one's will to god's orders; the motive for doing god's will is not a moral motive. Kant states that only good will is good in the moral sense of the word, the strict sense. Moreover, there is only one motive which is morally good and that is the will to act according to duty as expressed in a general principle. Thus an act is morally (in the strict sense of the word) praiseworthy if it is done out of a sense of duty as such, and not, for instance, from mere inclination or compassion. If what is my duty happens to coincide with what I will spontaneously, my act is morally empty (in the strict sense); a duty should be performed merely because it is duty and not for any other reason. Kant also realized that people being what they are may act from various motives. Thus the rational act performed out of a sense of moral duty is the supreme ideal of moral acts.

It is the task of modern investigation into the evolution of the human psyche to illuminate ultimately the co-ordination between nature and freedom, between the human being as part of the natural world and a free agent, and between the moral and natural ends of mankind.[470]

Kantian morality has a supreme normative principle, the Categorical Imperative, recommending us to act in such a way that we would wish the particular rule governing a given action to become a universal law. This principle has a formal character and it states the condition on which any particular moral rule may claim to be valid.

---

470 Robert Wright, *The Moral Animal. Evolutionary Psychology of Everyday Life*. (New York: Vintage Books, 1995). Mary Midgley, "The Evolution of Ethics." In P. Singer, *op. cit.*, pp. 3-13. Michael Ruse, "The Significance of Evolution." In P. Singer, *op. cit.*, pp. 500-510. Marc D. Hauser, *Moral Minds. How Nature Designed Our Universal sense of Right and Wrong*, (New York: HarperCollins Publishers, 2006). Walter Sinnott-Armstrong, ed., *Moral Psychology, Vol. 1: The Evolution of Morality: Adaptations and Innateness. Vol. 2: The Cognitive Science of Morality: Intuition and Diversity. Vol. 3: The Neuroscience of Morality: Emotion, Brain Disorders, and Development*, (Cambridge, MA; London, UK: The MIT Press, 2008).

VII. ISSUES IN PRACTICAL ETHICS

PHILOSOPHERS AND THE ISSUE OF ABORTION[471]

The following article is adapted from a talk given October 19, 1996, at the Ethics 96, University Humanist Conference, *University of Houston central campus, as part of a forum entitled* Are Traditional Moral Standards Inadequate for Modern Medical Practice ?

Introduction

Abortion remains one of the most hotly debated social and moral issues. Both sides present powerful arguments for and against abortion. The pro-life group emphasizes the argument of preserving human life since conception at any cost, to the point of giving absolute priority to the life of the unborn fetus over the life of the mother. The pro-choice group emphasizes the argument that a woman should have a right to control her body to the point of absolutizing her right over the natural phenomenon of development of a new being.

The problem in debate is that both sides are extremely dogmatic and defensive presenting arguments from one perspective only and fail to see the whole issue in its biological, psychological, moral, and societal complexity. The issue is difficult but we shall argue that it can be solved if the both sides show good will and work together for a common good. We, as humanists, should not allow ourselves to follow the demagogic slogans of politically influential groups, but we should take a rational moral stand.

Views of philosophers on abortion

The fundamental problem with respect to justifying abortion is the moral status of the fetus. There are basically three types of positions: liberal, conservative, and moderate.

Extreme position
A. Liberals

The liberal position is represented by Judith Jarvis Thomson, who assuming a conservative position for the sake of argument shows

471   Published in *Essays in the Philosophy of Humanism,* American Humanist Association, Houston, 1997, pp. 131-140.

that such a view does not lead to consequences its supporters assume. Taking the conservative position on the moral status of the fetus, she argues that even granting the assumption, abortion is still justified in a wide range of cases. She creates a fantasized situation asking us to imagine that we are kidnapped for the purpose of preserving the life of unconscious violinist. We are connected to him so that he may share the use of our kidneys. If we disconnect the violinist before nine months elapse, the violinist will die. Thomson thinks that it is obvious that we have no obligation to share our kidneys with the violinist in such a case. Now she makes her case claiming that in an analogous situation the fetus is using his mother's body. Hence she argues, in an analogous case, abortion can be justified in practically all cases: a woman has a right to abortion in cases involving rape, in cases where the woman's life is endangered and in cases in which the woman had taken reasonable precautions to avoid becoming pregnant.

Obviously the analogy is exaggerated and patently false. Thomson refuses to recognize the special character of the growing fetus and that the fetus is a result of a previous conscious act with predictable outcome. Even in the case of rape, the killing of the fetus is not morally acceptable, though rape itself was morally condemnable.

Another liberal position is argued by Mary Ann Warren, who arrives at her conclusions by analysis of the concept of personhood. She claims, for the sake of argument, that if the fetus is a person, then indeed there is a wide range of cases in which abortion is not permitted. But all depends on what a person is. So she wants to build a consensus by proposing a set of criteria for being a person with full moral status that she thinks both pro-abortionists and anti-abortionists could accept:

1. consciousness of objects and events external and internal to the being, and in particular the capacity to feel pain;

2. reasoning -- the capacity to solve new and relatively complex problems;

3. self-motivated activity;

4. a capacity to communicate;

5. the presence of self-concept and self-awareness.

Using these criteria Warren now contends that fetuses, even with their potentiality to become a person, do not sufficiently resemble a person to have a right to life. Thus she holds that, at least until birth, the fetus has no moral status and lacks a serious right to life. But she herself realizes that her argument, if logically followed, would justify infanticide. Although, according to her criteria the newborn infant would not have a significant right to life, she would not permit infanticide so long as, according to her, there are people who are willing to care and provide for the child's well being. But then why permit abortion if there are people who want to adopt and take care of the new born?

Though we may agree with her criteria of personhood, this personhood is a very special case of how the law treats personhood. The concept of personhood is derived from the Roman law and obviously the definition is modeled on the examples of adult individuals in a social context. Such a definition may have legal value in a societal setting as it is applied to fully grown and functional members of society. Even, according to Warren herself, the argument from personhood would lead to infanticide as morally acceptable practice. Thus the argument using the "personhood," unless one believes in some supernatural "rational substance," is totally irrelevant with respect to children or to human developmental forms. It does not recognize the potentiality and special unique qualitative status of the embryo.

Conservatives

The conservative position contends that from conception the fetus has full moral status; hence a serious right to life. John Noonan objects to the example of the unconscious violinist of Thomson's model and offers a more realistic example. It is a case of a family who was found to be liable for a frostbite suffered by a dinner guest whom they refused to allow to stay overnight, though it was very cold outside and the guest showed signs of being sick. His model is not a true analogy either. But Noonan examines various models and methods used in the analysis of the abortion question. He rejects the argument of development in stages -- because they are arbitrary and there is a continuity in development of the human being. He correctly states that the line can be drawn only at conception. The fetus has an absolute right to life from conception.

He objects to any attempt to make exceptions for abortion when e.g. the fetus is known to be seriously defective or the result of a rape -- such exceptions, according to him, would "eat up the rule." He rejects the application of the "doctrine of double effects" to cases of ectopic pregnancy and the removal of a cancerous uterus containing a fetus. The physician "necessarily intends to perform the abortion, he necessarily intends to kill." In such cases, abortion is permissible on the grounds of self-defense only when the fetus is a danger to the life of the mother.

Moderate Position

The moderate position is represented by Jane English, who questions the concept of personhood assumed by Warren, and assumes both positions for the sake of argument and comes to conclusions supporting the U.S. Supreme Court Decision Roe vs. Wade (1973). She argues that the concept of personhood is not sharp enough and decisive to have an impact on a solution to the controversy. She argues that if we assume the conservative view that the fetus is a full-fledged person, then there are still cases where abortion would be justified to prevent serious harm or death to the woman. Similarly, she argues that even if we accept the liberal view that the fetus is not a person, there are still cases, at least in the late months of pregnancy, where abortion would not be justified, because of the fetus resemblance to a "person" (for reasons of our psychological conditioning). She concludes: "In the early months of pregnancy when the fetus hardly resembles a baby at all, then, abortion is permissible whenever it is in the interests of the pregnant woman or her family. The reasons would only need to outweigh the pain and inconvenience of the abortion itself. In the middle months, when the fetus comes to resemble a person, abortion would be justifiable only when the continuation of the pregnancy or the birth of the child would cause harm -- physical, psychological, economic or social -- to the woman. In the late months of pregnancy, even on our current assumption that a fetus is not a person, abortion seems to be wrong except to save a woman from significant injury or death." The moderate position found its expression in the abortion law of 1973 of the United States Supreme Court.

Solution: Naturalistic Perspective of Moral and Biological Commitment

The sexual act is a conscious human activity with several purposes that developed during the evolution of the human psyche. Its biological function is preservation of the species, but it is also associated with several psychological conditions:

1. It serves as a bonding between committed individuals (as in a family) which developed as a mechanism to secure the care of the helpless infant. Not every act leads, is intended to or must be intended to lead to pregnancy. Therefore it is morally justified to prevent any unwanted pregnancy by techniques preventing the fertilization of the oocyte. Once, however, the fertilization of the oocyte took place, we are faced with a new situation.

2. The sexual act satisfies our psychological needs when it is associated with long – lasting commitment and responsibility. Otherwise it is a dehumanizing exploitation and, though it may provide temporary sensual gratification it can lead to a sense of frustration, dissatisfaction, cynicism and even psychological aberrations and neurotic disturbances. The traditional form of long-lasting commitment is the institution of marriage, in which involved partners build psychological relationship of mutual support and responsibility.

3. Commitment is necessary also for responsible sexual activity. Since sex, even with utilization of preventive measures, may predictably lead to unwanted pregnancy and development of a new life, responsible sex must take such a possibility into consideration. Therefore every sexual act outside the institution of marriage or similar arrangement, guaranteeing lasting commitment, is morally unacceptable.

4. Evolution of the human psyche developed a need for human interaction: such a need is primarily satisfied between individuals in a family, then between individuals in a larger group or society. When the sexual urge is suppressed, this need for companionship still remains and can be partially fulfilled by vicarious mechanisms (e.g. group living in a tight community as among monks or nuns

or development of intense and long-lasting special interests and preoccupations). That need is so strong that, in the extreme cases, social isolation may result in psychological disturbances such as the pathological conditions observed in clinical psychiatry. Thus the pope is wrong in his assertion that every act must be open to produce progeny.

5. The phenomenon of homosexuality is a condition in which the psychological need for companionship does not correspond to the sexual compatibility of the partners. Nevertheless, though it is certainly a rare type of biological phenomenon, it is natural and morally correct since it is driven by biologically conditioned impulse the same way as the heterosexual drive. The moral aspect of it consists again in the mutual long-lasting commitment. Even homosexuals may have a family life (and they need it too) with adopted children (at least from one partner's side). Heterosexual individuals do not understand psychology of the homosexuals because they do not have the same urge, The condemnation and persecution of homosexuals is one of the last moral aberrations imposed by erroneous religious doctrines.

Very important argument often used by the proponents of the abortion is based on the observation that the human development takes place in stages, therefore, they argue, there are some stages in which "personhood" is absent or less developed and hence abortion is then permitted. For better understanding of the biological process of gestation and human development, we will briefly summarize the biological stages that take place.

The fertilized oocyte develops through the second meiotic division into ovum and undergoes several developmental stages. Cleavage is the stage in which the single fertilized cell called zygote is converted into a multicellular ball called morula. Morula in turn implants in the uterus and is transformed into a hollow ball, blastocyst, in which a surface layer of cells, called trophoblast, differentiates from the rest of the inner cells called the inner cell mass. The implantation takes place usually one week after fertilization. The trophoblast will develop into part of the placenta and the inner cell mass will be transformed into embryonic disk.

The embryonic disk, during the week after the implantation, will develop into gastrula -- a stage with three layers of cells: ectoderm, mesoderm, and endoderm. From these three layers of cells, during the next six weeks, will develop embryonic organ systems in a process called organogenesis. The ectoderm, the layer of cells remaining at the surface, will give rise to the nervous system and certain glands; endoderm, the inner layer of cells, will give rise to parts of the respiratory and digestive systems; the mesoderm, the intermediary layer of cells, will develop into the heart, muscles, bones and other internal organs. The nervous system begins to develop through the process of neurulation. During this process, the ectoderm cells in the midline of the embryo elongate and form a neural plate which folds to form a tube running through the length of embryo, the so-called neural tube. Mesoderm and endoderm develop into other organs and the embryo assumes, at this stage, segmented appearance common to all vertebrate embryos. Between the fourth and the sixth week arms, legs, fingers and toes develop. By the eighth week the embryo resembles a human figure which looks like a human in miniature and is designated a fetus. During the first three months, in more than 20 % of all conceptions, spontaneous expulsion of the uterine contents may take place (miscarriage) or may be a result of genetic disorders that prevent normal development. Fetuses born before the seventh month of gestation are not ready for independent living outside the womb and rarely survive, even with the intensive medical support.

The brain develops between the ninth and sixteenth weeks of gestation. The development of the new life, though artificially presented in stages, is a continuous process from the moment of fertilization. Fertilization is thus a crucial step which determines a new quality for the fertilized oocyte. Until that moment oocyte is one of the cells in the body, not committed and not determined. The developing zygote, however, becomes a unique cell in the body with a very specific function. Thus the determining factor for a new human being is not the "personhood." "Personhood," as we have seen, has no application for the embryos, small children and even young adults. The embryo of four weeks, the fetus of four months or the new born have the same quantity of "personhood." But the embryonic cells cannot be classified just as any "clump of cells" like liver cells or kidney cells. The role of these embryonic cells is absolutely different and they acquired a new quality and potential unlike any other cells in the body. They cannot be compared to the cancer cells either, because they are not abnormal cells and they do not destroy the host. Moreover they arose by a conscious act with predictable consequences and our moral responsibility demands that we recognize their unique and specific potential. Our moral responsibility begins with the sexual act itself. That responsibility should be inculcated in young individuals through the process of moral education.

The fact that pro-abortionists do not see any moral harm in abortion during the first two and a half months of gestation is based only on our psychological conditioning -- the embryo does not look yet like a human, therefore intuitively and psychically we feel less objection to destroying it. The same psychological mechanism prevents us from destroying the new born -- since, as I indicated previously, there is no difference in "personhood" between these stages of human life.

Abortion thus may be justified in cases threatening the life of the pregnant woman and for medical reasons with defective embryos.

In other cases (e.g. in cases of rape and social hardship) it is a moral question depending on the decision of the pregnant woman within her immediate social and economic milieu. No state/government should be allowed to control woman's decision by restrictive laws or legal regulations.[472]

Addendum
The United States Supreme Court Roe versus Wade Decision (1973).

The court decided that the constitutional right to privacy, protected by the due process clause of the Fourteenth Amendment entails:

1. No law may restrict the right of a woman to be aborted by a physician during the first three months of her pregnancy.

---

[472] Most recently Chris Meyers, a professor of philosophy, wrote a most comprehensive book on the issue of abortion anal analyzed the most common arguments for and against abortion and presented to the reader pertinent philosophical arguments on its moral aspect. Though he does not give explicit conclusion and leaves it to the reader, it is clear that abortion cannot be justified on moral grounds. Chris Meyers, *The Fetal Position. A Rational Approach to the Abortion Issue*, (Amherst, NY: Prometheus Books, 2010).

2. During the second trimester, abortion may be regulated by the law only to the extent that the regulation is reasonably related to the preservation and protection of maternal health.

3. When the fetus becomes viable (not before the beginning of the third trimester) a law may prohibit abortion, but only subject to an exception permitting abortion whenever necessary to protect the woman's life or health.

Bibliography

Robert Wright, *The Moral Animal. Evolutionary Psychology and Everyday Life,*(New York: Vintage Book, 1994).

Cecie Starr and Beverly McMillan, *Human Biology,* (Belmont, CA: Wadsworth, 1995). Karol Wojtyła, *Miłość i odpowiedzialność,* (Kraków: Wydawnictwo Znak, 1962).

Antony Flew, *An Introduction to Western Philosophy,* (New York: Thames and Hudson, 1989). Judith Jarvis Thomson, "A Defense of Abortion", *Philosophy & Public Affairs,* No 1, 1971. Reprinted in James P. Sterba, ed. *Morality in Practice,* second edition, (Belmont, CA: Wadsworth Publishing Company, 1988) pp. 140-148.

John Noonan, "Responding to Person: Methods of Moral Argument in Debate over Abortion,"
Theology Digest, 1973, pp. 291-307. Reprinted in James P. Sterba, *op. cit.,* pp. 149-159.

Mary Anne Warren, "On the Moral and Legal Status of Abortion," *The Monist,* Vol. 57, no. 4, 1973. Reprinted in James P. Sterba, *op. cit.,* pp. 159-168.

Mary Anne Warren, "Postscript on Infanticide," in *Today's Moral Problems,* Richard Wasserstrom, ed., pp. 135-136, 1979. Reprinted in James P. Sterba, *op. cit.,* pp. 168-169.

Jane English, "Abortion and the Concept of a Person," *Canadian Journal of Philosophy,* Vol. 5, no.2, pp. 233-243, 1975. Reprinted in James P. Sterba, *op. cit.,* pp. 170-176.

LIBERATION THEOLOGY:
A RELIGIOUS RESPONSE TO SOCIAL
PROBLEMS. A SURVEY[473]

INTRODUCTION

In the late 60s a new social and intellectual movement appeared on the Latin American continent. The movement is rooted in the Christian faith and Scriptures and seeks its ideological superstructure based on the religious reflection in close association with the Church organization[474]. It is typical not only of Latin America but also of the entire Third World and any social situation of oppression.

Members of the religious orders are committed to the vow of poverty and do not own property individually, nevertheless they enjoy a standard of living and security that separates them from the daily agony of the poor. The question then arose for some of them what is the ideal of poverty in a situation where most are suffering dehumanizing poverty, and what should the Church and Christians do about it?

Liberation theology thus emerged as a result of a systematic, disciplined reflection on Christian faith and its implications. The theologians who formulated liberation theology usually do not teach in universities and seminaries, they are a small group of Catholic or Protestant clergy and have direct contact with the grass-roots groups as advisors to priests, sisters or pastors. Since they spend at least some time working directly with the poor themselves[475], the questions they deal with arise out of their direct contact with the poor. Liberation theology interprets the Bible and the key Christian doctrines through the experiences of the poor. It also helps the poor to interpret their own faith in a new way. It deals with Jesus's life and message. The poor learn to read the Scripture in a way that affirms their dignity and self

---

473 Published in *Humanism and Social Issues. Anthology of Essays.* American Humanist Association, Houston, 1993, pp. 35-52.

474 Phillip Berryman *"Liberation Theology. Essential Facts About the Revolutionary Movement in Latin America and Beyond".* New York: Pantheon Books, 1987. Michael Novak *"Will it Liberate? Questions About Liberation Theology".* New York: Paulist Press, 1986. J. A. O. Preus, III *"Liberation theology: basic themes and methodology"* in *Concordia Journal,* Vol. 13, No. 1, Jan. 1987, pp. 6-26. Paul L. Schrieber *"Liberation theology and the Old Testament: an exegetical critique",* in *Concordia Journal,* Vol. 13, No. 1, Jan. 1987, pp. 27-46.

475 Clodovis Boff *"Feet-on-the Ground Theology: a Brazilian Journal."* Translated from the Portuguese by Phillip Berryman. Maryknoll, New York: Orbis Boks, 1987

worth and their right to struggle together for a more decent life. The poverty of people is largely a product of the way society is organized therefore liberation theology is a "critique of economic structures". Phillip Berryman described the liberation theology in the following terms:

"Liberation theology is:

1. An interpretation of Christian faith out of the suffering, struggle, and hope of the poor;

2. A critique of society and the ideologies sustaining it;

3. A critique of the activity of the church and of Christians from the angle of the poor.

NORTH AND SOUTH

Unlike in North America the Catholic Church was a major part of the machinery of conquest nd colonization of in Latin America. It all began with a decree from pope Alexander VI who, in 1492, divided the world not yet under the Christian rule between the Spanish and Portuguese monarchs and conferred to them the right and duty to propagate the Christian faith. The conquest was done with unbelievable cruelty and complete disregard to any human decency to say nothing of the presumed ethical values of Christianity. There were only sporadic individual protests from some missionaries of conquest like Bartolomé de las Casas in Hispaniola (XVIth century) or from the bishop of Nicaragua, Antonio de Valdivieso (stabbed to death in 1550). The conquistadores imposed a model of Christendom where civil and religious authorities were connected - religious authority being a ruling one and the civil authority executing the orders of the religious one. Clergy remained predominantly in the cities and towns serving primarily the ruling class (e.g., in schools) and enjoyed all the comforts provided by a privileged status and the ownership of land. During the independence movement in the 19th century, bishops sided with the Spanish crown, and popes made pronouncements against the struggle for independence.[476]

---

476   Enrique Dussell "*A History of the Church in Latin America. Colonialism to Liberation 1492 - 1979*". Translated and revised by Alan Neely. Grand Rapids, Michigan: William B. Eerd-man's Publishing Co., 1981.

The social and political structure imposed on the continent had its roots in the ecclesial doctrines formulated by Thomas Aquinas. In such a religiously dominated society there was no room for innovation, for social mobility, for free and spontaneous thinking, for democracy and democratic institutions. Society represented a rigid, hierarchical, feudal structure fixed once forever, resembling the ecclesiastical institution. All this was quite opposite to the society developed in the North.

SOCIAL AND RELIGIOUS ROOTS OF LIBERATION THEOLOGY

The theology of liberation, though explicitly mentioned for the first time in 1968 in a speech by a Peruvian theologian delivered in the fishing port of Chimbate, has roots in religious and social movements that swept the Latin American continent in the 50s. Catholic bishops were concerned with the increasing influence of Protestant missionaries, the growing secularization of the population and the spreading of communist ideas (these were topics of the first plenary meeting of CELAM - Latin American Bishops' Conference - in 1955 in Río de Janeiro). Church problems were aggravated by the lack of clergy to serve poor people in the country and the visible complicity of the Church with an unjust social order. The social situation in Latin American countries gave rise to revolutionary movements in Cuba, Venezuela, Guatemala, and Peru. In Brazil, peasants became militant, and the radicalized middle-class people went to work directly with the poor. A Brazilian educator, Paulo Freire[477], developed a new method for teaching literacy to the masses of peasants through the process of "conscientizaçao", consciousness-raising. All these movements and problems arose directly from the conditions of abject poverty, how 70% of the population lived. In a socio-economic analysis of the structure of Latin American society, some Christians and missionaries began to utilize Marxist tools[478] without, of course, embracing the philosophy of dialectical materialism.

The missionaries raised questions of the theological significance of a social revolution. On the religious plane, a strong impetus for changes and new vision of the world came from the documents of the Second

---

477 Paulo Freire *"Pedagogy of the Oppressed"*. New York: Seabury, 1970.
478 José Porfirio Miranda *"Marx and the Bible. A Critique of the Philosophy of Oppression."* Translated by John Eagleson. Maryknoll, New York: Orbis Books, 1974

Vatican Council (1962-1965).[479] Latin American bishops insisted that the final documents should deal with the issues of development and human progress as a historical imperative. One statement of a Latin American bishop is especially significant: "Authentic socialism is Christianity lived to the full, in basic equality and with a fair distribution of goods"[480]. Father Camilo Torres exemplifies this new attitude. He realized the need for a United Front linking together peasants, workers, slum dwellers, and professionals for basic changes. He expressed the need of revolution for implementing the fundamental changes in the economic, social and political structures. The essence of revolution was the removal of power from the privileged to the poor majorities. Revolution could be peaceful if the privileged elites did not put up a violent resistance, and the Christians should become involved. He sacrificed his own life in the struggle in 1966. On the international plane, social scientists emphasized that underdevelopment was structurally conditioned by the exploitation by foreign economic powers maintaining Latin America in a system of dependency on hegemonic centers. Such a system of oppression calls for ethical indignation. The encyclical of pope Paul VI *"Populorum Progressio"* (1967)[481] critiqued the international economic order, explicitly condemned the capitalistic system as presently known for the social evils and called for development through consensus rather than struggle:

> "[It is a system] ... which considers profit as the key motive for economic progress, competition as the supreme law of economics, and private ownership of the means of production as an absolute right that has no limits and carries no corresponding social obligation".

> "We know ... that revolutionary uprising - save where there is manifest long-standing tyranny which would do great damage to fundamental personal rights and dangerous harm to the common good of the country - produces new injustices, throws more elements out of balance and brings on new disasters".

479 *"The Documents of Vatican II. In a New and Definitive Translation with Commentaries and Notes by Catholic, Protestant and Orthodox Authorities."* Walter M. Abbott, S.J., general editor. Introduction by Lawrence Cardinal Shehan. Translation directed by Joseph Gallagher. Herder and Herder, Association Press, 1966.

480 Phillip Berryman, *op. cit.*, 1987.

481 *"Populorum Progressio"* in Joseph Gremillion, ed., *"The Gospel of Peace and Justice"*. Maryknoll, New York: Orbis Books, 1976.

The Magna Charta of the new pastoral approach to social problems became the documents of the second plenary meeting of CELAM convened in Medellín[482], Colombia (1968). They called for the Christians to be involved in the transformation of society; denounced institutionalized violence and named it a "situation of sin"; called for renovating societal changes; called for the defense of human rights; called for consciousness-raising evangelization and spoke of "comunidades de base" - lay-led groups of Christians as basic organic units of society and pastoral activity. The documents often used the term liberation and spoke of the interrelationship between liberation and evangelization:

"The Church ... has the duty to proclaim the liberation of millions of human beings, many of whom are her own children ... This is not foreign to evangelization."

The general assumption was that basic changes would come through a conversion on the part of the privileged and powerful. Revolutionaries were defined as those who sought radical changes and who believed that people should chart their own course and not as those who were using violence.

BASIC PRINCIPLES OF THEOLOGY OF LIBERATION

Facing enormous problems in the society, some theologians realized that the traditional theology concerned with religious dogmas and abstract religious concepts lost any relevance. It became an abstract speculation removed from the original spirit of the Gospel message and out of touch with real life. On the social level it served the rich. They realized that if one really cared for and believed in the Christian ideals, one had to answer the question: how to be a Christian in a concrete historical situation? The basic concerns in Latin America shifted thus from "whether one can believe what Christianity affirms to what relevance Christianity has in the struggle for a more just world."[483] Out of such considerations was born "liberation theology," outlined for the first time by a Peruvian theologian Gustavo Gutierrez a few weeks before the Medellínn conference. Gutierrez[484] defined theology

---

482   CELAM *"La Iglesia en la Actual Transformación de América Latina a la Luz del Concilio"*, Bogota: CELAM, 1969.
483   Phillip Berryman, *op. cit.*, 1987.
484   Gustavo Gutierrez *"A Theology of Liberation"*. Maryknoll, New York: Orbis Books, 1973.

as a "critical reflection on praxis in the light of the word of God." Liberation theology has two basic principles: first, it recognizes a need for liberation from any kind of oppression - political, economic, social, sexual, racial, religious; second, it asserts that the theology must grow out of the basic Christian communities and should not be imposed from above, that is, from the infallible source book or from the magisterium of an infallible Church. It explores the theological meaning of human activities:

1. It interprets Christian faith out of the suffering, struggle, and hope of the poor;

2. It critiques society and ideologies sustaining it, pretends not to lay down specific rules for how to struggle for justice, but stresses that a responsible commitment with class conflict is an expression of love for one's neighbor. Through solidarity with the poor theologians of liberation advocate the transcendence from class division to a new type of society;

3. It critiques the activity of the Church from the angle of the poor.

The main theme, liberation, is considered at three levels of meaning which are interconnected. At the social and political level liberation is an expression of aspirations of the oppressed classes and peoples. This liberation emphasizes the conflict in the economical, social and political process between the oppressed and the oppressors. At the human level the liberation is conceived as a historical process in which people develop consciously their own destiny through the social changes. At the religious, salvific level the liberation means liberation from sin, the ultimate source of all deviation from fraternity, of all injustice and oppression. It brings man back into communion with God and fellow men, which is the radical, total liberation. These three processes cannot be separated, they form a unique, complex process ("proceso unico y complejo"). For the first time sin was formulated in social terms as a concrete social act and not in traditional way as an abstract, and even an allegoric personification in the person of satan, or at best, a personal act. For the first time the religious, salvific plan was explicitly linked to the human experience in a society.

PRIORITY OF PRAXIS OVER THEORY

Direct source of liberation theology was the personal experience of many priests, pastoral workers and sisters who in the 60s made an effort and came close to the poor. It grew out of their reflections. E.g. Brazilian theologian Clodovis Boff spends half a year working among the poor in the state of Acre.[485] Theologians of liberation are thus "organic intellectuals" who can bridge the sharp class barrier in Latin American society. Gutierrez and other liberation theologians[486] insist that theology is a secondary reflection, the first commitment being the work among the poor. The shift is from the abstract speculation to living one's faith. This emphasis on the primacy of praxis over the abstract contrasts with the Catholic orthodoxy. Traditionally, priests preached resignation to "God's will" in a way that it reinforced the belief that the present distribution of wealth and power comes from God. Peasant society indoctrinated this way tended to internalize a fixed and even fatalistic view of the universe with symbols and rationalizations.

Gutierrez[487] found three meanings of poverty: the dehumanizing lack of material goods, the openness to God and commitment to solidarity. The Bible understands material poverty as an evil resulting from the oppression of some people by others. Therefore the Medellín document[488] suggests that a poor Church denounces the unjust lack of goods in this world and the sin that causes it, preaches and lives spiritual poverty as an attitude of spiritual openness to God and commits itself to poverty. Voluntary poverty is considered an act of love and liberation, of solidarity with the poor and those who suffer injustice. This commitment calls for giving up the relatively comfortable life and going to a barrio or a rural area to live with the people. By this act the clergy still would not become poor themselves. Next they have to develop a model of activities based on the work of Paulo Freire. The

---

485   Clodovis Boff *"Feet-on-the Ground Theology: a Brazilian Journal."* Translated from the Portuguese by Phillip Berryman. Maryknoll, New York: Orbis Boks, 1987.
486   Gustavo Gutierrez *"A Theology of Liberation".* Maryknoll, New York: Orbis Books, 1973. Leonardo and Clodovis Boff *"Salvation and Liberation".* Translated from the Portuguese by Robert R. Barr, Maryknoll, New York: Orbis Books, 1984. Leonardo Boff *"Liberation Theology: from Confrontation to Dialogue".* Translated from the Portuguese by Robert R. Barr, San Francisco: Harper & Row, 1986. Leonardo Boff *"Church, Charism and Power: Liberation Theology and the Institutional Church".* Translated from the Portuguese by John W. Diercksmeier, New York, Crssroad, 1985. Clodovis Boff *"Theology and Praxis. Epistemological Foundations".* Translated from the Portuguese by Robert R. Barr, Maryknoll, New York: Orbis Books, 1987.
487   Gustavo Gutierez, *op. cit.*, 1973.
488   CELAM, *op. cit.*, 1969.

encyclical "Redemptor Hominis"[489] is pervaded by the perspective of liberation:

> "Injustice, the exploitation of some human beings by others, the exploitation of the human being by the state, institutions, and mechanisms of economic systems, must be called by their name". "... liberation must be inserted into the entire contemporary reality of human life".
> ... liberation is a faith reality, one of the basic biblical themes, deeply inscribed in the salvific mission of Christ, in the work of redemption, and in his teaching".

The praxis of liberation theology finds its embodiment in the Christian ecclesial base communities. They are small, lay-led groups of Christians that see themselves as part of the Church and work together to improve their lot and establish a more just society. Base communities were a result of pastoral problems related to the lack of clergy in the country. They had their antecedents in the activity of Catholic Action in Belgium and in "cursillos de Cristianidad" - a kind of weekend retreats - in Spain. In Latin America they combined the social an educational function with the pastoral activity. Their primary motivation is religious based on popular religiosity embodying the cults of the saints and Virgin Mary. (This popular religiosity may be an uncorrupted illustration of Karl Barth's definition of religion: all religions in history represent human effort to reach God and in fact are forms of idolatry). They were modeled on the work of Paulo Freire. They include several activities like teaching peasants to read and write, organize self-help, and raising their self-consciousness.[490] Slowly, some clergy adopted this method for the "re-evangelization of adults" meaning by this term the spreading of Christ's message to its fullness. Such an evangelization covered the topics like sources of poverty and social injustice, community questions in human relations, religious tenets and assertions etc., all this in close connection with the Bible. Base communities have an enormous impact on society. They constitute the initial step in raising the consciousness of the people by giving them a broad perspective on their role and place in the society, they help people to project their vision of life and motivate them for

---

489   John Paul II *"Redemptor Hominis (Redeemer of Man)"*. Washington, DC: USCC, 1979.
490   Oralia Cardenas Zacarias y Salvador García Angulo *"Autodidactismo solidario. Una experiencia de autoeducación de adultos en el Valle del Mezquital."* Ixmiquilpan, Mexico: Sevicios de Educación de Adultos, A.C. (SEDAC), 1987.

involvement. Such communities develop a sense of solidarity within the group and generate mutual aid and support; they serve as a training ground for the experience of democracy and direct their social and political actions.

As a whole, these communities do not fit into the traditional vertical, hierarchical authority system of the Catholic Church. At some point the powerful and the Church hierarchy itself saw the community as a threat to its domination[491] and used intimidation and violence against them. However, there is no way now to turn the clock back, therefore some bishops opted to include base communities in the overall ecclesial structure and subordinate them to their rule and control as a cell in their organization. The conclusions of the Medellín conference were confirmed by CELAM meeting in Puebla (1979)[492]:

> "We see the growing gap between rich and poor as a scandal and a contradiction to Christian existence. The luxury of a few becomes an insult to the wretched poverty of the vast masses".

> "Analyzing this situation more deeply, we discover that this poverty is not a passing phase. Instead it is the product of economic, social, and political situations and structures, though there are also other causes for the state of misery.

> In many instances this state of poverty within our countries finds its origin and support in mechanisms which, because they are impregnated with materialism rather than any authentic humanism, create a situation on the international level where the rich get richer at the expense of the poor who get ever poorer".

It was a great victory for the theologians of liberation when the Puebla conference adopted the vocabulary and the themes of liberation theology.

---

491   Leonardo Boff, *op. cit.*, 1986.
492   John Eagleson and Philip Scharper, eds. *"Puebla and Beyond: Documentation and Commentary"*. Translated by John Drury, Maryknoll, New York: Orbis Books, 1979.

HISTORY AS A FOCUS OF THEOLOGY

The liberating message of the Gospel does not identify any social form as just. It permeates the total historical realization and places it in a broader perspective of the radical salvation. Only when the Gospel message is not implemented in life then it becomes inevitable to search for an ideology that would justify a determined social situation. For believers, therefore, the evangelization is liberating since it announces the radical liberation that includes the transformation of historical and political conditions in which they live. But without considering the social and political reality, the analysis would lack the depth and would fall into another extreme of spiritual reductionism equally erroneous, according to the theologians of the liberation theology. For many theologians appeals to eschatological "beyond" have no relevance, they must be rooted in the historical present or rejected.

In the theological literature one can find frequent references and allusions to Marxism and Marx, in the social and economical analysis. It does not mean the acceptance of Marxism, and especially, of course, its concept of life, or its philosophy to the exclusion of the Christian faith. Some go so far as to affirm that there is no systematic theology in North America today without the analysis of Marx.

In the realm of international relations the theologians of liberation adopt, in a somewhat naïve and simplistic way, the dependence theory which maintains that the underdeveloped countries were set up as main producers of raw materials and agricultural products by an international division of labor[493]. It entails also the political dependence. Medellín Conference (1968) and Secretariat General of Celam (1973) accepted the dependence as a fact. "Nos referimos aquí, particularmente, a las consecuencias que entreña para nuestros países su dependencia de un centro de poder económico, en torno al cual gravitan. De allí resulta que nuestras naciones, con frecuencia, no son dueñas de sus bienes ni de sus decisiones económicas. Como es obvio, esto no deja de tener sus incidencias en lo politico, dada la interdependencia que existe entre ambos campos." And: "... la dependencia parece como un hecho ... sobre ese hecho se elabora una teoría que esta en búsqueda, que se critica a sí misma ... La teología de la liberación tiene en cuenta la teoría de la dependencia y es imposible, al mismo tiempo, no tener en

---

493 Michael Novak, *op. cit.*, 1986.

cuenta la teoría de la dependencia. Y la tiene en cuenta con su sentido crítico, sin embargo, la teología de la liberación debe ser más atenta a estas variaciones y a estas críticas en la teoría de la dependencia, evitar generalización, enriquecerse con otro tipo de análisis y de niveles."[494]

READING THE BIBLE

Reading the Bible and interpreting it from the viewpoint of the poor is an essential element in the theology of liberation[495]. Without that religious aspect, the theology of liberation would be just an extension of social analysis. A few examples will give a clear idea of what is involved in here. In the story of Genesis, creationism is not an issue. The peasant masses are able to appreciate the poetical account of creation better than anyone else since it deals with the objects of their everyday experience. Liberation theology stresses the goodness of creation, the dignity of the poor as God's image and their dominion over the earth and their rights to its fruits (it cannot escape in this analysis that only few own the land - "tierra"). Sin assumes social dimensions in the story of Cain and Abel and is not rooted in the story of Adam and Eve (the traditional basis of the abstract and mythical concept of the sin). The story of Exodus becomes a prototype of liberation constituting a basic paradigm of God's saving action. Little attention is given to the miraculous, the emphasis being put on the oppressive rule and liberation. Prophets and prophecies are seen as conscientizers of the people. Christ is a figure representing struggle, death, and vindication - in short - liberation:

> "The spirit of the Lord is upon me; therefore, he has anointed me. He has sent me to bring glad tidings to the poor, to proclaim liberty to captives, recovery of sight to the blind and release to prisoners, to announce a year of favor from the Lord." (Luke 4:18-19)

No doubt this reads like a social manifesto! Jesus himself lived like a poor person, in real material poverty, not a spiritual one. His criterion of a just life was practical material aid for one's neighbor! Jesus made enemies by denouncing the organized and ritualized religion of his time that was not committed to the love of one's neighbor. He was executed by the order of the Church authority that felt threatened in its organization and power. The New Testamental communities of the

---

494 CELAM, *op. cit.*, 1969.
495 Paul L. Schreiber, *op. cit.*, 1987.

faithful are seen as the first "comunidades de base". How revealing this reading of the Bible is in the light of the fact that the Catholic Church also felt that its power was threatened by the base communities and objected to that aspect of the theology of liberation. It did not hesitate to use intimidation and silencing on the most prominent expounder of liberation theology, Leonardo Boff[496]. Also as an excuse for persecution of the theologians of liberation the Church hierarchy used their presumed espousal of the Marxist doctrines. Liberation theology is thus based on the Bible. However, Bible is not taken literally, but symbolically as a sign.

METHODOLOGY

From the discussion as presented we deduce three basic planes of operation or mediation of liberation theology[497]:

1. The socio-analytical i.e., the perception of social reality. In this context it is the condemnation of the capitalistic system as the source of evils (explicitly expressed in the quoted fragment of *"Populorum Progressio"*);

2. The hermeneutic i.e., the theological reading of social reality in the light of faith based on the Bible.

Leonardo and Clodovis Boff[498] succinctly formulated it in this way:

... Faith helps the Christian endorse and support those historical movements that have a greater affinity with the ideals of the gospel. Today, for example, we perceive that the Christian ideal is closer to socialism than to capitalism. It is not a matter of creating a Christian socialism. It is a matter of being able to say that the socialist system, when actually carried out in reality, enables Christians better to live the humanitarian and divine ideals of their faith";

---

496   Leonardo Boff, *op. cit.*, 1986. Joseph Ratzinger *"Carta a L. Boff"* in *"Mision Abierta al Sevicio de la Fe,"* 1/1985, Febrero, pp. 9-13. Leonardo Boff *"Datos basicos de mi llamada a Roma"* in *"Mision Abierta al Servicio de la Fe",* 1/1985, Febrero, pp. 14-30. *"Observaciones sobre la teologia de la liberacion de Gustavo Gutierrez",* Sagrada Congregacion para la Doctrina de la Fe, in *"Mision Abierta al Servicio de la Fe,"* 1 /1985, Febrero, pp. 33-35. Gustavo Gutierrez *"Respuesta a las observaciones"* in *"Mision Abierta al Servicio de la Fe,"* 1/1985, Febrero, pp. 36-76, Leonardo Boff *"Ante el nuevo documento vaticano sobre la teologia de la liberación"* in *Mision Abierta al Servicio de la Fe",* 1/1985, Febrero, pp. 124-136. Juan Luis Segundo *"Teologia de la liberacion. Respuesta al Cardenal Ratzinger,"* Madrid: Ediciones Cristiandad, 1985. Clodovis Boff, *op. cit.*, 1987.
497   Clodovis Boff, *op. cit.*, 1987.
498   Leonardo and Clodovis Boff, *op. cit.*, 1984.

3. The pastoral service, the praxis i.e. search for the viable avenues for the praxis and embodiment of the theology of liberation in pastoral activity. Again we find a formulation of it in the Boffs' work:

"... Church has the duty to act as agent of liberation. It must attempt to articulate its words, its catechesis, its liturgy, its community action, and its interventions with established authority, in the direction of liberation.

CONCLUSIONS

The analysis of the social situation by concerned Church workers leads to the formulation of a social theory and provides a tool for liberation theology. The social theory becomes dialectical if it envisions the possibility of a systematic change.

Liberation theology too opts for the social changes. Often the Marxist analysis is selected as the best suited tool to describe the socio-economic situation.

The Church hierarchy itself has difficulty in choosing either the socialist or the capitalistic system, both with their advantages and limitations, as the model to be propagated for current economic structures.

It is interesting that throughout all the deliberations and sincerity of the theologians of liberation, not a single word was said about the disparity between the overgrowth of population and the economic growth in countries with endemic poverty.

In the realm of international relations the theology of liberation adopts, not without a certain naïveté, after certain Church pronouncements, the dependence theory which maintains that the underdeveloped countries were set up as the main producers of raw materials and agricultural products by an international division of labor.

The main theme of the theology of liberation - liberation - is understood as a break with the present order, an integral development, and an embracing of its three levels of meaning (Gutierrez)[499]:

---

499   Gustavo Gutierrez, *op. cit.*, 1973.

1. an aspiration of the poor and liberation from oppression;

2. gradual expansion of freedom and actualization of the ability of human beings to take charge of their own destiny;

3. on the religious level, attainment of freedom of Christ as a communion with God and with other human beings.

The liberation thus is a complex process and for a liberation theologian it has human, historical and political dimensions of salvation. For an atheist, agnostic or Marxist, the liberation process has a purely historical sense and nothing else. Salvation is the artificial transcendent dimension of liberation. The traditional Catholic view was that our earthly life is a transitory phase to the way of heaven, treated as a trial. This tradition is reversed by the theology of liberation which asserts that there is continuity between the temporal process and ultimate transcendence. The Church and Christians should be involved in human history - the one human history where people are shaping their destiny! The theology of liberation says that politics is the most important dominant dimension today. After the Medellín meeting, the reactionary forces mounted an offensive against the new way of thinking. The attack came from the CIA and conservative, traditional circles of the Church. Bishop Alfonso Trujillo and Belgian Jesuit Roger Vekemans organized a campaign and eventually bishop Trujillo became elected the secretary of the CELAM. The encyclical of Paul VI *"Octogesima Adveniens"*[500] (1971) suggested caution and restrain. At the same time repression against progressive clergy and archbishop Helder Camara, later also against Gustavo Gutierrez, Leonardo Boff, and others,[501] was instigated by the Congregation for the Doctrine of the Faith.

During the preparation for the CELAM conference in Puebla, the preparatory document was rejected by the conservative bishops.

---

500 Paul VI *"Octogesima Adveniens."* in Joseph Gremillion, ed. *"The Gospel of Peace and Justice."* Maryknoll, New York: Orbis Books, 1976.

501 Norbert Greinacher in Hans Küng and Leonard Swidler, eds. *"The Church in Anguish. Has Vatican Betrayed Vatican II?"* pp. 144 - 162. San Francisco: Harper and Row, 1987. Joseph Ratzinger *"Carta a L. Boff"* in *"Mision Abierta al Sevicio de la Fe",* 1/1985, Febrero, pp. 9-13. Leonardo Boff *"Datos basicos de mi llamada a Roma"* in *"Mision Abierta al Servicio de la Fe",* 1/1985, Febrero, pp. 14-30. *"Observaciones sobre la teologia de la liberacion de Gustavo Gutierrez",* Sagrada Congregacion para la Doctrina de la Fe, in *"Mision Abierta al Servicio de la Fe,"* 1/1985, Febrero, pp. 33-35. Gustavo Gutierrez *"Respuesta a las observaciones",* in *"Mision Abierta al Servicio de la Fe,"* 1/1985, Febrero, pp. 36-76. Leonardo Boff *"Ante el nuevo documento vaticano sobre la teologia de la liberacion",* in *"Mision Abierta al Servicio de la Fe",* 1/1985, Febrero, pp. 124-136. Juan Luis Segundo *"Teologia de la liberacion. Respuesta al Cardenal Ratzinger,"* Madrid: Ediciones Cristiandad, 1985.

However, the final document was accepted upon the insistence of the Latin American bishops. The document is rather inconclusive, and tries to replace the liberation theology terminology. In 1973, Trilateral Commission was instituted in the U.S., primarily as a means to making imperial domination function more smoothly under the cover of the advocacy of human rights and the ideology of national security[502]. The Church hierarchy shows essentially a devious character. It claims not to be involved in politics, however, it sides explicitly with one side only depending on the convenience of the situation. In a new situation in the modern world and the new Church-State relationship, the Church is losing control over societies. This new situation is sometimes defined as the end of Christendom understood as the unity of Church and State. The Church therefore feels threatened and some members of its hierarchy are searching for a new justification of its existence.

Liberation theology may be the solution. It happens that the Marxist analysis serves heuristically to discern the evil of the social injustice and pose the questions. Some see the convergence between the Marxist analysis and the original Christian ideals. Both ideologies are striving for a utopia, one for a classless society, the other for a Kingdom of God. Thus Marxist socio-economical analysis is fully vindicated in liberation theology. Traditionally, the Church claimed to be the Kingdom of God. Liberation theology redresses the errors of the Church, reminding it to serve the Kingdom of God, but understood as an earthly affair. Its service should consist of the ongoing humanization of the human realm at every level and in every situation.

The theology of liberation is not unique to Central and South America. Parallel movements exist in Africa and Asia and in various cultures with various religions or ideologies. They represent a reaction against the European and North American theological establishment. In Asian cultures, people talk about "liberation both human and cosmic" which represents a struggle for a full humanity. The foundation is cosmic religion - the attitude of all human beings vis-à-vis Nature. Non-Christian religions do not envision the ultimate reality as a "personal being", therefore are metatheistic or nontheistic. The starting

---

502   Phillip Berryman, *op. cit.*, 1987.

point for collaboration between the Christians and non-Christians is liberation.[503]

As the Protestant Reformation began as a revolt against corrupt practices in the Roman Catholic Church stressing the personal convictions and was more in tune with the modern age than Roman Catholicism, so the liberation theology is also a manifestation of a new worldwide movement for human emancipation. It constitutes a new, timely phenomenon and strives to implement the full realization of a human being in harmony with the Nature and for the believer, in harmony with the original Christian message.

---

503 Choan-Seng Song *"Third-Eye Theology. Theology in Formation in Asian Settings."* Maryknoll, New York: Orbis Books, 1979.

Index